For Mr. Woodard

All the best ——

Joe

# Under-standing Modern China

# Under-standing standing Modern China

Edited with an Introduction by Joseph M. Kitagawa

Quadrangle Books Chicago 1969

Library of Congress Catalog Card Number: 70–78310

Erwin Riasz *Landform Map of China* on pages 44–45
from *Land of the 500 Million* by G. B. Cressey.
Copyright 1955 by McGraw-Hill, Inc.
Used with permission of McGraw-Hill Book Co.

TYPOGRAPHY BY LAWRENCE LEVY

# Preface

Much has been written in recent years on various aspects of China, and yet there remains a great discrepancy between our knowledge about and our "understanding" of China. We are all aware that China has preserved one of the oldest and most enduring forms of civilization in the history of mankind. But, ironically, for centuries the popular imagination of the West portrayed China primarily as an exotic never-never land. Unfortunately, the West came into direct contact with China only in the last two centuries when China was steadily losing its power and prestige due to internal disintegration and external aggression. Since the turn of the century China has made serious and agonizing efforts to regain its past glory while simultaneously trying to modernize its culture and society. Meanwhile, the rise of the Communist regime in Peking after World War II, which resulted in the flight of the Nationalist government to the island of Taiwan, marked a decisive turning point in the modern history of China and, to a significant degree, of the rest of the world. So today many people ask: "What is happening to China?" "What might happen to Mainland China and Taiwan in the foreseeable future?" And "How can average Westerners, especially Americans, understand the seemingly incomprehensible and perhaps irremediable problems posed by China?" It is our modest hope that this small book may provide some clues.

These essays developed out of a seminar held at Solvang, California, in March 1968 on the theme: "After Mao and Chiang: Two Chinas?" This seminar, like others sponsored by the Council on Religion and International Affairs (CRIA), was designed to stimulate public discussion on a timely subject by concerned laymen, rather than to arrive at agreements or solutions by learned specialists. The program of the conference was planned by William J. Cook, then the National Field Director of the CRIA; I served as special consultant. The participants in the seminar appreciated the fact that the speakers, who were specialists in their respective fields, presented complex and technical subjects in a succinct and meaningful way, and they enthusiastically sought to make available those materials in book form for the benefit of a wider reading public.

Grateful acknowledgment is made to the editors of *Asian Survey* for permitting us to include Professor Yuan-li Wu's article, originally entitled "Economics, Ideology and the Cultural Revolution," which appeared in Vol. VIII, No. 3 (March 1968), of that journal. Dr. Wu has added to it a new introduction in which he discusses the general background of modern Chinese economics.

It is a pleasant duty to thank all those who have made the publication of this book possible—the contributors, the staff of the CRIA, and all the participants in the seminar. I owe special thanks to my research associates, Lowell W. Bloss and Winston B. Davis, for their editorial assistance; to Mrs. Doris Dawson and Mrs. Lillian Hopkins for typing and retyping the manuscript; and to Ivan R. Dee, managing editor of Quadrangle Books, for his careful editing and insightful suggestions. Finally, much of the credit for this book must go to William J. Cook, the real architect of the Solvang Seminar.

J. M. K.

*The University of Chicago*
*April 1969*

# A note on transliteration

The problem of romanizing Chinese place names is a difficult one. Solutions differ from language to language, and there are several so-called "systems" used even in the English-speaking world.

The system most widely accepted by professionals is the Wade-Giles system. One of its key advantages is that it permits the reader to check back to the original Chinese characters, since most dictionaries are arranged according to this romanization system. Norton Ginsburg's chapter on the geography of China uses this system throughout—except for a few commonly used place names, such as Canton, for which the Wade-Giles equivalent might be unfamiliar to the average reader. The map which shows administrative entities and railway lines in China (pages 16–17) also follows the Wade-Giles system.

A common way of romanizing Chinese place names, though

technically not a true "system," is often referred to as the "Postal Atlas" system. Most of the place names used in this book which do not conform to the Wade-Giles system use the conventional Postal Atlas spellings. The physiographic diagram of China (pages 44–45) uses this type of spelling.

The government of the People's Republic of China has developed its own romanization system, known as the "Pin-yin," which is widely used in the communist world but rarely used in the West.

The contributors to this book have been free to use whichever method of transliteration they prefer, which accounts for some of the inconsistencies in spelling from essay to essay.

# Contents

# An Outline of Chinese History

| | | |
|---|---|---|
| **B.C.** | ca 3000 | Beginning of prehistoric civilization along the Yellow River. |
| | ca 1800–ca 1500 | Hsia dynasty. |
| | ca 1500–ca 1100 | Shang (later called Yin) dynasty. |
| | 1122–256 | Chou dynasty |
| | | Spring and Autumn period (722–481). |
| | | Age of Classical Philosophers—Lao Tzu, Confucius, Mo Tzu, Mencius, etc. (550–230). |
| | | Warring States period (403–221). |
| | 221–207 | Ch'in dynasty—unification of China. |
| | 202–A.D. 9 | Former Han dynasty—contacts with Middle East and Roman empire begin. |
| **A.D.** | 25–220 | Later Han dynasty. |
| | | Introduction of Buddhism (A.D. 68 ?). |

| | |
|---|---|
| 220–280 | Period of the Three Kingdoms (Wei, Shu, and Wu). |
| 280–420 | Chin dynasty. |
| | Chinese pilgrim, Fa-hsien, visits Central Asia and India (399–414). |
| | State patronage of Taoism (440). |
| 589–618 | Sui dynasty. |
| 618–906 | T'ang dynasty. |
| | Chinese pilgrim, Hsüan-tsang, visits India (629–645). |
| | Chinese pilgrim, I-ching, visits India (671–695). |
| | Official persecution of Buddhism (845). |
| 907–960 | Period of Five dynasties and Ten States, following the collapse of T'ang dynasty. |
| 960–1279 | Sung dynasty (Northern Sung, 960–1127; Southern Sung, 1127–1279). |
| | Revival of Confucianism (11th century A.D.). |
| | Unification of the Mongolian tribes of Chinghis (Genghis) Khan (1206). |
| | Mongol invasion of Eastern Europe (1236–1242). |
| | Baghdad captured by the Mongol forces (1258). |
| 1260–1368 | China ruled by Yüan (Mongol) dynasty. |
| | Marco Polo in the service of the Mongol court (1271–1295). |
| 1368–1644 | Ming dynasty. |
| | Unification of Korea under the Yi dynasty (1392). |
| | Vasco da Gama reaches India (1498). |
| | Arrival of the Portuguese at Canton (1517). |
| | Portuguese embassy to Peking (1520). |
| | Spaniards occupy the Philippines (1565). |
| | Portuguese establish the port of Macao (1566). |
| | Italian Jesuit, Matteo Ricci, arrives at Macao (1582). |
| 1644–1912 | Ch'ing (Manchu) dynasty. |
| | British trade at Canton begins (1699). |
| | Anglo-Chinese (Opium) War (1839–1842). |
| | T'aip'ing Rebellion (1850–1864). |
| | Arrow War and Treaty revisions (1858–1860). |

American minister, Anson Burlingame, in China (1861–1867).

France establishes French Indo-China (1887).

Sino-Japanese War (1894–1895).

| | |
|---|---|
| 1898 | The Hundred Days of Reform. |
| 1900 | Boxer Rebellion. |
| 1905 | Three People's Principles of Sun Yat-sen (1866–1925) issued. |
| 1906 | Civil service examination system ends. |
| 1908 | Constitution proclaimed. |
| 1911 | Manchu dynasty overthrown by revolution; republic proclaimed. |
| 1915 | Japan makes Twenty-one Demands on China. |
| 1917 | Hu Shih (1891–1962) advocates literary renaissance. |
| 1919 | May Fourth Movement begins. |
| 1921 | First National Congress of the Chinese Communist party. |
| 1923 | Sun Yat-sen and A. Joffee issue Joint Manifesto. Nationalist party reorganized with the help of the USSR. Peking-Hankow Railway workers strike. |
| 1924 | First Congress of the Nationalist party (Kuomintang). |
| 1926–1928 | Northern expedition by the Nationalist regime, following Chiang Kai-shek's coup against the Communists. |
| 1927 | Nationalist-Communist alliance ends. Mao Tse-tung's "Autumn Harvest Insurrection" in Hunan fails. |
| 1931 | Japanese expansion in Manchuria begins. Chinese Soviet Republic organized with Mao Tse-tung as chairman. |
| 1932 | Manchuko established. |
| 1934 | Long March of Communists begins. Chiang Kai-shek's "New Life Movement" inaugurated. |
| 1935 | Communist headquarters established at Yenan. |
| 1936 | Sian incident. |
| 1937 | Japanese invasion of coastal China following the Marco Polo Bridge incident. Nationalist-Communist alliance. |

| | |
|---|---|
| 1938 | Capital moved to Chungking. |
| 1940 | Japanese invasion of French Indo-China. |
| 1941 | Pacific War begins. |
| 1942 | Treaty revisions. |
| 1943 | Chinese Communist party begins reform at Yenan. |
| 1945 | Pacific War ends. |
| 1946 | Philippines achieve independence. |
| 1947 | India and Pakistan achieve independence. |
| 1948 | Burma, North and South Korea achieve independence. |
| 1949 | Communists' People's Republic established on mainland; flight of Nationalist regime to Taiwan (Formosa). Republic formed in Indonesia. |
| 1950 | Korean War begins. |
| 1953 | Cease-fire in Korea. |
| 1955 | Bandung Conference held. |
| 1957 | "Hundred Flowers" campaign inaugurated by Mao Tse-tung. |
| 1958 | Withdrawal of Chinese forces from Korea. Both Nationalist China and Communist China sever commercial relations with Japan. Communist China signs agreement for a 50,000,000 rupee loan to Ceylon. Mao Tse-tung retires as chairman of Chinese People's Republic. Commune system inaugurated. |
| 1959 | Dalai Lama escapes from Tibet. Liu Shao-ch'i becomes chairman (president) of Communist China. Communist Chinese forces invade Ladakh area of India. |
| 1960 | Chiang Kai-shek elected to a third six-year term as president of Nationalist China. International Commission of Jurists declares China guilty of trying to exterminate Buddhism in Tibet. Laos adopts good-neighbor policy with Communist China. Famine hits mainland China. |
| 1961 | Peking and North Korea sign military assistance treaty. Communist China and Cuba declare everlasting friendship. |
| 1962 | India charges new Communist Chinese invasion into Ladakh area. |
| | Hong Kong government returns ten thousand refugees to Communist China. Communist Chinese |

forces occupy Indian town of Towang, situated on Indian-Tibetan border. India assured of U.S. military assistance in defense against Communist China.

Cease-fire on Indian-Chinese border.

1963    Soviet-Chinese Communist ideological discussion fails. Peking denounces nuclear test-ban treaty. Peking charges USSR failed to keep pledge to help China develop atomic bombs. Peking and Pakistan sign air transport agreement. C. K. Yen succeeds Ch'en Ch'eng as premier of Nationalist China.

1964    Peking accuses Khrushchev of collaborating with U.S. Peking grants Kenya interest-free loan of $15,000,000 and gift of $3,000,000 and pledges military aid to Cambodia. Peking announces successful explosion of its first atomic bomb.

1965    Peking signs five-year trade agreement with Cuba, pledges economic and technical assistance to North Vietnam, and offers $28 million to Nepal for highway construction. Pro-Chinese Indonesian Communist party overthrown and President Sukarno taken into protective custody.

1966    Anti-Chinese violence breaks out in Indonesia. Peking halts economic and technical assistance to Indonesia. Peking rejects all-Asian peace conference on Vietnam. CCP Central Committee endorses "great proletarian cultural revolution." Defense Minister Lin Piao designated as Mao's heir apparent. Red Guards begin anti-Western campaigns. Peking announces new nuclear explosion.

1967    Premier Chou En-lai calls for moderation in Cultural Revolution. Chinese army mobilizes to defend Cultural Revolution. Red Guards ordered to return home. Peking announces explosion of hydrogen bomb.

1968    Rail bridge over Yangtze at Nanking, a ten-year project, completed. Liu Shao-Ch'i dismissed from government offices and expelled from party. Proposal to seat Communist China in United Nations defeated. Peking announces explosion of hydrogen bomb on Mao's birthday.

1969    Sino-Soviet border incidents.

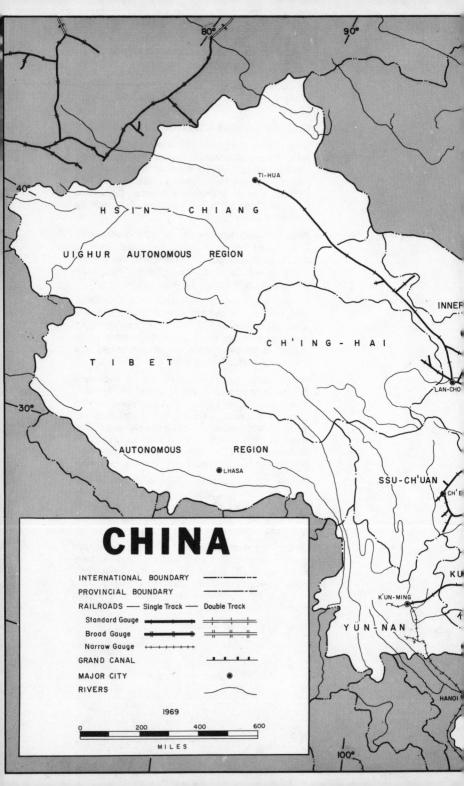

# Under-
# standing
# Modern
# China

# Introduction: Western Understanding of the East

On January 1, 1968, the president of Nationalist China, Chiang Kai-shek, issued his customary New Year's message, reiterating his now-familiar theme of delivering his 700 million compatriots on the mainland from the "Communist Hell." On this occasion President Chiang indulged in a bitter personal attack on Mao Tse-tung as an archcriminal, a notorious liar, an egocentric, a devil-tyrant, and a self-centered bandit-chief. He went so far as to say that the seventy-four-year-old Mao was "crazed and struggling in his death throes."[1] Of course, given the political situation of Formosa and mainland China, no one expected Chiang to send a get-well greeting to Mao in Peking. But many people felt that Chiang, himself not in robust health and no longer young at the age of eighty-one, was hardly in a position to comment about Mao's declining age. Meanwhile, we are all aware that the future of the world will be greatly affected by the passing of both these men.

What may happen in China after Mao and Chiang, important though it may be, is only one dimension of the monstrous global puzzle confronting us. We must be reasonably prepared for various eventualities, yet perhaps the best we can hope to do is reflect on the main thrusts of our historic experiences and assess the dynamics of the present situation, recognizing that new factors can radically alter the course of history. The most precarious aspect of such a reflection is the ambiguity of our own perspectives. This is particularly true in analyzing the encounter of the East and the West.

## FOUR ANCIENT CULTURAL TRADITIONS

The so-called meeting of the East and West—that is, the encounter of the cultural traditions of Europe and Asia[2]—is a relatively modern phenomenon. All the civilizations of the ancient world—those of Mesopotamia, Egypt, Crete, India, China, Mexico, Peru, and Palestine—considered themselves as exclusive and self-sufficient ways of life. It was taken for granted in the ancient period that the migration of an ethnic group into certain areas, such as the penetration of the Aryans into India, Persia, and Europe, or the settlement of the Scandinavians in Iceland, implied the wholesale transplantation of the civilization of the invading group over the entire region. In the course of time there developed several great empires, some of which competed with rival powers in expanding their political and cultural influences over wider territories. For instance, the ancient Babylonian empire was conquered by the rising Persian empire, which extended its hegemony to Asia Minor, Egypt, and the border of India around the fifth century B.C. It was the obscure Macedonian king, Alexander (356–323 B.C.), a one-time disciple of Aristotle, who during his short life established a vast cultural, political, and economic network stretching from western Macedonia to the Punjab region of India in the East, which was administered by a series of Greek territorial monarchies.

Alexander's audacious dream to unify the whole world was doomed to failure. Shortly after his death even his own empire lost its political unity. In the East, half a century after Alexander's departure from Indian soil, King Asoka (r., 274–232 B.C.) unified the Indian subcontinent and ushered in a glorious age of Buddhist expansion, not only within his own realm but also into India's neighboring countries as well. In the Far East the third century B.C. witnessed the unification of China for the first time under the "First Emperor" (Shih Huang Ti) of the Ch'in dynasty, which was followed shortly afterward by a more stable Han rule. (During the Han empire, which lasted over four centuries, Confucianism established itself as the dominant ideological system in China.) In the West the Roman empire began to expand during the first century B.C. and reigned over the Mediterranean world for centuries to come. It was to provide the medieval foundations of Western civilization, blending within it Judeo-Christian religious tradition, Greek philosophy, and Roman jurisprudence. Thus by the beginning of the Christian era there emerged at least four major cultural spheres in the world, namely, China, which considered itself the Middle Kingdom with its Confucian universalism; India, with its cosmic vision as expressed in Hinduism as well as in Buddhism and Jainism; the Middle East, which was the cradle of great world religions (Zoroastrianism, Judaism, Christianity, and later Islam); and Rome, which inherited and amplified Hellenistic cosmopolitanism.

Unfortunately, our knowledge of the relationships among these four great ancient cultural spheres is quite fragmentary. We do know that there was active trade between Rome and China via the overland caravan route, as well as between India, Iran, and the Mediterranean world by means of ocean routes, whereby gold from Siberia, amber from Northern Europe, pepper from India, and silk from China, for example, found their ways into all corners of the known world. The commercial traffic between Europe and Asia was such that as early as the first century B.C. Cicero warned his fellow Romans that if the Chinese government were to pursue an adverse trade policy, it could easily result in a financial panic in Rome. But the interrelationship between Europe and Asia was not confined to trade. Frederick Teggart, who studied the relationship between Rome and China during the period from 58 B.C. to 107 A.D., reminds us that "of the forty occasions on which outbreaks [of war] took place in Europe, twenty-seven were traceable to the policy, or rather changes of policy, of the Han [Chinese] government."[3] While active commercial trade across the steppes and desert began to wane after the third century A.D. because of the internal decay of China and of Rome, religious and cultural intercourse continued for some time. Among the consequences were the penetration of the Middle Eastern mystery cults and Christianity into the Roman empire, establishment of Syrian Christian communities in South India and northwestern China, spread of Manicheanism throughout Central Asia, and expansion of Buddhism into various corners of Asia.

ISLAMIC EXPANSION

The historic East-West relationship was greatly affected by the rise of Islam in the Middle East in the seventh century. Within ten years after the death of Muhammad, Syria, Iraq, and Egypt were claimed by the Muslim empire. In less than a century Islam conquered the Christian belt of North Africa, the home of St. Augustine and many other eminent Christian saints and patriarchs, and reached the Iberian peninsula. In the eighth century Muslim forces crossed the Pyrenees into France. The Muslim traders were soon found in Canton as well as in northern China, and they began to settle in the islands of the East Indies, now known as Indonesia, shortly afterward. Nor did Islam leave India untouched. As early as 712 the Sind region was conquered by Muslim invaders. It took three more centuries before the Punjab was added to Muslim rule, but after 1526 the whole of India came under the control of the Muslim Mughal dynasty. Understandably, such a rapid and widespread expansion of Islam sharply disrupted the historic intercourse between Europe and Asia.

The vitality of Islam was not confined only to its military and political domains during the first four centuries after its inception. The world of Islam, under the Abbasid rulers in Baghdad (in the present Iraq), the Umayyad rulers in Cordova, Spain, and the Fatimad rulers in Egypt, made extraordinary progress in commerce, industry, and culture. For instance, thanks largely to enlightened Muslim rule, Spain became one of the richest European nations during the Middle Ages. The intellectual life of the Muslims was greatly enriched by the translation of Greek philosophical works and Persian and Indian scientific books into Arabic. Muslim universities in Cordova and Granada, as well as other schools and libraries in Spain, attracted Muslim, Jewish, and Christian students from other parts of Europe and Africa. Significantly, Christian Europe first became acquainted with the major works of Plato and Aristotle through the writings of Muslim scholars.

The balance of power between the world of Islam and Christian Europe began to shift around the eleventh century, when Christian forces regained control of Sicily, Sardinia, and later the Iberian peninsula. Meanwhile, the Seljuq Turks, a nomadic group from the Turkestan steppes, migrated westward and defeated the Byzantine forces. The Turks' mistreatment of Christian pilgrims to Jerusalem provided a ready excuse for European Christendom to undertake a series of bloody Crusades between 1096 and 1291. Actually, the Crusades, in which saints and scoundrels fought side by side with a mixture of spiritual and mundane motives, failed to dislodge Muslim power, although they left unpleasant memories of European Christendom in the minds of the Muslims. On the other hand, the two centuries of fanatic campaign propaganda, sanctioned by the papacy which was then consolidating its political power, greatly distorted the Europeans' image of non-Europeans, much to the detriment of East-West relations for centuries to come. Indeed, as Edwin Calverley points out, "The false reports brought back by those who returned from the wars filled the West with popular mis-information about Islam that Western mass education has not yet been able to remove."[4] Subsequent religious developments in Europe—the Reformation, the Counter-Reformation, and the rise of Pietism—only added more fuel to Europeans' prejudice against non-Western religions and cultures, and this in turn hardened the attitudes of the Muslims and other non-Western peoples toward "Christian" Europe. As Norman Daniel observes, once a normal and peaceful channel of communication is broken down,

> under the pressure of their sense of danger, whether real or imagined, a deformed image of their enemy's beliefs takes shape in men's minds. By misapprehension and mis-representation an idea of the beliefs and practices of one society can pass into the accepted myths of another society in a form so distorted that its relation to the original facts is sometimes barely discernible.[5]

The East-West relationship, which deteriorated on account of the Crusades, was further strained by the dramatic appearance of the tribes from the Central Asian steppes onto the world scene beginning in the thirteenth century. The first to be mentioned are the Mongols, who not only conquered China but quickly overpowered Muslims from the Oxus frontier to the Euphrates, and subjugated all of Russia. Around 1241 the Mongol hordes devastated southern Poland and Hungary. Only the death of the son of Jenghiz Khan saved Western Europe from their onslaught. After the Mongols, the Mamluks, originally a Turkish slave family, established a dynasty in Egypt and dominated international commerce during the fourteenth and fifteenth centuries. Not until 1498, when Vasco da Gama discovered the sea route to India by the Cape of Good Hope, could Europe challenge the commanding position of the Mamluks' Egypt in international commerce. The Ottomans, too, a tribe of the Ghuzz Turks which had earlier been driven from their homes in Central Asia by the Mongols, moved westward. In 1453 they defeated the forces of Byzantine Christendom and established the vast Ottoman empire, embracing within it a large portion of the Eastern Orthodox as well as Arab Muslim territories. The Ottoman's attempted siege of Vienna in the seventeenth century frightened European nations, especially Austria, Venice, Poland, Russia, and the papacy, which formed an alliance to check the advance of Turkish power.

WESTERN DOMINANCE

Even this superficial account of the historic relationship between East and West enables us to appreciate the intensity of emotion that has been involved in the encounter since the sixteenth century. There is much truth in Toynbee's observation that "in the encounter between the [non-Western] world and the West that has been going on by now for four or five hundred years . . . it has not been the West that has been hit by the world; it is the [non-Western] world that has been hit—and hit hard—by the West."[6] A new page of history was turned when the Mongol rule of Russia came to an end in 1480, followed by the expulsion of the Moors from Granada, Spain, in 1492. In contrast to China, India, and the Middle East, which were then showing signs of stagnation, the enormous vitality of Europe was apparent in the emergence of modern nation states, economic nationalism and a new social structure as well as the Renaissance in the cultural domain, and the Reformation and Counter-Reformation in the religious domain. The self-confidence of the new Europe was also evidenced in the aspiration of new maritime powers of Europe, such as Portugal and Spain, which tried to control vast territories in the non-Western world. This colonial expansion brought two kinds of results. First, the new continents of North and South America, and later Australia, were completely colonized by Europeans and became for all intents and purposes an extension of Europe, culturally and religiously. Second, many parts of Asia and Africa were subjugated, politically and economically, by the European powers, but they were not heavily colonized, except in certain areas, and as such their cultural and religious traditions were not replaced by those of the Europeans.

The phenomenal colonial expansion of the West during the sixteenth century may be graphically seen in the Spanish conquest of Mexico (1520), Peru (1531), Argentina (1535), the Rio Grande territory (1540), Florida (1565), and Manila, Philippines (1571). Soon Portugal colonized Brazil and established settlements on the west coast of India and in the Spice Islands. In all these ventures the most blatant form of economic exploitation was mixed with fanatic religious motivation. "In fact," says William Sweet, "the early Spanish *conquistadores* considered themselves Christian crusaders and brought over to the New World the ideas which had grown up in the long wars which they had fought against the Moors in Spain, using the same battle cries and evoking the same saints in the New World that had served them in the old."[7] The Portuguese, with similar fanatic zeal, tried to root out "infidels" in their colonies. Thus, for example, "Hindu temples in Goa were destroyed and their property distributed to religious orders [like the Franciscans] in 1540, [and even] the Inquisition was established in 1560."[8]

In the meantime Great Britain, which defeated the "invincible Armada" of Spain in 1588, and France and the Netherlands began to compete with Spain and Portugal for the control of North America, the West Indies, Africa, and Asia. In the north, Russia expanded eastward along the Amur River and established a settlement in the port of Okhotsk in 1638. Belgium, Germany, and other

European nations also pursued their own colonial policies. By the end of the nineteenth century much of the non-Western world was under the yoke of Western colonial imperialism, which sought new markets and new fields of profitable investment in an aggressive manner. It is reported that King Leopold II of Belgium and his associates "reaped a fortune in the Congo, but the cruelty of their methods of exploitation shocked the conscience of the entire civilized world."[9] Other nations were not much better in this respect. After the infamous Opium War (1840–1842), China was penetrated by British, French, Russian, and German as well as by Japanese interests. Before the turn of the twentieth century, Indo-China was taken by the French; the islands of Java, Sumatra, Celebes, parts of Borneo and New Guinea were taken by the Dutch; the Bismarck Archipelago, the Ladrone Islands, and some islands of Samoa were occupied by the Germans; and the islands of Hawaii, the Philippines, Guam, and Wake came under American control. Much of the Middle East and the continent of Africa were also divided into spheres of interest by various colonial powers.

There is no intent here to discuss the pros and cons of colonialism, except to point out that under colonial rule the initiative was completely in the hands of the West. Those who came under the rule of the colonial powers had nothing to say about the handling of their own affairs. In such a situation it was impossible to achieve a genuine encounter between the East and the West. To be sure, a few European thinkers from the time of the Enlightenment voiced their admiration for the ancient wisdom of China and India, and some liberal churchmen and humanists in Europe criticized Western political and economic imperialism and crude forms of Christian missionary activities. But their voices were not listened to by men of practical affairs. Rather, the prosperity brought by colonial policies led many Westerners to feel that their culture, religion, technology, and socio-economic and political systems must be successful precisely because they were attributes of a superior race. Many Europeans took it for granted that "biology and sociology point to the superiority of the Caucasian or white races over the coloured races of the earth. Superiority in physical and mental constitution, together with superiority in civilization and organization entail responsibility as well as privilege."[10]

Thus many came to accept an oversimplified formula: European equals Christian equals superior race *versus* non-Westerner equals pagan equals inferior race. Otherwise it would have been difficult to comprehend how Bartolomé de las Casas, known as the "Apostle to the Indians" in Latin America, was instrumental in initiating slavery in the sixteenth century, and how modern European nations which advocated the importance of human dignity, welfare, and freedom at home did not even bother to conceal their contempt for the natives in their colonies. The so-called "pig trade," which kidnaped and illegally shipped Chinese laborers in the mid-nineteenth century, was no less cruel than the earlier slave trade of the African natives. It is reported that "to San Francisco alone 108,471 Chinese laborers had been taken before 1863."[11] Lord Elgin, who ordered the burning of the Summer Palace in Peking, undoubtedly acted with the mistaken notion, prevalent among the colonial rulers, that international morality was not applicable in the West's dealings with non-Western peoples.[12] In short, the East-West relationship, which historically had been understood as the confrontation on the same plane of two rival groups, each with its peculiar beliefs, cultural traditions, and ways of life, even during the bloodiest period of the Crusades, came to be seen by many Europeans as a vertical relationship, with the superior European race destined to conquer, rule, or enlighten the poor natives in the non-Western world. Conversely, there developed a strong suspicion among non-Westerners that Westerners were aggressors and exploiters without regard for human welfare, coupled with a conviction that the only effective means to deal with the Westerners was to adopt their ways—and especially their technical know-how—in order to resist their further encroachment and eventually to be emancipated from their yoke.

SELF–FULFILLING PROPHECY

The development of seemingly irrational and tragic relations between East and West during the modern colonial period amply supports the well-known sociological theory of the "self-fulfilling prophecy," which tells us that if men define situations as real, they often become real in their own minds regardless of the objective features of situations. According to Robert K. Merton: "The self-fulfilling prophecy is, in the beginning, a *false* definition of the situation evoking a new behavior which makes the original false conception come true." This leads Merton to conclude that "social beliefs father social reality."[13] Often, those who fail to understand that they can hypnotize themselves by their own deep-seated racial prejudices or cultural prejudgments regard their distorted views as the only objective view of social realities. In difficult circumstances like colonial rule, both the Western colonial masters and their non-Western subjects became easy victims of self-fulfilling prophecies.

One of the common by-products of the self-fulfilling prophecy is the practice of "typing" and "categorizing" things and people, often in sharp dichotomy. Indeed, the diaries and letters of many nineteenth-century Western colonial officials, army personnel, missionaries, and business representatives who lived in the Eastern world betray how pervasive such easy categories were. In most cases Westerners portrayed themselves as civilized, honest, hard-working, fair, generous, kind, and reasonable, while the "natives," to use a word which acquired ugly connotations during the colonial period, were characterized as superstitious, dishonest, lazy, cunning, ungrateful, cruel and irrational, and so forth. Conversely, many Easterners who resented colonial rule and the penetration of Western ways indulged in similar oversimplifications—in reverse order. When the two sides "typed" each other, responding not to the reality of the situation but to the meaning this situation had for each side respectively, their "antagonistic cooperation" became a vicious circle.

The self-fulfilling prophecy was built into the very structure of colonial rule. In colonial administration there was, generally speaking, under the throne or the home government, something like a colonial office which functioned to supervise the viceroy or governor-general of a given colony. Usually the latter official ruled the colony, not directly but through a kind of nominal legislative body that embraced a few "representatives" of the colonial subjects. By far the most complex colonial administrative machine was developed in India under British rule. According to Sir Reginald Coupland, the main strength of the British *raj* was the Indian Civil Service, which attracted the cream of English youth, usually those who were educated in Oxford and Cambridge. Next in importance to the Indian Civil Service (ICS) was the Indian Police Service (IP). There were other technical services, such as education, agriculture, and forestry, which were considered less important than the ICS and the IP, and these permitted a substantial number of native Indians to enter their ranks. Under these so-called All-India Services, there were also many Provincial Services which were staffed almost entirely by non-British personnel. It was reported that as early as 1900 the British *raj* employed over 500,000 Indian and 4,000 British personnel.[14] Britishers often cited this type of statistic to illustrate the magnanimity of enlightened British colonial policy, following Queen Victoria's proclamation: "that, so far as may be, our subjects of whatever race or creed be freely and impartially admitted to offices in our service, the duties of which they may be qualified by their education, ability, and integrity duly to discharge." Such an interpretation of statistics never impressed the Indians, because they knew too well that the best-paid jobs and decision-making posts were almost completely in the hands of British personnel, while their Indian counterparts were relegated to minor positions with meager pay.

Defenders of colonial policy can find many reasons for a certain amount of inevitable inequality in such arrangements, and they cite the recent examples of some European nations which under the Allied Occupation after World War II were also subjected to unequal treatment. But the real tragedy of the colonial period is that the inequality and lack of social contact between Westerners and Easterners were rationalized not on the grounds of political and military necessity or cultural differences but on racial grounds. On this ground, for example, Rabindranath Tagore, the Bengali poet who received various international honors including the Nobel Prize, or Dr. Sarvepalli Radhakrishnan, renowned professor of All Souls, Oxford, and later President of India, were not permitted to step into many of the social clubs in their own homeland, even as guests of the Britishers.

The ugly practice of discrimination based on color and race, which spread like a contagious disease in the modern period wherever the West was in political or economic control—in Africa, the Middle East, Asia, the Americas, and Australia—poisoned the wellspring of mutual understanding between Westerners and non-

Westerners. After all, no gesture of good will toward the Chinese on the part of Westerners, for example, was effective when the Chinese were not even allowed to enter the exclusive parks in the foreign concessions on Chinese soil. Long before apartheid became the adopted policy in South Africa, the "white Australia" of the later decades of the nineteenth century excluded all "colored" immigrants; this policy was liberalized somewhat only in the early 1960's. The United States, too, during the first quarter of the twentieth century excluded immigrants from India, Siam, Arabia, Indo-China, the Malay Peninsula, Afghanistan, New Guinea, Borneo, Java, Ceylon, Sumatra, the Celebes, China, and Japan on the grounds of race or color. As late as 1922 Mr. Justice Sutherland, speaking for a unanimous Supreme Court, interpreted the wording of the 1790 Naturalization Act—that "any free white alien was eligible to become a citizen of this republic"—to mean that only members of the white "race" were eligible, and insisted that the test was membership in the Caucasian "race," regardless of color. In that same year, in dealing with a high-caste Hindu, Justice Sutherland, again speaking for a unanimous Court, concluded that a person may be a member of the Caucasian "race" and yet not "white," on the grounds that "the words of the statute are to be interpreted in accordance with the understanding of the common man from whose vocabulary they were taken." This unusual legal logic was later extended to the extreme by Mr. Justice Cardozo, who stated: "Men are not white if the strain of colored blood in them is a half or a quarter, or, not improbably, even less. . . ."[15]

Apparently the encounter of the modern West and the Eastern world, coming as it did immediately after Europe's centuries-old struggle against the world of Islam, had an unfortunate beginning. The phenomenal expansion of the West, which came to control a vast portion of the non-Western world, convinced many Europeans of their superiority, not only militarily, politically, and economically but also "racially." Inevitably they looked at the non-Western world from this perspective, which in turn prompted non-Westerners to react against racism as the most intolerable component of modern Western colonial imperialism. To complicate the matter further, mutual suspicion and hostility were kept alive by the "self-fulfilling prophecies" of both sides, so that both Westerners and

Easterners regarded each other not as living human beings but as complexes of virtues, vices, types, and categories.

As far as non-Westerners are concerned, their worst suspicion—that Westerners are imperialists and racists—is firmly confirmed by their experiences at home and by the behavior of Western nations in other parts of the world. Much of the thinking and behavior of the people in the East has been rooted in this reading of the modern world situation in which they find themselves. For their part, Westerners have their share of self-fulfilling prophecies. Their self-confidence as masters of the world is confirmed by their economic, political, technological, and military achievements; it is their manifest destiny to reshape the world according to their own image. Whether or not this view coincides with the reality of history is not questioned; they have defined it as real, and thus it has become real in their own minds.

## UNFINISHED DRAMA

While formal colonialism came to an end in many parts of the world by the middle of the twentieth century, the drama of the East-West encounter continues. It has so far seen three distinct phases in modern times. In the West these were (1) economic and political control of the East, (2) Westernization of the East, and (3) permanent tutelage over the East. In the East the corresponding phases were (1) passive resignation, (2) aspiration for modernization and equality with the West, and (3) an anti-Western campaign and the independence of the East.

Little need be said about the first phase of the drama, in which the West decisively took the initiative. Overwhelmed by the military, economic, and technological superiority of the West, the bewildered East could only accept the situation with passive resignation. In turn, the West took this as a sign of the political and cultural weakness of the East. There were, to be sure, different kinds of initiatives taken by different Western nations. For example, the earlier colonial empires, such as Spain and Portugal, which were motivated both by economic exploitation and religious enthusiasm, tried to superimpose their political, economic, and religious systems on the Eastern world. Nevertheless they were determined not to enlighten the Easterners too much. For example, when the

Jesuits arranged a European tour (1582–1586) for a few Japanese Catholics, "they were not to learn anything of Christian divisions and especially nothing about Protestantism. Their tour was carefully chaperoned and of limited duration so that they would receive only the best possible impression of Catholic Europe."[16] The later colonial powers adopted a much more explicit policy, at least initially, of concentrating on economic gains, with no attempt to introduce Western culture and religion to their colonies. Thus when the Moravian mission began its work in the jungle of Dutch Guiana, "the Dutch government issued orders forbidding the Indians to join any Moravian settlement."[17] Similarly, the British East India Company took the position during the eighteenth century that "to hold India in subjection Christian missionaries must be excluded. It was not only that the arrival of Protestant emissaries of this faith might anger Hindu priests and Muhammadan mullahs, but *it would open the eyes of the Hindus and Hindis to the great facts of the world.*"[18]

This attitude began to change during the second phase of the colonial period. By that time the colonial powers, ostensibly to expedite the importing of raw materials from and the exporting of merchandise to the colonies, established harbors, roads, railroads, banks, and telecommunications. They were compelled to train a corps of minor officials, for which they had to provide a degree of Westernized education and streamline the administrative structure. This development coincided with the growth of a messianic complex coupled with feelings of racial superiority among Europeans, which in turn resulted in a policy of Westernization of their colonies and spheres of interest in the non-Western world. Some of the colonial officials even boasted with an air of self-righteousness of the tangible benefits of colonialism to the East. This shift in the Western attitude toward the East was epitomized by the famous British policy, advocated by Macaulay in 1834, to create "Indians in blood and color, but English in taste, in opinion, in morals, and in intellect." With this shift the colonial administrators, who had been hostile earlier toward Christian missionary work, began to welcome missionary activities—educational, medical, and other philanthropic as well as evangelistic programs. And Western missionary societies, unconsciously if not consciously, began to cooperate with the aims and policies of the colonial administrators.

Meanwhile, the East began to recover from the shock of the onslaught of the West. Progressive elements in the Eastern world, especially the iconoclastic youth, were attracted by certain features of Western civilization. They were instrumental in writing in the East the second phase of the confrontation, advocating the modernization of social, economic, and political institutions as well as humanistic and scientific education. In so doing they hoped that the East would be accepted as an equal by the West. To be sure, they championed "modernization" and not "Westernization" of Eastern society. Ironically, their dedicated effort to reform Eastern society by appropriating some Western ways appeared very much as though they were advocating Westernization of the East—at least it appeared so to Westerners—and their enthusiasm, which the conservative majority by no means shared, nevertheless encouraged the West to promote a wholesale Westernization of Eastern societies and cultures. The large number of Eastern students who flocked to Western universities in the nineteenth and twentieth centuries convinced many Westerners that while the East had everything to learn from the West, the West had nothing to learn from the East. Thus many Westerners came to believe that ancient cultural traditions were doomed to extinction, despite a small number of scholars and romanticists who appreciated Eastern religions and cultures. The expectation of the decline of the East also encouraged Christian missions, as illustrated by the motto of the Student Volunteer Movement around the turn of the century: "The evangelization of the whole world in this generation." As late as 1928 a spokesman of Western Christendom went so far as to say, "These [Eastern religions and cultures] are going to be smashed anyhow, perhaps not quickly, but surely, and what is going to do it . . . is modern science, modern commerce, and modern political organization."[19]

During and immediately following World War I a marked change took place in the attitudes of East and West toward each other. Leaders in the Middle East and India, for example, who advocated cooperation with the West with the hope of gaining the West's respect for their causes, were disillusioned by the postwar settlement. On the other hand, the dreams of Westerners who crusaded for rapid Westernization of the East, gave way to a series of disappointments because of the tenacity of the indigenous Eastern way of life which stubbornly resisted the influence of the West. As a consequence, the new Eastern stance was formulated by those who espoused the cause of national independence. In the words of H. A. R. Gibb: "Western political and economic controls in the Near and Middle East, and the disregard of Western political leaders for human and social interests, forced the nationalist leaders to devote all their energies to the struggle against Western domination."[20] In India and many other parts of Asia developments followed the same pattern. Anti-Western sentiments in the East quickly united diverse social and religious reform movements which otherwise had little in common. Undoubtedly the most dramatic Asian figure to emerge in this period was Mahatma Gandhi, whose shrewd political strategy and profound dedication to religious ideals enabled him to lead India to political independence.

As for the West, World War I revealed the bankruptcy of the European state system which had existed since the sixteenth century. The façade of European cultural, religious, and moral unity was shattered, and two new powers, the United States and Soviet Russia, stepped into the forefront of world history, each claiming universal validity for democracy or communism. The fragile fraternity of the West could not prevent the emergence of Nazi Germany and fascist Italy, which together with Japanese militarists brought about World War II. The power vacuum thus created in the East after the war made it possible for non-Western nations to achieve political independence. Nevertheless, many Westerners still assume that the West will remain as the model and provide tutelage for generations to come, if not permanently, in the less advanced nations of the non-Western world.

DIMENSIONS OF UNDERSTANDING

The end of World War II ushered in a new phase of modern world history. The lofty dreams of "one world," four freedoms, and the rest which had given hope to millions of people during the postwar period were rudely shattered by a series of breathtaking events, including the Cold War and crises in the Middle East, Africa, South America, and Asia, which continue today. In each of the three generally accepted divisions of the world, namely, the "Free

World," the "Communist World," and the "Uncommitted World" of Asia and Africa, life has become infinitely more complex than before. The West's expectation that it would remain the tutor of the non-Western world has eroded in the face of the independence of former colonies in Asia and Africa and the emergence of Communist China. The East is disillusioned because the end of colonial rule did not solve all its problems. Soviet Russia, a wayward cousin of the West, which has tried to identify itself with the causes of Asians and Africans with some measure of success, is no longer certain how long it can maintain even nominal alliance with Communist groups in Asia and Africa.

Nevertheless, all segments of the divided world of our time have something in common. Whether we like it or not, we must acknowledge that the four-centuries-old dominance of the West has left lasting imprints on economic, political, and technological developments in every corner of the earth. It is hard to deny that worldwide trade and transportation and communication systems have helped to break down historic barriers which had kept peoples and nations apart. Realizing this, many dreamy-eyed idealists chant the litany of "mutual understanding," which according to their oversimplified logic will follow automatically the shrinkage of physical distance. This theme has been enthusiastically espoused by Westerners recently because they find in the non-Western world many things familiar to them—airlines, automobiles, universities, hospitals, and modernized defense systems—except at less advanced levels of development. Ironically, these idealists fail to see that under a surface which appears similar, the world is divided culturally. The basic issue, to quote Toynbee, is the fact that "while the economic and political maps have now been Westernized, the cultural map remains substantially what it was before our Western society started on its career of economic and political conquest. On the cultural plane, for those who have eyes to see, the lineaments of the four living non-Western civilizations are still clear."[21]

This does not imply that traditional cultures of the Middle East, India, and China, for example, have remained unchanged. Indeed, the spirit of modernity, which had earlier shaken the foundation of traditional Western culture, has greatly stimulated and rejuvenated Eastern cultures. But the effects of modernity have been different in the East and in the West. That is to say, the impact of modernity has compelled every one of the Eastern cultures, each in its own way, to come to terms with some of the significant features of the Western culture, whereas the West, which has developed global systems of economics, politics, and technology, has preserved its own "provincial" cultural outlook without being exposed to serious dimensions of non-Western cultures. This fact has deep implications for the present and future interplay of, and mutual understanding between, the East and the West. In this context, says Barbara Ward:

> . . . it may well be that we in the West may have more to learn at this stage because the patient assimilation of other peoples' ideas is not something that "comes naturally." Our brothers in Asia have undergone for centuries the immense battering impact of western ideas, and they have had time, as it were, to sit and sort them out, to consider them, to compare and weigh them, whereas we have not given ourselves comparable opportunity to live with eastern ideas or assimilate the great traditions of Asia.[22]

Cora DuBois makes the same point equally emphatically in terms of languages:

> To the extent that the Asians know our language but we do not know theirs, they are in a better position to understand us than we to understand them. To the extent that Asians know English and we are ignorant of their language and literature, they have the right-of-way in travelling what the State Department likes to call "that two way traffic."[23]

Happily there are more Westerners today than ever before who are concerned with the study of non-Western languages, ideas, religions, and cultures. Even so, the West's effort is very limited. Many Westerners, impressed as they are by the West's contribution to world economic, political, and technological development, still are tempted to think that what is required for mutual understanding between East and West is simply the propagation and extension of the "provincial" Western culture to the rest of the world. The Western perspective has been so shaped and conditioned by its last four centuries of experience that nations and peoples in the West think of the non-Western world primarily in terms of order and security; Easterners, who view the past four centuries from an opposite perspective, are passionately concerned with freedom and welfare, though they also recognize the importance of order and security as necessary prerequisites. This difference in perspective has been a major factor hindering the development of mutual respect and understanding between the East and West in our time. In the main, when crucial decisions are to be made, Western policymakers, who advocate mutual respect and mutual understanding in their oratory, would rather settle for order and security even at the expense of the freedom and welfare of the peoples involved. Conversely, emotional and often irrational criticisms of Western policies by vocal minorities in the East, motivated as they are by a genuine concern for the freedom and welfare of the people, show little sympathy for the anguish of great powers who shoulder the main burden of international peace and security.

The events of our time do not encourage optimism about the future of the world. We sense that we are in a new era of world history, in which problems must be seen from a new perspective. Already we have some notions as to the new modes and styles of man's thinking and behavior, cultural, religious, and moral sensitivities, or lack of them, which will affect the course of the future as much as economic, political, technological, and military factors. For one thing, we are beginning to learn by bitter experience that in this post-imperialist era no great power, Western, Communist, or Eastern, can in the long run dictate the destiny of others, including "less developed" nations. Increasingly, military intervention, however necessary, will have to be regarded only as a temporary measure, for, as Walter Lippmann succinctly points out, "supreme military power and political mastery do not necessarily go together."[24] We have also come to accept the idea of regional or global economic cooperation and assistance, although existing programs may fall far short of our ideals.

More basically, we are beginning to realize that our common habit of polarizing the world into East and West, a habit which has been deeply ingrained in us, is based on a relatively modern phenomenon in the history of the world. We are also beginning to appreciate the tenacity of cultural and religious traditions which condition and color the perspectives of peoples, who in turn draw the meaning of a situation from their own perspectives and act according to the principle of the self-fulfilling prophecy. Our realization of these factors will help us develop a more adequate perspective for the West's understanding of the East and the East's understanding of the West, as much as for self-understanding on both sides.

NOTES

1. Quoted in *Chicago Sun-Times,* January 2, 1968.

2. See my article "East and West: A Dialogue," *Perspectives,* VI, no. 1 (January–February 1961), 19–38.

3. Frederick J. Teggart, *Rome and China: A Study of Correlations in Historical Events* (Berkeley, 1939), p. vii.

4. Edwin E. Calverley, "Islamic Religion," in T. Cuyler Young, ed., *Near Eastern Culture and Society* (Princeton, 1951), p. 103.

5. Norman Daniel, *Islam and the West: The Making of an Image* (Edinburgh, 1960), p. 2.

6. Arnold Toynbee, *The World and the West* (New York, 1953), pp. 1–2.

7. William W. Sweet, "Christianity in the Americas," in Archibald G. Baker, ed., *A Short History of Christianity* (Chicago, 1940), p. 227.

8. K. M. Panikkar, *Asia and Western Dominance* (London, 1959 ed.), p. 280.

9. Henry W. Littlefield, *New Outline History of Europe, 1815–1949* (New York, 1949), p. 137.

10. A. J. Macdonald, *Trade Politics and Christianity in Africa and the East* (London, 1916), p. 270.

11. Panikkar, *Asia and Western Dominance,* p. 141.

12. *Ibid.,* p. 104. Panikkar writes: "The burning of the Summer Palace has not been forgotten and the present writer was told by a high official of the Central People's Government in 1951 that the account is still left open and awaits settlement."

13. Robert K. Merton, *Social Theory and Social Structure* (Glencoe, Ill., 1949), pp. 182ff.

14. Sir Reginald Coupland, *India, A Re-Statement* (New York, 1945), pp. 42–70.

15. See Milton R. Konvitz, *The Alien and the Asiatic in American Law* (Ithaca, 1946), pp. 81, 88, 89, 95. The racial aspect of the qualification for U.S. citizenship was modified by the McCarran-Walter Act, or the Immigration and Nationality Act, of 1952, which was passed over presidential veto.

16. Donald F. Lach, *Asia in the Making of Europe,* I, Part II (Chicago, 1965), 691.

17. Charles H. Robinson, *History of Christian Missions* (New York, 1915), p. 53.

18. Macdonald, *Trade Politics,* pp. ix–x, italics added.

19. The Jerusalem Conference of the I.M.C., *The Christian Life and Message in Relation to Non-Christian Systems of Thought and Life,* I (New York and London, 1928), 366.

20. H. A. R. Gibb, "Near Eastern Perspective: The Present and the Future,"

in Young, ed., *Near Eastern Culture and Society*, p. 230.

21. Arnold J. Toynbee, *A Study of History*, abridgement of Vols. I–VI by D. C. Somervell (New York, 1947), p. 36.

22. Barbara Ward, "A Summing Up," in Cora DuBois, *et al.*, *The East and West Must Meet: A Symposium* (East Lansing, Mich., 1959), p. 130.

23. Cora DuBois, "The Cultural Interplay Between East and West," in *ibid.*, p. 10.

24. Walter Lippmann, "Superpowers Can't Govern World," *Chicago Sun-Times*, July 23, 1967.

# The Geography of China

Norton Ginsburg

I t is paradoxical that India is known as a "subcontinent" in Asia, when China is twice as large, and the term "subcontinent" is never used to describe it. Perhaps the reason is India's separation from the rest of Asia by formidable, though not impenetrable, orographic barriers, of which the Himalayan mountain system is the most conspicuous. Yet China too is separated from the rest of Asia by similar, though perhaps less imposing, physiographic elements. To the southwest is the Tibetan plateau and the same Himalayan ranges south of it which mark India's northern boundaries; to the west are the high Pamirs—roof of the world—and their derivative ranges, the T'ien Shan and Karakorum, as well as lesser ranges, which encompass great deserts; to the northwest lies the Mongolian plateau, much of which is occupied by the Gobi—the Great Desert—and by extensive high steppes; and to the north is the formidable *taiga* of eastern Siberia. Although all of these natural frontier zones have long impeded access to China, they have never substantially prevented it, and, in fact, from very ancient times the passages through the western mountains and the Mongolian steppes and deserts have been well-used passages which linked China with the lands of the Middle and Near East and the Mediterranean. Subcontinentality, therefore, appears to have been more a matter of landward inaccessibility than of territorial size alone.

By any standard, China is huge, with its 3,692,000 square miles being slightly larger than the United States. Although commonly described as being in East Asia, as opposed to South and Southeast Asia, China extends westward almost as far as all of India, and it shares a short stretch of boundary with Afghanistan. From south to north it covers thirty-six degrees of latitude, from 18° North to 54° North, or the equivalent in North America of the range from Jamaica to Newfoundland. Thus, like all large countries, but even more than some, China encompasses an enormous variety of natural conditions, and these are associated with an equal heterogeneity of land uses and occupance patterns.

These patterns can be grouped into those that are basically Chinese and those that are not. The eastern third of the country has long been occupied by so-called Han-Chinese, persons of Chinese culture and language; the western two-thirds has long been occupied by non-Chinese peoples, although Chinese settlers have made their way to the far corners of contemporary Chinese territory and in increasing numbers in recent years. Thus there are two Chinas, one almost exclusively Chinese, another not. For centuries, moreover, despite the ebb and flow of Chinese power, the frontiers of China, though not specifically her formal boundaries, have remained relatively stable.

It is true, however, that China has occupied territories beyond her present boundaries. These lie chiefly to the west and northwest, rather than to the south and southeast. In Southeast Asia, only what is now northern and central Vietnam had ever been under Chinese hegemony for any length of time; but under the Manchu or Ch'ing Dynasty, which lasted from 1644 until 1911, China also controlled large territories which are now included within the Soviet Union and the Mongolian People's Republic. These included parts

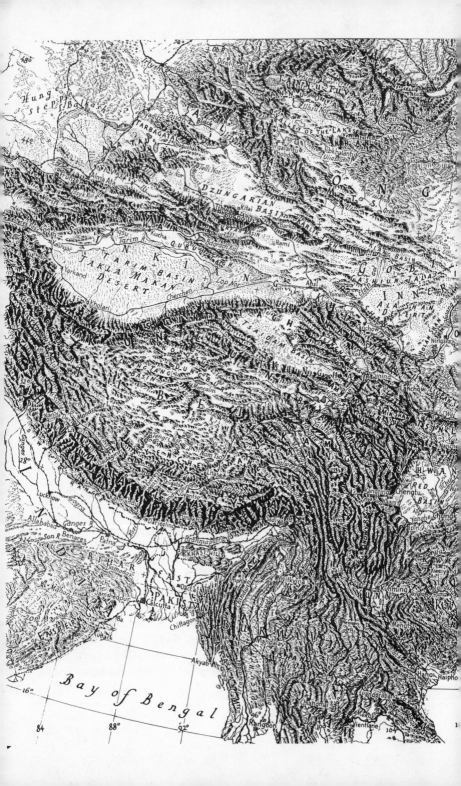

# Landforms of China

Scale 0 |———|———|———|———| 500 Miles

by Erwin Raisz 1955

*from G.B. Cressey: Land of the 500 Million,*
*McGraw-Hill Book Co, 1955*

of Soviet Central Asia as well as most of central and eastern Siberia south of the *taiga* and the Soviet Maritime provinces. Most of these territories are considered by Chinese today as *terrae irridentae,* lost territories to be regained at some future date. On the other hand, Chinese formal power never extended into South Asia nor directly for any length of time into other parts of Southeast Asia, although several of the Southeast Asian states such as Burma and Thailand, as well as Korea, were long regarded as client states, tributary to the Chinese court. In this sense, the Chinese regarded their country as the Central State *(Chung-kuo),* that is, central to a system of loosely held territories or tributary states which behaved as satellites to the largest, longest-lived empire the world has ever known. Even today China claims special interests in these former tributary areas, and these interests extend also over the adjacent seas, not only the East China Sea but also the South China Sea over most of which China still claims hegemony.

ASPECTS OF PHYSICAL GEOGRAPHY

*Surface Configuration.* The grain of country in China for the most part is latitudinal rather than meridional. This is a consequence of the physiographic structure and the broad hydrologic patterns associated with it. On the national scale, orography displays a marked east-west orientation. The great Plateau of Tibet, with an average elevation of over twelve thousand feet, itself is elongated from west to east, and it is associated with ranges such as the Karakorum, K'un-lun, and Altyn Tagh which border it on the north and which also have this orientation. To the north of these, but spinning out from the same Pamir Knot to which the Karakoram are tied, is the T'ien Shan, or Mountains of Heaven, and between them lies the elongated Tarim basin of western Hsinchiang. North of the T'ien Shan is the Dzungarian basin, roughly paralleling the mountains, and to the north of it the Altai ranges of western Mongolia. The Mongolian plateau itself extends over thirty degrees of longitude and extends well into Chinese territory. Perhaps most important is the extension eastward of the K'un-lun and Altyn Tagh ranges into China Proper at about 35° North Latitude as the Ch'in Ling, which forms a major physiographic and climatic divide between the northern and southern portions of eastern China. In Far West China, then, a traverse from south to north, beginning with the northern slopes of the Great Himalaya, would show: highest mountains—plateau-*cum*-mountains—high mountains—basin—high mountains—basin—plateau—low mountains. This descriptive model overlooks such important physiographic features in the area as the Tsaidam basin northeast of the Tibetan plateau, and the below-sea-level Turfan depression at the eastern tip of the T'ien Shan, nor does it include reference to the corridor which lies between the northeastern Tibetan plateau and the Mongolian plateau, the so-called Kan-su corridor. All of these also are elongated from east to west and serve to accentuate the predominant grain of country in the West.

The Tibetan plateau extends eastward to about 102° East Longitude, near the western border of Ssu-ch'uan Province, but well before that meridian its grain has taken on a southerly component as a series of ranges thrust southward from it to form the highlands of the several mainland Southeast Asian countries. Eastward into China itself, the High Plateau and its surface ranges descend into southern China via a series of plateaux steps—the Yün-nan and Kuei-chou plateaux—which in turn merge eastward into the hills of southern China, sometimes known collectively as the Nan Shan, the Mountains of the South, and thence into the sea.

In middle China, the Ch'in Ling extension of the northern edge of the Tibetan highlands carries eastward through a series of rapidly declining ranges, such as the Ta-pieh Shan, well into the lower Yangtze basin. To the north, two main meridionally trending lines of highlands appear. The western of these marks the eastern edge of the Mongolian plateau and is marked by two north-south ranges, the T'ai-hang Shan just west of the North China plain and the Ta-hsing-an (the Great Khingan) range west of the Central Manchurian lowland. The eastern line of highlands runs northwest-southeast along the Manchurian-Korean frontier through the Liao-tung peninsula under the Yellow Sea and into eastern Shan-tung Province.

The eastern third of China, that which is occupied predominantly by Chinese, is dominated by two great river systems which have their origins in the Tibetan plateau. The northernmost of these is the Huang Ho basin, covering an area of 298,000 square miles, the master stream of which is 2,900 miles long. The Huang (Yellow) rises in the eastern portion of the K'un-lun range, where it is snow-fed, and flows northward then eastward and southward in a great bend that encloses the Ordos desert. During most of its upper course, once it leaves the highlands, the Huang is an exotic stream which receives no major tributaries. As it approaches the Ch'in Ling and just before its diversion by that range eastward, it receives a major tributary on its left bank, the Fen, which flows southward through central Shan-hsi Province, and then the historic Wei, the valley of which runs just north of and parallel to the Ch'in Ling. These tributaries drain extensive areas of loess, or wind-blown silt, deposits, and they carry heavy loads which they pass on to the Huang as it turns eastward through narrow gorges for about one hundred miles before it debouches onto the North China or Yellow plain, a great alluvial lowland largely of its own making. Thence it flows northeastward across the plain until it enters the Po Hai or Gulf of Chih-li, a westward extension of the Yellow Sea.

The Huang is an extraordinary river in every respect. Not only is it long and possessed of an enormous catchment area, but it also is characterized by extreme variations of flow. Most of its catchment area receives less than twenty inches of rainfall each year, and that precipitation is extremely variable, though concentrated during the summer months. The maximum discharge recorded is 883,000 cubic feet per second, the minimum 8,650 c.f.s.—both at the point near its entry onto the plain. The extreme range of discharge marks the propensity of the river to flood once it reaches the plain, and it does. More than fifteen hundred floods have been recorded over a three-thousand-year period, some of them devastating. For this reason the river has been named "China's Sorrow." The flood potential is increased by the fact that the bed (or beds) of the river rises above the level of the plain, since it is the bed of the stream that receives much of the deposition that results when the river's gradient decreases as it reaches the plain. With each flood has come huge deposits of alluvium, mostly fluvial-worked loess. Normally the river carries about two billion tons of silt annually, and at low water the solid matter in the stream may account for up to 46 per cent of its weight. Deposition of this silt in the long run has resulted in the rapid extension of the Yellow plain and some renewal of fertility, but in the short run it also has meant destruction of crops and fields. So unstable is the lower Huang that its mouth has shifted as much as five hundred miles from north to south at various periods in its known history, that is, from north of the Shantung peninsula to south of it and back again. In 1938 the great stream was deflected to the south by the Chinese in a misplaced effort to delay the advance of Japanese forces moving southward from T'ien-ching (Tientsin) and Pei-ching (Peking); and it flowed southeastward into the Huai river system and thence through a series of lakes and the Grand Canal down into the Yangtze drainage area. In 1947 the river was again deflected northeastward into its present channel.

From very ancient times the natural levees of the river have been raised by artificial levees built on top of them, and, in addition, dikes several miles away from the main stream at any given time also have been constructed in an attempt to contain the river. But these efforts have been only palliatives and indeed have contributed to the further instability of the river, since the partial containment of the stream through levees and dikes has resulted in the even more rapid elevation of the stream bed and thereby an increase in flood potentials. For this reason, the present regime has placed high priority on the construction of a system of multi-purpose river-basin facilities designed to control floods, generate hydroelectric power, expand the irrigated area, and improve the navigability of what has been in large part a river unfit for navigation. A series of forty-six dams is projected, several of the smaller of which have been completed and the largest of which probably has been completed at San-men (Three Gates) in the gorge area just west of the plain; but all of these are threatened with rapid silting and with consequent shortness of life, until the entire system has been completed and supported by extensive programs of reforestation and other types of soil-erosion control in the uplands through which the tributaries Wei and Fen flow.

The second great river of China also flows from west to east, also rises in the eastern Tibetan plateau, also is characterized by great variations in flow, also is associated with great lowlands, densely occupied and productive; but many of its characteristics are markedly different from those of the Huang. The Yangtze is an even longer stream than the Huang, with 3,470 miles, and its catchment area of 706,000 square miles is much larger. That area receives considerably greater average precipitation (38 inches annually) than the Huang's; the volume of meltwater from glaciers and surface snow is greater; and the great size of the catchment area, with several very large tributary streams such as the Han from the north and the Yuan, Hsiang, and Kan from the south, has meant a considerably more even flow of water into the main stream. Furthermore, there are two natural lakes associated with the right bank (southern) tributaries, Tung-t'ing lake and Po-yang lake, which act as natural flood detention reservoirs when the river is high, expanding as the river discharge increases, contracting as it declines. In general, too, the silt load is less than that of the Huang, and the Yangtze does not flow in an elevated bed. Nevertheless, the flood potential of the stream also is very high, and a maximum flow of 2.5 million c.f.s. has been recorded at Wu-han. When the normal flow is enlarged by heavy rainfall associated with the passage of weak fronts in mid-summer, the results can be catastrophic. Thus, flood control also is a major problem in the Yangtze basin, and over two thousand miles of dikes have been constructed over the centuries, augmented recently, to help prevent or lessen flood damage, together with flood-retention basins to supplement those provided by nature. Plans also exist to construct a gigantic dam in the Yangtze gorges above I-chang, which would even out the seasonal flow, provide flood control and hydroelectric energy, and above all improve navigability. Even at present, the Yangtze, unlike the Huang, is navigable for smaller ocean-going vessels much of the year as far as Wu-han, and at high water sizable river crafts can pass through the gorges westward, despite the swift currents, into Ssu-ch'uan Province to Ch'ung-ch'ing (Chungking); but at low water the gorges can be passed only by shallow-draft vessels drawn by trackers on the banks. Because of its great width and depth in its middle and lower course, the Yangtze has been a major barrier to overland communications throughout Chinese history, and not until 1957 was it crossed by a railway and highway bridge at Wu-han. On the other hand, its year-round navigability, at least to the gorges, for smaller craft throughout the year has made it the major line of entry into what is termed Middle China, one of the richest areas of the country and roughly coterminous with the boundaries of the Yangtze drainage system other than its headwaters.

Between the two great master streams is a lesser one, the Huai, about 680 miles long, which rises in the eastward extensions of the Ch'in Ling and flows across a portion of the North China plain south of the Shantung peninsula. Although the Huai drainage area is estimated at about 67,000 square miles, in fact that area is barely distinguishable from either the Huang drainage area to the north or the Yangtze area to the south. At times the Huai has carried much of the water of the Huang and become a distributary for it when the Huang has swung its lower courses and mouth southeastward. At other times Huai waters have flowed southward through a number of lakes and man-made channels, such as the Imperial Canal, into the Yangtze estuary. The Huai is the nearest thing to a stream that is not a stream, to a drainage basin that is not a basin at all; it illustrates the difficulties of separating the North China plain from the lower Yangtze lowland to the south. However, its crucial position between the two, the longevity and intensity of occupance within the area concerned, and the ever-present problems of flood and drainage, especially following the deflection of the Huang back to its northeasterly course in 1947, have made the Huai a particular focus of attention for the Communist regime after its rise to power in 1949. The Huai was given the highest priority in river-basin development in 1950, and thereafter its drainage system was transformed into a largely artificial one, dotted with barrages, highly canalized, with an extensive dike system, and with a largely new outlet cut through to the sea.

In the far north there is only one stream at all comparable to the Huang and the Yangtze, the Amur or Hei-lung river, but it is shared with the Soviet Union, as it, together with its right-bank tributary the Ussuri, forms much of the boundary between northern Manchuria and eastern Siberia, and its lower course is entirely within Russian territory. The Amur headwaters rise on the eastern slopes of the Yablonovyy mountains in Siberia and on the eastern Mongolian plateau. It flows eastward in an S-shaped course which brings it to the Okhotsk Sea after 2,700 miles. The river is navigable for about 1,700 miles during the summer months, but it is closed by ice during the cold northern winters. Most important from the

Chinese standpoint is its longest right-bank tributary, the Sung-hua or Sungari river, 1,200 miles in length, which drains central and northern Manchuria, is a major navigation route for summer traffic, and also is a major source of hydroelectric energy from a great dam built by the Japanese before the Pacific War, upstream from Chi-lin (Kirin).

In the far South the major drainage area is that of the Hsi river which rises in eastern Yün-nan Province and flows southeastward for 1,200 miles into the South China Sea just west of Hongkong. Its lower course, after it is joined near Canton (Kuang-chou) by the Pei and Tung rivers, is known as the Pearl river. Although a lesser stream than the others, it still carries enormous quantities of water during the wet season. On the other hand, it is associated with no large alluvial lowlands as are the Huang and the Yangtze, although in its lower course it drains a substantial lowland broken by hilly outliers and crossed by innumerable canalized distributaries.

Associated with these and lesser streams are the several great lowlands of eastern China, where most of the population of the country and most of China's agricultural activity is concentrated. All but one of these major fluvial lowlands is alluvial and aggradational in nature. The largest by far is the North China plain, largely the product of the Yellow river, the Huang, and sometimes known as the Yellow plain. Covering an area of 125,000 square miles, the plain is composed of yellow-grey sediments in places three thousand feet or more in depth and derived from loessial materials carried down by the river and its tributaries from the uplands of its middle course. These materials originally were of high natural fertility, though they have been used so long that their fertility has declined substantially, and near the sea intrusions of brackish water have made cultivation difficult. Yet this remains one of the great agricultural areas of China and potentially the most productive.

The middle and lower Yangtze lowlands also are alluvial, are composed of somewhat less fertile materials, but still highly productive for agriculture, and cover an estimated 76,000 square miles. Except for the Yangtze delta, however, these lowlands are fragmented by hilly outliers of the southern China hill lands to the south and the extensions of the Ch'in Ling to the north. Between the Yellow and Yangtze lowlands are the Huai lowlands which form a region of transition from northern to more southerly climatic and agricultural conditions.

In the south are the Hsi river lowlands, the chief portion of which, the Canton delta, covers some three thousand square miles and is densely settled and developed. Along the southeastern coast are a number of lesser lowlands associated with the four principal rivers that drain the southern hill lands, but none of these is comparable to the others noted.

Among all the major lowlands, only one is predominantly alluvial—the Central Manchurian, or Liao-Sung, plain of the Northeast. Covering about 138,000 square miles, this lowland is drained by two river systems separated by an inconspicuous divide, the Sung-hua or Sungari, a tributary of the Amur, to the north and the smaller Liao to the south. Most of it is an erosional plain rather than an alluvial one, and the lowland soils of central and northern Manchuria are largely grassland soils similar to those in parts of the Midwestern United States. But the lower Liao basin is alluvial, and it is interesting to note that this was the area known as the "Chinese Pale," the part of Manchuria long settled by Chinese as far back as the Han period.

Two other major areas in the eastern third of China require special mention. The first of these is the so-called Red basin of Ssu-ch'uan, drained by the Yangtze and certain of its tributaries, and located west of the Yangtze gorges. Encompassing an area of about 75,000 square miles, the basin is far from flat, but instead has rugged terrain and high relief associated with the broad, deep-cut valleys of four rivers (therefore the name Ssu-ch'uan or "four rivers") which drain southward into the east-flowing Yangtze. The term "red" is derived from the deep reddish sandstones widely distributed throughout the basin. For the most part its elevations range downward from about three thousand to one thousand feet, but it is surrounded by mountains on all sides—on the west by the Min Shan and the Azure Wall mountains, of which Minya Konka (24,900 feet) is perhaps the best known, on the north by the Mi-tsang and the Ta-pa Shan just south of the Ch'in Ling, and to the south by the highlands marking the edges of the Yün-nan and Kuei-chou plateaux. To the east are the Yangtze gorges.

The second major area, other than the lowlands, worthy of note is the loess highlands of Kan-su, Shen-hsi, and Shan-hsi, and western Ho-non provinces, extending over some 120,000 square miles and covered by a mantle of fine aeolian silt, or loess, which is believed to have originated either in the Gobi or in the nearer Ordos. The rate of its deposition probably was greatest in the immediate post-glacial period, but it still is going on. Deposits vary from a few feet to over 250 feet, and the mantle covers a highly irregular subsurface of which most had been uplands of three to four thousand feet elevation. This area is the source of most of the silt carried and partly deposited downstream by the Yellow river. The loess itself, calcareous and rich in humus, is fertile, though prone to severe erosion and vertical cleavage, and that in an area where precipitation is for the most part well below twenty inches annually and highly erratic. Despite these limitations, it, like the other areas referred to, is a long and densely settled portion of the Chinese ecumene.

*Climate.* The climate of China is as diversified as its size and physiographic diversity would suggest. Its primary characteristics can be discussed under the following headings: latitude, continentality (including air-mass analysis), surface configuration, and maritime influence.

Perhaps the most readily comprehensible element in explaining China's climatic variations is latitudinal range. As expected in a country extending from 18° North Latitude to 54° North, temperature differences are marked from north to south. Although midsummer temperatures are relatively high through the country, except at higher elevations, winter temperatures vary enormously from north to south. In northern Manchuria, for example, winters are exceedingly harsh, and mean temperatures for January may be below zero. In the North China plain, winters are harsh again, but less so, and January temperatures are below freezing. In the central and lower Yangtze basin, mean January temperatures are above freezing, about 40° F, and in southern China, say at Canton, they are in the mid-fifties. Similarly, growing seasons vary from about three months in the northern Manchurian lowland to about seven months in the North China plain, eight to nine months in the Lower Yangtze area, and eleven to twelve months in southernmost China. These generalizations hold chiefly for eastern China.

Western China displays markedly greater continentality and therefore greater ranges of seasonal temperatures, but these are also affected by altitudinal differences. In eastern China during the winter months the area is dominated by outflows of cold to cool continental air which emanates from a semi-permanent high pressure belt formed over Lake Baykal and eastern Siberia. Conversely, in summer most of the area is dominated by tropical maritime air moving in two major streams from the south and from the southeast. These are associated with the break-up of the intertropical front as it moves northward from the equator in the spring and with the shift of the northeast trade winds of the western Pacific to a southeasterly direction. The tropical maritime air masses, however, move less forcefully toward the continental low pressure area over the Gobi in summer than do the continental flows outward from the high-pressure belt in winter. Thus, some mechanisms are required to release moisture from the humid air as it moves into the warm interior and as its capacity for retaining moisture increases. These mechanisms are of two sorts. The first is elevation, and in selected areas orographic precipitation is common. The second and more important is frontogenesis and cyclonic air movements, and these are associated with latitudinal shifts in the eastward-moving jet stream which flows at altitudes over ten thousand feet over most of Asia. In summer the jet stream has moved far enough southward to have been bifurcated by the Tibetan plateau, one stream moving south of the plateau, the other north. Both streams converge over Middle China, and this convergence is associated with numerous cyclonic movements through the Yangtze valley and out over East China and toward Japan. In the course of frontogenesis associated with these movements, warm air is lifted over intruding cooler air from the north, and the result is massive precipitation. In winter the jet stream moves northward and very little maritime air reaches the continent, even though frontogenesis takes place as cold continental air moves outward and eastward over northern and northeastern China and the Sea of Japan. Thus the summers are wet and the winters are dry, although not absolutely so, and snow is common enough in northern and northeastern China, even at lower altitudes. On the other hand, except for the highlands, most of the Far West is dry in winter and indeed most of the year, but what moisture reaches it is more likely to be associated with North Atlantic cool maritime air that has crossed Europe and western Asia or with cold maritime air moved southward from the Arctic. In addition, part of southwestern China, Yün-nan and Ssu-ch'uan, seem to draw much of their moisture from tropical maritime air of Indian Ocean origin which has crossed Assam and Burma into China.

These basic elements are conditioned by surface configuration. In the simplest case, the Tibetan plateau resembles the tundra of northern Siberia in climate by virtue of its elevation, as do the higher portions of the mountain ranges of western China. Lowland basins protected from air movements by prominent orographic barriers, such as the Tarim basin, are rain-shadow as well as continental deserts. More important, in eastern China, the Ch'in Ling and associated ranges act as a prominent barrier to the movement of the relatively thin tongues of cold continental air that move southeastward from the Baykal high-pressure zone in winter. Thus, the areas to the south of them, conspicuously the Ssu-ch'uan basin but also most of southeastern China, on the average display milder winter temperatures than they would otherwise. On the other hand, these ranges have a much less significant effect on summer precipitation for the areas north of them. Equally important is the lack of a north-south trending lowland in southern China, similar to that of the Mississippi lowland in North America, that would provide ready access into the interior of eastern China from the south. Here the east-west grain of country again plays an important role. Finally, the seas off the coasts of northern China are shallow continental-shelf seas, the temperatures of which vary as does land, and in summer they have a warming effect on in-drifting tropical maritime air from the southeast, which makes for greater stability of that air. Thus, in climatic terms, many coastal stations in northern China display characteristics of inland stations; T'ien-ching, for example, lies about five hundred miles from the Pacific edge of the continental shelf East China sea, and is in effect, then, five hundred miles "inland." As compared with the south, relatively little unstable air reaches northern China even in the summer months, although that is the period during which almost all precipitation takes place.

Direct maritime influences are strong in the coastal areas particularly south of the Huai river. These are of two sorts. First, the warm Japan Current, analogous to the Gulf Stream of North America, washes the shores of southeastern China and Taiwan, and exerts a markedly ameliorative effect on winter temperatures. Thus, Taiwan, cut through by the Tropic of Cancer, has a year-round growing season. Second, between May and November, but particularly in the early autumn, southeastern China is affected by typhonic storms which bring heavy rainfall to areas as much as several hundred miles away from the eyes of the storms. Thus many stations show late summer or early fall rainfall maxima, even though they may seldom be hit directly by typhoons.

Finally, it is well to recall that rainfall variability is a partial function both of low rainfall and of greater continentality, although variability occurs everywhere. Thus, in areas where rainfall is light, as in the North China plain and the loess highlands, variability is very great, and the threat of famine is ever present. In the desert and steppe interior and Far West, the range of variability is even greater, but agriculture is less directly affected because unirrigated cultivation is uncommon there.

*Soils and Vegetation.* The soils in China that count the most are, for the most part, "nonsoils"; that is, they are classified under the International Soil Classification System as "azonal." These are in contrast to the "zonal" categories, each of which is identified by a well-developed soil profile generally formed in place and not unduly influenced by local parent materials, slope, and drainage conditions, but reflecting prevailing climatic conditions, age, and dominant vegetation. So-called "alluvial soils" fall into the azonal category. These are in fact more soil materials than soils; they lack well-developed profiles and are transported rather than formed in place. They also tend to be relatively fertile, since they often are renewed by flooding. Most of the best and most intensively used soils in China fall into this category. All of the North China plain, the Middle and Lower Yangtze plain, the Hsi lowland, and the lower Liao valley, as well as countless lesser floodplains, are examples. They probably account for less than 15 per cent of the total land area of the country. Of course, not all alluvials are alike. Those derived from loess, for example, are likely to be more fertile, especially in drier areas, than those derived from the weathering of crystalline rock, but such differences vary in importance with the length of cultivation and the crop associations used. In addition, loess "soils" also are azonal, but rather than of fluvial origin, they are aeolian. Rich in calcium, the deep, unstratified loessial materials permit cultivation for indefinite periods with little loss of inherent fertility.

In the Central Manchurian lowland, soils have been formed under grass, are deep, dark, calcareous, and productive, similar to the prairie soils of the Corn Belt in the United States, though not as rich. Other grassland soils, formed under drier conditions, are found beyond the Great Wall northwest of the Loess highlands and the North China plain. Like those of the Great Plains in North America, these grassland soils present both opportunities and risks for continuous cultivation. Beyond them are soils formed under dry steppe and desert conditions, potentially cultivable, but not without controlled irrigation and even then subject to salification and water-logging. In the desert interior of the western basins, such as the Tarim, alluvial materials in compound deltaic fans of streams drain-ing the slopes of the T'ien Shan and Karakoram ranges, form the basis for productive oasis agriculture which depends wholly on irrigation.

The remaining soils of China were formed under forest cover. In the north these for the most part are podzolics of various colors, depths, and fertility, and they are little used by virtue largely of inaccessibility. In the south, however, are extensive areas of slope covered by red and yellow lateritics, similar to those in the south-eastern United States, rich in iron and aluminum acidic oxides, and requiring careful management to maintain productivity and resist erosion. In some cases, parent materials strongly affect both the podzolics and the lateritics, as in the case of the so-called Brown Soils of the Shantung uplands and the Purple Soils of the Ssu-ch'uan basin.

The natural vegetation of eastern China is difficult to determine in much of the region, so long and intensively has it been utilized. The natural vegetation of the alluvial lowlands probably was marsh and grass, although some evidence of forest cover also exists, par-ticularly in the North China plain. That of central Manchuria undoubtedly was tall grass, blending into shorter grasses in the drier areas to the west and on the Mongolian plateau. The loess lands may have been grass-covered, but there is evidence also of deciduous forests. The forests of Manchuria are largely coniferous, especially at higher altitudes, with larch, fir, spruce, and pines. Farther south, such forests as remain are largely deciduous except at higher altitudes; and in the south these become increasingly broad-leaved evergreen forests, with conifers at higher altitudes. In places where rainfall is particularly heavy in the far south, on the Hai-nan and Taiwan islands, tropical rain forest appears, but with species such as the camphor tree not normally found in it. In the highlands, mountain grasslands also are found, but these are of uncertain origin. In the Far West, xerophytic and short-grass vegetation is most common, except on higher slopes where coniferous forests dominate, as is the case in the western United States for example; and in much of the Tibetan plateau, stunted tundra vegetation is characteristic.

Only a small proportion, perhaps 5 per cent, of all of China's territory is now forested, whereas it is estimated that perhaps half might have been under forest at one time and about 30 per cent would be desirable for reasonable supplies of firewood to be available and for proper soil and water management.

## LAND USE AND AGRICULTURE

Most of the land of China is not used or is used sparingly. If this seems paradoxical, it is because what is used is on the whole used very intensively, but only a small proportion of the total land area of the country actually is under cultivation, and agriculture is the most extensive user of land in any country. The key lies in the characteristics of China's resource endowment. Most of its territory is too dry, too cold, too hot, too high, or too wet for continuous and productive human occupance. Ninety-five per cent of the cultivated area of the country lies east of a line drawn from Tsitsihar (Ch'i-ch'i-ha-erh) in northern Manchuria to K'un-ming in Yün-nan Province. This is eastern China, and within it is the Chinese ecumene.

The land that is intensively used amounts only to about 10 per cent of the area of the country, and is that associated with alluvial lowlands of the river basins large and small, with the erosional plains of central Manchuria, with the loess lands of Shan-hsi and

Shen-hsi, and with the Red basin of Ssu-ch'uan. Particularly in
southern China higher hill slopes also are used, though not intensively, for forage, firewood, and brushwood, and for some shifting
cultivation. There, natural cover has long since been removed, but
little is regularly grown there to replace it, with the exception of
tea in the south and the rare stands of planted timber forced upon
the peasantry by authoritarian governments. Some slopelands also
are used, however, for regular cultivation—lower slopes in many
areas for dry crops of grain or vegetables; higher slopes as in the
Red basin and on the Kuei-chou plateau where the growing season
is long and the returns on dry cultivation relatively high.

Eastern China can be divided into a number of agricultural regions based on the types of crop associations found. The primary
division, however, is between the north and the south, and the line
of division is approximately that of the Ch'in Ling and its southeasterly extensions, or roughly the 33rd parallel. North of that line
wheat, *kao-liang,* and other dry grains predominate; south of that
line rice is the grain of primary importance. Thus it appears that
China can be divided not only into an eastern ecumene and a much
larger West, but also the ecumene itself can be divided into a North
and a South on the basis of the importance of rice in the agricultural
system. Of course, there are overlappings of crops in all the major
agricultural regions, and changes have taken place of uncertain dimensions since the basic survey of Chinese agriculture was made
by J. Lossing Buck in the early 1930's, but the broad regional
patterns remain clear.

*North China.* North China is a region in which dry-cropping, as
opposed to irrigation, prevails. The basic grains are wheat, both
spring and winter, *kao-liang* (a grain sorghum), small millets, and
maize. In the driest areas northwest of the Great Wall, spring wheat
is the chief crop. In the next drier areas, the small millets prevail as
a summer crop, but where moisture and fertilizer availability permit, winter wheat also will be raised. *Kao-liang* is found almost
everywhere, and it is one of the two main crops in both the North
China plain and in the Central Manchurian lowland, in the first case
in association with winter wheat, in the second with soybeans. On
the other hand, soybeans also are widely grown as a summer crop,
and corn is of increasing importance in some droughty areas. Other
crops of lesser importance are nonetheless worth noting. Cotton is

a major crop in the southern portions of the northern zone. Rice is widely grown on the North China plain and in Manchuria, where short-maturing varieties provide generous yields, but regional convention militates against its cultivation, and it is a water-hungry crop in areas where water is scarce. Peanuts, sesame seeds, and cotton seeds are important sources of cooking oils, in addition to soybeans. Vegetables are grown everywhere. Although double-cropping is rare in Manchuria and in the drier areas, it is not so uncommon on the North China plain, where summer vegetables may rotate with winter wheat, the chief cash crop of the area. Some irrigation is practiced, chiefly from wells, and increased acreages of irrigated land are likely from the major river-basin developments on the Yellow river and the Huai. Cotton and tobacco, as important cash crops, are likely to be the chief initial recipients of benefits from these developments, but enlarged rice acreages may also be a consequence.

The sweet potato has become an increasingly important crop in much of the region other than Manchuria, and especially in cultivated hill lands like those in Shan-tung. A poor man's crop, it nevertheless compares favorably with rice and maize as a source of carbohydrates and can be raised on relatively steep slopes if necessary.

*South China.* In South China, rice is the single most important crop. Double-cropping ratios are everywhere high and provide a measure of the intensity with which land is cultivated. As one moves from the Huai river toward the Yangtze, winter wheat alternates with rice on summer-irrigated fields. But cotton (on the saline soils near the sea), peanuts, rape, sesame, and soybeans, among the oil-producing crops, and tobacco, corn, barley, and sweet potatoes also are important, although *kao-liang* and the small millets are not. South of the Yangtze double-cropping ratios approach 200, wheat declines in importance as does corn in the lowlands at least, but oil seeds, tea on slopelands, beans and peas, and sweet potatoes continue to be important. In the far southern areas the double-cropping of rice becomes common, double-cropping ratios frequently exceed 200, and controlled irrigation, usually from traditional small-scale sources, is practiced wherever possible. Some terracing of both paddy lands and uplands becomes an important part of the landscape, and citrus fruit, tung (oil) trees, and tea also are part of the crop associations. In general, the size of farms in the pre-Communist period decreased as one moved southward, and it appears probable that even under a collective system of agriculture this is still the case. In Taiwan, double-cropping of paddy is ubiquitous, and in southwestern Taiwan it is rotated with sugar cane in a system of small holdings linked by contract with sugar mills operated by a government corporation.

Conditions in the South are, of course, exceedingly diverse. In Ssu-ch'uan, with its growing season of more than three hundred days despite its inland situation, is found one of the great rice granaries of China. Terracing is conspicuous and irrigation ubiquitous. The double-cropping ratio approaches 200, with paddy the chief summer crop and wheat the chief winter grain, but maize, barley, and sweet potatoes are other major sources of carbohydrates, and, as in the Southeast, mulberry is important for silkworm feed. On the southwestern plateaux of Yün-nan and Kuei-chou, where there is relatively little arable land available, some double-cropping of rice is practiced, but double-cropping more commonly is that of paddy alternating with other grains or oilseeds and vegetables during the drier part of the year.

In all regions livestock are an important adjunct to cultivation. Swine are found everywhere, as are poultry, especially ducks, chickens, and geese, but also turkeys. Cattle, horses, and mules in the North and West are beasts of burden, and beef is not a common part of the diet anywhere in China. In the Far West, sheep and goats are widely distributed, as are horses and Bactrian camels as beasts of burden, and in the south the water buffalo is the most common type of farm work animal. Animal manure is a common form of natural fertilizer on the farm, and the cost of this valuable material is low, since most animals that provide it, such as swine, are scavengers or virtually so. One of the appeals of raising sweet potatoes is the use of the vines themselves as swine food.

*Agricultural Production and Organization.* The productivity of Chinese agriculture is high and has been for centuries. Careful husbandry, as compared with Southeast Asia and India, have made for yields perhaps two to three times as high as in those areas; but when compared with Japan, yields per crop are modest, perhaps two-thirds as high at best. On the other hand, where rice is double-cropped, as in southernmost China, total per-unit area yields are as high or higher than those in Japan. Thus, raising productivity in Chinese agriculture on a unit area basis may be difficult, since the existing level is already high; but improved strains, better water control, the selective use of mechanical aids to improve labor efficiency, particularly at planting and harvesting times, and the increased use of commercial fertilizers to supplement the traditional use of animal and human wastes and green manures, may well lead to substantial increases in total output, and at the same time release some labor for employment in other types of occupations, whether as unskilled workers in public works projects or as skilled workers in the expanding industrial sector of the economy.

It is probable that about 200 million metric tons of grains and starchy tubers are produced annually in China, although precise data are not available. Of this tonnage, rice probably accounts for about 40 per cent, wheat for some 25 per cent, other grains for about 25 per cent, and sweet potatoes and other starchy tubers for the remainder. Whatever the correct data, China is self-sufficient, though at a low level of consumption, in foodstuffs, and in recent years has even been an exporter; but then her food imports always have been minute when compared with her enormous production.

In pre-Communist China, agriculture was, for the most part, associated with small farms, individually owned, of about five acres in the North and half that area in the South, organized into agglomerated villages, fairly evenly spaced, where surface conditions permitted, over the surface of the land. Tenancy was common, but higher in some areas, particularly in the South, than in others. Rural indebtedness was high almost everywhere. To a considerable degree modern public works for agriculture were few, and the country lived off the enormous capital investment in such works made over millennia of Chinese history. The system was particularly vulnerable to natural disaster, and flood, drought, and famine, depending on locale, were major apocalyptic horsemen clouding the face of China.

Transportation and marketing systems were poorly developed by modern standards. Surplus foodstuffs from any one area could not readily be moved to areas of shortage. Marketing organization, in part a function of administrative organization, was associated with a honeycomb spatial structure in which each cluster of villages was relatively isolated from all the others and from the urban centers.

Only near these centers and in certain of the eastern provinces of what has been called the "Maritime Frontier" region was this structure modified.

The Communist regime moved very rapidly toward the collectivization of agriculture, partly no doubt for political expediency and control, certainly also to lessen the vulnerability of the system by enlarging the basic productive units and increasing their capabilities to improve infrastructure and take advantage of opportunities to produce more. In the course of this, the traditional marketing system, inadequate though it might have been, was adversely affected. Yet by 1958 almost all of rural China had been organized into some 24,000 communes, in effect, collective farms, which possessed both economic and administrative functions and thus conserved, among other things, scarce administrative manpower. Within several years most of these entities proved to be too large for efficient production, and their number was increased to 75,000. Moreover, most basic productive functions were delegated to so-called production brigades *within* the communes, each involving about one hundred families and two to five hundred acres, which are roughly equal to the size of pre-collectivized villages in many parts of the country.

It is still unclear what communization has meant for agricultural production in China. Certainly it has made for great control of production by provincial and central authorities, although private plots and local periodic markets still appear to be part of the commune scene. Theoretically, the greater control over productive resources by the commune ought to make for efficiencies in agricultural activity, especially in the development of infrastructural facilities such as irrigation and flood-control works, and in the mobilization and use of fertilizers. In fact, however, there is virtually no evidence to show any relationship one way or another, except that, despite some bad years of drought and flood, there have been no reliable reports of famine or mass malnutrition in mainland China for several years. The new system may not be working well, but it appears to be working well enough.

AREAL ORGANIZATION AND DEVELOPMENT

In China, as in most countries in Asia, the distributions of people and of agricultural land are virtually identical, at least in general pattern. If the agricultural land were weighted by its productivity, the fit between the two distributions would be even closer. Moreover, if Japan is a relevant example, this type of areal association is likely to continue. Thus, the Chinese ecumene, or densely inhabited area, is found in the eastern third of China, in which over 95 per cent of the agricultural land also is located. In the western areas, composed of the Hsin-chiang Uighur Autonomous Region, Tibet, the Inner Mongolian Autonomous Region, and about half of the province of Kan-su, lives only about 4 per cent of China's population, and the great majority of these people, even today, are not Chinese ethnically. The West is, however, a much more important region than its size and character of population would indicate. Although mineralogical exploration has been limited, the area clearly is metallurgically rich, and it contains many of the known oil reserves of China. Tibet itself is one of the great mineralogical unknowns left in the modern world; it would be astonishing if it were not mineralogically valuable. Moreover, the West could be a major source of specialized agricultural produce from irrigated oasis agriculture, as is the Imperial Valley of California, and it could provide quantities of animal products from its vast pastures and steppes. Strategically, its value is incalculable, for it borders on India, Pakistan, Nepal, Afghanistan, and the USSR and represents the major thrust of Chinese political power interests into the heart of the great continent. Thus the West receives greater investment from government sources than its population suggests, and an increasing number of Chinese are moving into the growing cities of the region, thus altering the composition of its population.

In the Chinese ecumene to the east, the higher densities of population coincide with the most productive agricultural areas—the lowlands and basins throughout eastern China and the loess highlands of its Northwest. Densities are somewhat lower in the North which, with the Northeast, contains about 40 per cent of the national population, than in the South, which, including the Yangtze lowlands, accounts for about 56 per cent of the national population. In fact, however, it may be more useful to think of the division of the ecumene into four regions rather than the two which were convenient for consideration of agriculture—the Northeast (Manchuria), the North, Middle China (essentially the Yangtze valley including Ssu-ch'uan), and the South. In general, overall densities of population increase from the Northeast southward, although the differences between Middle and South China are slight. However, physiological densities are much greater in the South than in any other parts of the country, with the possible exception of Ssu-ch'uan.

*Types of Settlement.* With the exception of the Central Manchurian lowland and parts of the loess lands and other lesser areas, the basic settlement unit in China is an agglomerated village surrounded by its lands or located on some eccentric topographic feature which draws it off the valuable arable land available to the village. Size of village has varied greatly in China, but normally a village would include several hundred persons and could reach as high as two or three thousand. Groups of such villages would be distributed about a marketing center, itself in part an agricultural village but larger, and with a periodic market. Groups of such village clusters about a marketing center would look to some larger town, perhaps one of about ten thousand population, which would have a daily market. Some of these might have administrative functions as well, but for the most part these functions would be associated with the next level in the hierarchy, the smaller city of China, often a *hsien* or county seat and serving a hinterland with upwards of 100,000 population. Above the *hsien* capitals would be the provincial capitals, and at the summit, the national capital, Peiching (Peking), or as it was under the Kuomintang regime, Nanching (Nanking). Despite communization, this hierarchy apparently continues to exist, and it describes one major dimension of the settlement pattern in China. One of its characteristics is that cities of under fifty thousand population are underrepresented, given the size of China's population. Settlement leaps quickly from the overgrown village to the sizeable *hsien* capital and beyond.

On the other hand, a stratum of cities exists in China which does not fit readily into this hierarchical structure. These are cities, mostly of considerable size, which have developed as a result of political considerations or as a consequence of contact with the West or more recently with Japan. The first of these are exemplified by cities which have served as capitals of China, but no longer do, such as Nan-ching and Ch'ung-ch'ing, or as capitals of major areas now within China, such as Feng-t'ien (Mukden), which was the capital of the Manchus before they conquered China, or Ch'ang-ch'un also in the Northeast, which, under the name Hsin-ching, was the capital of the puppet state of Manchukuo between 1933 and 1945.

Even more important perhaps than these are the so-called Treaty Ports, of which there were 119 in China about the time of World War I. These were cities, some of them river ports and some of them not actually ports at all, in which foreigners enjoyed special privileges and where they developed urban districts and urban elements which varied from Chinese traditional forms. Almost all of these cities had existed as part of the traditional settlement hierarchy; many of them were large and had a long tradition of external contact, such as Canton, but others originally were very small and developed largely as a result of Western enterprise. Of these, Shang-hai is by far the most significant. In effect the regional capital of Middle China, Shang-hai is the largest city in China with a population estimated at ten million. Although its growth was primarily as a commercial center, it rapidly took on industrial functions and now may well be the largest industrial center in China. Other cities of similar function, though lesser in size, are T'ien-ching, the port of entry into the northern part of the North China plain, and Ch'ing-tao, originally German-developed, the entry point for Shan-tung and the southern part of the plain. All of these places, but particularly Shang-hai, are in mainland Chinese eyes branded with the stigma of "imperialism." Attempts have been made to block migration to Shang-hai from other areas and to reduce its importance in the space-economy of China, but these attempts have failed. Indeed, it appears that the coastal cities, including the river ports of the "Maritime Frontier" such as Wu-han, together with Pei-ching (Peking) and the Manchurian cities, have become the major centers of urban development in the country as a whole.

The Manchurian cities represent a related but somewhat different situation. Most of them were developed less as commercial emporia, although this was true enough of Ta-lien (Dairen), than as industrial centers, particularly as Japanese interest in Manchuria increased after the Russo-Japanese war of 1905. Not only was Dairen developed further, as was nearby Port Arthur, previously a Russian naval base which now has been merged with Ta-lien as the metropolis of Lü-ta, but also several cities were expanded or developed *de novo* as specialized industrial cities utilizing the vast coal and iron resources of south-central Manchuria. Thus, cities like Fu-shun and An-shan came into being, and cities like Mukden enlarged their functions to include major industrial ones, as did Harbin, which was developed as a largely Russian city from which the Russian-built and then owned Chinese Eastern Railway was extended across northern Manchuria after 1898.

In short, there are at least two major discernible strata of cities in China, those that fit into the traditional settlement-*cum*-administrative hierarchy of the country, and those that developed largely as a result of foreign contact and enterprise, despite their predominantly Chinese population. Of course, the two strata are far from distinct in individual cases. All are Chinese cities. More important, under the Communist government, new specialized-function cities have developed, and older ones have taken on new functions. In the one case, the small frontier town of Pao-t'ou beyond the Great Wall in the Inner Mongolian Autonomous Region is, by virtue of nearby coking coal and iron-ore deposits, now one of the major industrial cities of China. The ancient city of Lan-chou guarding the Kan-su corridor to the West has become both a gateway city to the developing West and a major manufacturing center associated with oil-refining and petrochemical industries and with China's atomic energy program.

All of these cities taken together, whatever their functions, contain at least 100 million persons, perhaps more, even though only about 15 per cent of China's population is classifiable as "urban." This makes China the most highly urbanized country in the world in terms of size of urban population, though it ranks very low on a scale of urbanization defined as per cent of population urban. Yet China has always been urban in the sense that "urbanism as a way of life" and the upward mobility that goes with it has long been a part of Chinese culture. The city is not set against the country but is symbiotically related to it. This suggests that Chinese cities may grow even more rapidly than those elsewhere, and that they will be, even more than those in other developing countries, artifacts of Chinese culture, whatever its ideological phase.

Industrialization as a concomitant of urbanization has come to China late and then more in relation to the nontraditional stratum of cities than the traditional. The larger cities in the traditional hierarchy, of course, all have long been processing centers for agricultural produce—rice, wheat, and other grains, cotton, tobacco, oilseeds, silk and coarser fibers, animal products—as well as collecting and distribution centers; but modern manufacturing emerged primarily as an attribute of the Treaty Ports and of the specialized industrial cities developed by Europeans and later by the Japanese. The Treaty Port industries for the most part were not natural-resource oriented. Cotton mills, machine shops auxiliary to port activities, railway yards and repair facilities, tobacco-processing, egg-drying, all drew upon the products of rural areas, but their location was in relation to market and port facility rather than raw materials. This was not true of the specialized industrial cities which were located with an eye to raw materials, especially coal and ferrous metals. Such was the case with the Manchurian industrial cities and several others in North China, which were located on or near coal fields. Many of these were at or near enough to tidewater that foreign entrepreneurship could help develop them as adjuncts of Treaty Port and Japanese interests. Thus, although China has been a producer of coal for at least eight hundred years, most of the developed mines as recently as 1960 have been in the coastal regions, including southern Manchuria.

One of the major policies of the Communist government has been to encourage industries inland in areas away from the former Treaty Ports and in other resource-rich areas than those, such as southern Manchuria, which had previously been developed. Thus Pao-t'ou was developed as one of three great steel centers in China, and Lan-chou has been developed as a center of the petrochemical industry. This policy makes more sense in light of the distribution of mineral resources in China, although its success has yet to be determined.

*Mineral Resources.* Coal is the chief mineral fuel in China, and its reserves of 200 billion tons are among the largest in the world. Every province is said to contain some coal measures, but the best endowed are those in the loess region. The most extensively worked, however, are those in Manchuria and in Ho-pei and Shan-tung provinces; Shan-hsi, with the largest reserves, ranks well behind them, largely because of its relative inaccessibility. Iron-ore deposits, at least those known, are far less generous and more highly localized, chiefly in southern Manchuria and the former province of Je-ho north of Pei-ching (Peking) and the Great Wall, in the Pao-t'ou area, and in central China south of the Yangtze. Thus the three major iron-and-steel manufacturing areas are southern Manchuria, Pao-t'ou, and Wu-han, which is supplied by nearby coal measures as well as iron ore. The paucity of iron-ore deposits in South China and the relative inaccessibility of coal measures there have discouraged attempts to establish major ferrous metals industries in that region. Paradoxically, the official Communist policy of locating heavy industries near to resources and away from the coastal areas has, with regard to iron and steel, resulted in the development of only one very large new steel center, that at Pao-t'ou, and has at the same time greatly encouraged industrial activity in southern Manchuria and in Middle China, which had large industrial resources and potentials in any case. The latter two areas also contain very large markets for all sorts of producers' goods, as at Shang-hai, Nan-ching, Wu-han, Ch'ung-ch'ing, T'ien-ching, Ch'ingtao, Pei-ching (Peking), Mukden, Ch'ang-ch'un, and Harbin. As a result, an even greater concentration of industrial activity than ever before has taken place in the already developed areas.

Apart from Pao-t'ou, only with regard to petroleum resources have there been significant changes in the location of industry in China since the Communist regime came to power. Most of China's oil is in the Far West, in Hsin-chiang, with the exception of modest reserves in southern Ssu-ch'uan and northern Manchuria. That oil is brought from its sources in the Tsaidam basin and elsewhere by railroad and pipeline to Lan-chou, where it is processed and then transshipped to other parts of China. In general, China continues to be petroleum-short, and it very probably will in time have recourse to the enormous reserves of oil shales in southern Manchuria, associated with the coal measures there, which the Japanese had exploited during the Second World War when Southeast Asian sources of petroleum were no longer available to her.

A vast array of nonferrous metals are distributed about the country—manganese and bauxite in Manchuria (another resource factor in the location of industry there); tin, tungsten, zinc, lead, and antimony in the southwestern areas; and lesser deposits of almost all other known metallic minerals, although, oddly for a country which long relied on copper currency, copper is scarce. The great question remains concerning the mineral resources of the Far West. Tibet is unexplored; Hsin-chiang only partly. Should resources there be discovered as hoped, China may well be close to self-sufficiency in most mineral resources. To this end, the Far West as well as the South has been blanketed with mineralogical survey teams over the past fifteen years.

*The Transportation Network.* As a spatial system, China is poorly integrated by modern transportation, and it still relies heavily on traditional means of transportation, especially inland waterways. The Yangtze is the master stream and main transportation artery of Middle China. No railways or highways compete directly with it. Not only is the master river itself navigable (with limitations and inconveniences), but also most of the lower reaches of its tributaries. The lower Yangtze plain is covered with a maze of canalized distributaries, the effectiveness of which is measured by the fact that they were sufficient to supply Shang-hai with almost all of her foodstuffs virtually until the present. The lower Yangtze is connected with the Huai basin via the rebuilt Grand Canal and other canals built as part of the Huai basin development project.

The main land transportation network is built upon railways. China now has about 25,000 miles of main-line railways, an increase of about 40 per cent over the mileage that existed before 1949. Their functions are chiefly four: (1) to connect North with Middle and South China; (2) to link ecumenical China with the western areas; (3) to link interior areas inaccessible by inland waterways with the coasts; and (4) to service the Northeast and to link it with North China. The first function is provided by the trunk line between Pei-ching and Canton via Wu-han and the Yangtze bridge there. Most of this line has been double-tracked. Another line which serves a somewhat similar function is that from T'ien-ching to Shanghai and thence southwestward to the main north-south line. The second function is carried forward most dramatically by the Lung-hai railroad which runs east-west north of the Ch'in Ling range through Lan-chou to Ti-hua (Urumchi), the capital of the Hsin-chiang Autonomous Region. The western portion of this line was built since 1950, and it was supposed to have continued to the border of Soviet Central Asia, but that no longer is likely. Less dramatically but no less significantly, new lines have been constructed to link Pao-t'ou first with Pei-ching (Peking) and then with Lan-chou, and also to link Ssu-ch'uan with the Lung-hai railroad over the Ch'in Ling barrier. The third function is provided by several lines, of which a good example is the Shan-tung railroad built largely with German capital about the turn of the century. The fourth function is served by the highly developed Manchurian railway network, developed largely independently of the national grid but linked to it by the Pei-ching-Mukden line. The Manchurian network is the only part of the system that is reasonably well supplied with feeder lines. In the rest of the country the feeder system is either stunted or nonexistent, although the Yangtze artery and some of the other inland waterways serve a feeder function. In any case, the railways are vastly overburdened and appear to have a higher ratio of freight carried to length than any other railway system in the world, with the possible exception of the U.S.S.R.

The situation is beginning to be helped by an expansion of the highway system, but little is known of its effectiveness. What is known, however, is that Tibet is now tied to the rest of the country with an all-weather highway, and that other highways, presumably strategic, also have been constructed along China's frontiers.

On the international scale, China is linked by rail with northern Korea, and with the Soviet Union through the Manchurian grid, although there is a break-of-gauge at the border. In 1956 there was completed the broad-gauge Trans-Mongolian line which saved three days of train travel between Pei-ching and Moscow (despite another break of gauge) and also served to link China more effectively with the Mongolian People's Republic. Both of these connections were relatively little used after 1960, when Sino-Soviet relations began to cool. To the south, two lines provide links with North Vietnam, but again a break-of-gauge is involved, from Chinese standard gauge to the Vietnamese meter gauge. No railway connections exist with Laos, Burma, Pakistan, India, Nepal, and Afghanistan.

In short, China displays the same kind of "spatial stickiness" associated with all poorer countries, but in her case the situation is exacerbated on the one hand by the enormous territory to be consolidated, and ameliorated on the other by the existence of the Yangtze waterway. A special problem relates, moreover, to the traditional centrifugality of the South, with its predominantly non-Mandarin speaking populations and their fear of discrimination by Northerners. Similarly, the occupation of the West by non-Chinese presents a continuing centrifugal pressure upon the integrity of the contemporary Chinese state. Evidence of all these forces making for fragmentation is seen in the partial decentralization of much decision-making to the provinces and in the vagaries of the Cultural Revolution of 1966–1968, when areas less well integrated into the national spatial system seemed for a time to be beyond the control of Pei-ching's authority. In the long run, China's remarkable diversity should make for a more resourceful and powerful country; but in the short run that diversity will require a flexible system of regional checks and balances if China is not once again to be fragmented along its numerous lines of cultural and physical cleavage.

# The Unity
# of China

E. G. Pulleyblank

**M**en of good will in the West, particularly in the United States which bears the main responsibility, are anxiously looking for a way out of the impasse in which they find themselves with respect to China. The absurdity and danger of refusing to recognize the People's Republic of China, which has governed the destinies of a quarter of the human race for nearly twenty years, becomes daily more blatant. Yet it is difficult to get out from under the encumbrance of past commitments to the other "China," the rump of the former regime which maintains itself on the island of Taiwan, and perhaps even more difficult in the American context to free oneself from the bogies that have become associated with the whole question of China during the period of Cold War hostility. To a very large extent the problem has, in fact, little to do with China but is merely one aspect of the contradictions arising out of

America's own history and present situation and her emergence as the most powerful nation in the world, heir to the aggressive dominance that the West has exerted over the rest of the world for the last few hundred years. Another aspect of the problem is that because so little is known in the West about China's own traditions, there is little basis for a realistic appraisal of what to expect from her. Can one, for example, realistically think of a "Two Chinas" policy (the People's Republic *and* Taiwan) as a solution to the present dilemma concerning recognition? Must one assume that China, just because she is becoming a great power, is bound also to become an aggressive power?

Historians, of course, are not prophets. The lessons of the past seldom present themselves in such simple and clear ways that one can say with confidence that something will or will not happen. One of the lessons of the present century with regard to China has been that things that seem as unchanging and permanent as the annual flux of the seasons can crumble and vanish overnight. The monarchy is gone. Confucianism as a doctrine is at best a pale shadow, despite the fact that its basic attitudes may be imbedded in Chinese habits of thought and behavior. Still, some things endure. The trick is to recognize what is really enduring and what is an attribute of the past which need have no bearing on the present or future.

Having made these precautionary reservations, one must nevertheless admit that if one were to look for one characteristic of Chinese civilization that most distinguished it from others, one could hardly find anything more striking than the theme of unity, a unity that implied not merely the cultural unity of the Chinese people, like that of the Hellenes, but a political unity, always striven for as the norm even when not achieved in practice.

The earliest name for the Chinese is Hsia. This was the name of the first dynasty, whose historical existence has not yet been verified archaeologically but which, according to legend, ruled over the Chinese clans in the first half of the second millennium B.C. Later, in early historical times of the first half of the first millennium B.C., the Chinese states were known as *chu Hsia,* "All the Hsia," to distinguish them from their barbarian neighbors (those other inhabitants of north China who spoke different languages and were in other ways culturally distinct from the Chinese). Another form of the name Hsia is Hua, found in the official names of both "Chinas"—Chung-hua jen-min kung-ho kuo, "Chinese People's Republic," and Chung-hua min-kuo, "Republic of China."

What kind of political unity may have existed in the days of Hsia is impossible to know. It seems, however, that under the second dynasty, the Shang, for which we have contemporary documentary remains in the oracle bones of divination, as well as later historical traditions, the Shang king, or *wang*, already claimed supremacy over the other Chinese states. When we come down to the Chou dynasty (traditional dates 1122–256 B.C.) we are on firm ground. The Chou king, who was known as the Son of Heaven, was regarded as the supreme ruler on earth, entrusted with a Mandate from Heaven, the supreme ruler above. This Mandate had formerly been held by the Shang, whose last ruler had forfeited it by his wicked and licentious behavior. Though the Chou kings won their position in the end by military conquest, the new line really owed its success to its Virtue, accumulated by past generations of worthy ancestors, which had earned Heaven's favor. But just as Heaven's favor could be won, so it could be lost. The dangers of relaxation and lapsing into the errors of Shang are a frequent theme in the poetry of the dynasty.

Though the country was a feudal agglomeration rather than a unified state, it seems clear that in its first few centuries Chou exercised a real authority over its vassals, of whom the major ones were branches of the same royal house while others were descendants of the Shang or other "Hsia" clans. After 770 B.C., when the capital was moved eastward to Loyang under pressure from barbarian incursions, the royal domain was greatly reduced in size and Chou could no longer play a significant role as a military power. Nevertheless, the prestige of its name lingered on for several centuries more. The great feudatories that contended with one another for hegemony in the so-called Spring and Autumn Period were careful to make their claims in the name of the Chou king, for the sake of keeping the peace and defending the Central Hsia states against the barbarians.

By the fourth and third centuries B.C., the classical period of Chinese philosophy when the Hundred Schools really did contend, the Chou authority had ceased to command even lip service. The rulers of the Warring States, one after the other, usurped the old, sacred name of King and fought each other for supremacy with increasing ferocity. The striking thing about this situation is that no one seems to have regarded it as other than temporary. The universal assumption was that sooner or later one state would emerge victorious over all the others and restore the unity of All Under Heaven. The Mandate which had so manifestly been lost to Chou would fall to a new dynasty.

The political philosophies that competed for the allegiance of the men of those times, however varied were the means they advocated, all seem to have had this same basic assumption. The question at issue was never whether it was preferable to unite China under one ruler or whether there should be a permanent system of "sovereign" states, each developing its own individuality independent of the others. The only question was what were the most effective means of achieving and maintaining unity under a single ruler. This is obvious enough in a Confucian like Mencius, who was always trying to persuade rulers of the need to behave like the idealized Former Kings in order to be in a position to achieve the unification which those Former Kings had achieved. The Mohists also believed in unity as the sole means of ending warfare and restoring peace. The Legalists adopted the same principle, believing further that unity could only be brought about by a state which had itself been brought under the totalitarian control of a despotic ruler.

The long expected event took place in 221 B.C., when the King of Ch'in (whence our name China) defeated his last rival and proclaimed himself First Emperor. The thoroughness with which he set about imposing not merely unity but uniformity, abolishing the old feudal houses and placing the country under centralized bureaucratic control, suppressing all schools of thought except the Legalists and burning their books, including the Confucian classics, provoked a reaction; so that when the Ch'in dynasty collapsed as a result of popular uprisings after the First Emperor's death, attempts were made to revive some of the old feudal kingdoms. After prolonged civil war it was nevertheless a commoner who restored the empire under a new dynasty, the Han. Though at the beginning Han was forced to establish feudal principalities over two-thirds of its territory, in little more than half a century these had been greatly reduced in size and stripped of all effective independence. The empire was once more, as in Ch'in, governed by officials appointed from the capital. It was this Ch'in-Han empire that set the pattern for the Chinese state for the next two thousand years.

Under Han, with the supplanting of Legalism by Confucianism as the state orthodoxy (though the institutions of the empire retained their fundamental Legalist stamp to the end), there was a conscious identification with the ancient traditions of kingship of the Chou and prehistoric times. The idea of one Heaven ruling above and one Son of Heaven ruling on earth acquired a new and more potent force.

After the collapse of Han at the end of the second century A.D., and still more in the fourth century when Northern China fell to barbarian uprisings and invasions and a native Chinese dynasty survived only in the south, China entered a long period of effective disunity. The only acceptable political theory remained that of the Mandate of Heaven. No matter how little basis their claims to supremacy had in reality, each successive Chinese dynasty in Nanking claimed to be the legitimate rulers of the whole country. Similarly, the barbarian rulers of the north, taking on the trappings of Chinese imperial dignity, claimed the same universal authority and insisted on treating their Chinese rivals as usurpers. There was no room in the politics of those days, any more than there is in the twentieth century, for the idea of Two Chinas.

In practice, to be sure, there was not always open warfare between the northern and southern states, and for fairly long periods neither side harbored realistic ideas of conquering the other. As time went on the refugee aristocrats in the south became more and more absorbed in opening up their new lands and paid merely lip service to the idea of retaking the north. The barbarians, likewise, finding themselves at a disadvantage in the watery terrain of the Yangtze region, where their cavalry could not operate effectively, contented themselves with what they had and gave up the idea of further conquests. The stalemate persisted for over two centuries. If it had lasted some centuries more, one can suppose that something like the permanent splitting of the Roman empire into eastern and western branches might have occurred, and who knows what different political forms might have evolved?

What actually happened was the restoration of the unified empire as soon as the north came under the control of a dynasty of native Chinese origin. Sui (589–618), the dynasty that restored unity, collapsed in the second generation—a striking parallel to the fate of Ch'in—but the T'ang dynasty which followed (618–906) lasted for nearly three centuries. Thereafter, dynasty succeeded dynasty, sometimes with fairly protracted periods of warlordism in between, as in the Five Dynasties period (906–960) and in the civil wars at the end of Yuan (1351–1368), but never with any real disturbances to the idea of Chinese unity. The most serious threat was no doubt in the Southern Sung period (1126–1276), when Northern China was in the hands of the alien Jurchen dynasty of Chin, and subsequently, in a rather different way, in Yüan, when China under the Mongols was for a time part of a larger world empire. But even the Mongols in the end became Chinese-style emperors, and when they were driven out and Chinese rule was restored under the Ming, a turning back to traditional ways reinforced yet more strongly the ancient political theory. The replacement of the Ming by the Manchus in 1644 did nothing to change this, for the Manchus wanted nothing better than to be accepted as Chinese-style emperors.

The one China of All-Under-Heaven was, of course, not the same thing as one China, the nation state. The pre-eminence of the Chinese Son of Heaven over all surrounding rulers and their duty to offer him submission was part of the theory, which implied an innately hierarchical international order, rather than a system of equal sovereignties like that which grew up in Europe. The conflict between these two irreconcilable concepts was one of the main themes in Western relations with China from the sixteenth century onward. When Western might ultimately prevailed and China was forced to swallow her pride, the new concept of a Chinese nationality as one nationality among others began to emerge as part of the necessary adaptation to the new world in which China had to try to survive. The formulation of this concept, which did nothing to upset the old doctrine of Chinese unity but rather reinforced it and gave it new definition, was the work of the Nationalist revolutionaries.

Dr. Sun Yat-sen's Principle of Nationalism, the first of the Three People's Principles, was at first directed toward the liberation of the

Chinese from the yoke of foreign oppression under the Manchus. With the end of the Manchu dynasty, however, China became a multinational state, and Chinese nationality was redefined to include the minority peoples—Manchus, Mongols, Tibetans, Uigurs, and so forth. The spirit of nationalism was now directed against foreign encroachments on Chinese territory that had occurred during the nineteenth century, the foreign concessions and extraterritorial rights in Chinese ports, and, of course, the actual cessions of territory that had occurred, such as that of Hong Kong to Great Britain and that of Taiwan to Japan. The fact that, at least in its home territory, the Communist government has put an end to these humiliations has undoubtedly given quiet satisfaction to Chinese everywhere, even those who are totally out of sympathy with its political doctrines.

The enlargement of the concept of Chinese nationality to give it a geographical meaning coterminous with the boundaries of the old Manchu empire is no doubt an effect of superimposing Westernizing concepts on older and more basic feelings of identity based on language and culture. It has given rise to the claim, accepted as axiomatic by both "Chinas," that Tibet is an integral, inalienable part of China, whatever outsiders or the Tibetans themselves may think of the matter. There is indeed a close parallel with the new Indian spirit of nationalism, which makes its territorial claims on the basis of frontiers established by the British Raj and is, for example, as determined to keep the Nagas willy-nilly within the Indian federation as the Chinese are to keep the Tibetans.

In this respect, Mongolia illustrates what seems to me the crowning absurdity of the effects on American foreign policy of the twentieth-century Chinese doctrine of nationality as held, not by the Chinese Communists, but by the Nationalists on Formosa. Mongolia was part of the Manchu empire and as such was included in the new definition of the Chinese nation. Between the wars, however, the Mongolian People's Republic was established in Outer Mongolia under Soviet auspices. After the last war Chiang Kai-shek's government was prepared to recognize the independence of Outer Mongolia as part of its settlement with Russia; the Chinese People's Republic, of course, now does so. But the Nationalist government on Taiwan has withdrawn this recognition and insists that Outer Mongolia (like Tibet and Sinkiang) is an integral part of the China of which it claims to be the legitimate government. This claim would have little practical significance were it not that the United States has thereby also been inhibited from recognizing Outer Mongolia's independence. Those who know the situation in Mongolia have no doubt of the Mongols' desire for independence. They are inevitably under the shadow of Russia, but they are a proud people who run their own internal affairs and want nothing more than to be independent of both their powerful neighbors. One would have thought that it was obviously in America's interest to encourage this as much as possible, and that furthermore it would be clearly advantageous to have a diplomatic representative in such a strategic location. Nevertheless, all moves of the United States government toward recognizing the Mongolian People's Republic have been frustrated by objections emanating from Formosa (though admission to the United Nations was accepted a few years ago as part of a package deal).

To return to the main theme, it is clear that although a new concept of nationality on the Western model has been superimposed on the age-old idea of Chinese unity, it has done nothing to diminish this idea and has indeed strengthened it. It gives no comfort to the proposers of the Two Chinas idea.

One question which one should no doubt ask is whether there is, on the part of the Chinese at the present time, not merely a wish to assert their newly defined nationality among the nations of the world but also an atavistic desire to restore the old position in which China was at the center and summit of a world order, giving moral leadership and expecting submission from lesser peoples. This is the kind of historical analogy that appeals to journalists, and one sees it, or variations of it, from time to time used as an argument for the assumption that China is bound to be aggressive, and to justify aggressive measures to contain her. It implies that China, as China, has dreams of some kind of world domination and casts her by implication in the role of Napoleonic France or Hitler's Germany or prewar Japan under the militarists. It would be very hard to justify such an idea from any statements of Mao or his colleagues who do indeed, as good Communist revolutionaries, regard themselves as leaders in the struggle of all the oppressed peoples of the world against their oppressors, but certainly do not link this with any claim for inherent Chinese superiority. One may, to be sure, occasionally feel that traditional assumptions of natural superiority, particularly natural moral superiority, unconsciously color Chinese pronouncements; but this is surely a fairly universal human tendency. It would be at least as easy to make a case against England, or France, or India, or the United States.

If we consider actions as well as words, there is not, as far as I can see, the slightest evidence that China's recent foreign policy, however one may criticize it in certain respects, has been motivated either consciously or unconsciously by irrational dreams of conquest. Her intervention in the Korean War was evidence of an unwillingness to allow her Communist ally, North Korea, to be destroyed or to allow American troops to reach her frontiers. It can hardly be put down to a desire for territorial expansion. After all, Chinese troops have long since been withdrawn from North Korea, while American troops remain in the South; and North Korea has continued to be more in the Russian than the Chinese camp. The conquest of Tibet was looked on as aggression by the Tibetans but as an internal police action by the Chinese, who have never recognized the Tibetan claim to be an independent country. In this respect there is no difference in view between the Two Chinas. The dismal story of the frontier disputes between India and China, which no doubt came to a head as a result of Chinese irritation over the Indian attitude to Chinese actions in Tibet, made a sad end to the Bandung spirit of peace and friendship between the two countries; but, in spite of the hysterical reaction of the Indians to their humiliation, there is no evidence that the Chinese had any serious intention of invading the country.

China has, to be sure, given moral support to revolutionary movements in Southeast Asia, Africa, and elsewhere, but this, however reprehensible it may seem from an anti-communist point of view, has been motivated by the desire to assist those countries to "liberate" themselves, and to hurt the Americans, whom they regard, not unreasonably, as their chief enemy. It is the inverse of American foreign-aid programs. One can hardly see in it Chinese expansionism, still less anything deriving from atavistic tendencies.

The apprehensions of possible Chinese aggressiveness, in so far as this is taken to mean actual military threats to her neighbors, derive, it seems to me, more from a projection of Western attitudes onto the Chinese than from any evidence based on knowledge of Chinese history or an objective appraisal of her present attitudes. It is a Western assumption (well substantiated by the history of European nations) that great powers are naturally expansive. All the major European nations have traditions of military conquest; their periods of national greatness, that is, the times when they were able to lord it over their neighbors, are celebrated in their history books. European expansion over the rest of the world reached a frantic climax of competitive grabbing just before the First World War, barely half a century ago. During the same period America's expansion across the continent went on at an equally tumultuous pace and spilled over into the Pacific, to Hawaii and the Philippines. The heroic violence of that era has become *the* American myth, celebrated every day of the week on television, and supplanting to a frightening degree the older humane and rational ideals of the founding fathers.

The struggle for world domination among the Western European powers ended finally in disastrous internecine strife. All their empires have ebbed away. After the Second World War only America and Russia were left on the fringes of Europe with impressive power. It was natural and in keeping with the traditions of Western international politics that they should immediately square off against one another and become the leaders of rival power blocs. The fact that they represented opposing ideologies was also in the Western tradition, in which hostilities between rival states have regularly been exacerbated by religious animosities and crusading zeal. Now the emergence of China has frightened both Russia and America, and they would like to compose their differences in the face of this common menace. Is not the menace, however, the reflection of their own guilty faces, rather than a clear perception of the Chinese reality?

It would be ideal to pretend that China has never been militarily aggressive against her neighbors. Her record in this respect is nevertheless far better than that of most Western nations. War was never glorified in ancient China as it was, for example, in Rome, with her barbarous triumphs and her gladiatorial games, or in medieval

Europe, with her jousting knights, or in feudal Japan, with her samurai code. War was always a *hsiung-ch'i,* an ill-omened instrument, which might rebound on the one who resorted to it. Civil virtues always ranked higher than military ones. This was the constant theme of orthodox teachers from Confucius and Mencius onward, and though one may get tired of the priggish moral sentiments in traditional Chinese official pronouncements and historical evaluations, they are surely preferable to the glorification of national acts of violence.

There were few periods in history when the Chinese under a native dynasty made conquests beyond their frontiers. The Han (206 B.C.–200 A.D.) and T'ang (618–906) are the most notable examples. The latter (actually founded by a family of mixed Chinese and nomadic ancestry) subdued the Turks in what is now Mongolia; established briefly Chinese suzerainty as far west as Afghanistan; conquered, and for a short time occupied, Korea; and in the first half of the eighth century contended with the Arabs for mastery in what is now Russian Turkestan. In 755, however, a revolt by a leading general nearly overthrew the dynasty, and for the next two hundred years the country suffered grievously from warlordism. This bad experience of militarism made the succeeding Sung dynasty careful to curb the power of the army, so much so that it was always at a military disadvantage toward its much less populous and wealthy northern neighbors. North China was lost to the Jurchen from Manchuria in 1126, and the whole country was occupied by the Mongols in 1276.

The re-establishment of a native Chinese dynasty under the Ming in 1368 led to attempts, especially under the third emperor who reigned in the Yung-lo period (1403–1424), to subdue the Mongols, who remained a dangerous enemy, but for the most part the Chinese were content to defend the line of the Great Wall. At the beginning of the dynasty also, Annam (the northern part of modern Vietnam) was occupied. Annam had formed part of the Han and T'ang empires but had established its independence around 900 A.D. It was later conquered by the Mongols and formed part of their world empire. The Ming naturally first regarded it as part of their patrimony, and they incorporated it in their empire in 1407. But when they were driven out by a native revolt in 1427, they made no serious effort to recover the lost territory in spite of the humiliating loss of face. Thereafter they acknowledged the Vietnamese rulers as independent, tributary vassals on the same footing as the kings of Korea and other small neighbors. These rulers, for their part, were willing to play this game of nominal submission in return for the added prestige given to their authority by their investiture by the Chinese emperor and the material advantages that came from the trade that went with the tributary relationship. (It must be remembered that the cultures of Annam and Korea were deeply Sinicized and therefore under the influence of the Confucian worldview and the place it gave to the Son of Heaven.)

The expansion of China's borders to include Mongolia, Tibet, and Sinkiang in the seventeenth and eighteenth centuries was the work of her Manchu conquerors, not the Chinese themselves. Though, as shown above, these conquests established the boundaries for Chinese nationalist claims in the twentieth century, they do not give grounds for regarding the Chinese as naturally expansionist.

The fact that China always occupied the unrivaled central position in the Far Eastern world, a position dependent on her historic position as the fountainhead of civilization rather than on her military power, meant that it was never necessary to go to war to demonstrate her superiority. Even when militarily weak, even when conquered by nomads from the north, China's cultural ascendancy was axiomatic. There was therefore never the tendency that constantly recurred in Europe for more or less equally matched power blocs to contend for leadership. This could only have come about if China herself had been divided into rival states instead of being a single imperium. No doubt the competition between separate states in Europe has been a stimulus to progress, but it has been dearly bought in blood.

True to our own traditions, we expect the new, emergent China, remade as a Western-style state, to enter the same competition and to demonstrate her strength by attacking her small neighbors. Is there any evidence to justify this expectation, apart from our apprehensions based on our own history? There are of course apprehensions of a different kind among ruling classes in some of the smaller Asian countries, based on their fears of the effect of the Chinese example on revolutionaries in their own countries, and there is xenophobia in Southeast Asia against the industrious and successful Chinese merchants in their midst. But this is hardly the same thing as a rational fear of military aggression.

China does not wish to be dominated by anybody, but there is little, if anything, to suggest that she is motivated by a desire to dominate others. Rather she seems inclined to withdraw more and more into her shell, concentrating on her own internal affairs, with little real interest in the outside world. Her mistakes in foreign policy in recent years seem to be primarily the result of this, rather than of aggressiveness. Recent visitors have remarked that within China even the Vietnam War is seen mainly in terms of the threat it brings of an American invasion of their own country. If China's traditional view of her position in the world has any bearing on her present attitudes, it seems that it is in this direction, encouraging withdrawal and self-absorption, not in the direction of self-assertive expansion. This Middle Kingdom is still very much the real center of what matters. Ideological leadership of revolutionary movements in other parts of the world is important as a part of the Maoists' self-image in their internal struggles, but it seems to have less and less to do with real assistance to foreign revolutions.

As China's political tradition clearly affects her present attitudes, so China's culture has helped create its tradition of unity. It is obvious that more than the mere idea of unity is involved here, for the idea of the unity of Christendom under the papacy and the Holy Roman empire did not prevent the fragmentation of Europe, nor did the idea of the unity of Islam under the caliphate ever lead to a restoration of political unity once the first wave of Arab expansion had subsided.

The greatest binding force in traditional Chinese civilization, responsible more than anything else for its remarkable stability and resiliency even when in temporary breakdown, was undoubtedly the role played by the Confucian literati. They virtually monopolized the civil side of government and occupied an unchallenged position at the top of society in terms of intellectual and artistic creativity at most periods of Chinese history. They gave Chinese civilization such a uniform Confucian cast, not only in its high culture but also seeping down and deeply permeating the illiterate subcultures as well, that one must sometimes look very hard before perceiving the importance of other strains—Legalist, Taoist, Buddhist. United in the first place by the same long and arduous education in the Confucian classics, and indelibly stamped from their early childhood by Confucian morality, Confucian rationalism and humanism, and the Confucian world-view embracing All Under Heaven in one hierarchical order, the Chinese literati were a powerful balance wheel, always trying to restore society to its accustomed paths no matter what temporary disasters might befall it from internal collapse or invasions from outside. In this endeavor the literati achieved a truly extraordinary degree of success.

The shock of the Western impact in the nineteenth century was in the end too much for this well-tried mechanism, and in the twentieth century the Confucian order has collapsed and disintegrated utterly beyond repair. Confucius himself was dethroned and cast aside by the iconoclasts of the May Fourth Movement, and whatever reverence he may receive at times from Communists as well as non-Communists as a historical figure, it is impossible to suppose that he could ever be restored to his position as the one Sage. The acceptance of modern science, imported from the West but based on universal principles, is in itself enough to rule that out. Nevertheless, there may still be ways in which the ingrained habits of the Confucian past are still very much alive in the Chinese today.

In the first place, one must stress the basic importance of the Chinese language as a unifying factor, not only in providing a focus of identity of unique strength for present-day Chinese but also as a pervasive link, consciously and unconsciously, with the common Chinese past. The peculiarity of Chinese linguistic unity is, of course, its dependence on the written rather than the spoken language. As long as the ancient script remains in use, literate Chinese, no matter where they come from or what their native dialect, will be able to communicate with one another and, moreover, will have an awareness of a common history and a common cultural heritage that is much more vivid than that of Europeans.

The nature of the Chinese script is often misunderstood. It is not really pictographic or ideographic. That is, it does not directly represent objects or ideas without the mediation of language. The characters stand for meaningful words or word elements which existed in the ancient language and have been inherited by the modern spoken dialects, though they are now pronounced very differently from the way they once were. The same character can therefore be read with the same meaning but with quite different pronunciation by a man from Peking and a man from Canton, who could not understand each other's speech at all. In the past this common script created a linguistic unity that was enhanced by the fact that every one also wrote in the old classical form of the language, which therefore played a role like that of Latin in premodern Europe. This is no longer the case since the so-called *pai-hua,* "plain speech," revolution which occurred at the end of the First World War. Nevertheless, abandonment of classical Chinese has not meant the emergence of a whole series of new vernacular literatures in the dialects of Canton, Shanghai, Amoy, and so forth, as happened in Europe with the decline of Latin. The new literary movement has gone hand in hand with the movement to establish a standard form of spoken language based on Peking, and this has provided the basis for the new literary language.

This Common Speech (*p'u-t'ung-hua*), as it is called on the mainland, or National Language (*kuo-yu*), as it is called in Taiwan, already had a basis in the Officials' Speech (*kuan-hua*), that is, the common spoken language based on the dialect of the capital. Officials had to learn it in order to communicate when they came from other parts of the country to Peking. It is therefore often still referred to as Mandarin. About four-fifths of the whole Chinese population, from Manchuria in the far north to Yun-nan in the far south, actually speak what are collectively referred to as Mandarin dialects. They are dialects no more distantly related to one another than, say, the dialects of English. It is only in the coastal regions from Shanghai to Canton (and including the native population on Taiwan, as opposed to the mainland refugees) that dialects are spoken which differ from one another as widely as the Romance languages do among themselves.

Mandarin is now being promoted as the standard form of Chinese both on the mainland and in Taiwan (and also in many overseas communities in Southeast Asia). It is propagated through the schools and through the press and radio. If and when it really becomes universally understood and used, it may become possible to take the next great step of abandoning the characters and going over to an alphabetic script. Although an official romanization has been adopted in Peking and is used to a very limited extent, mainly as an aid to teaching Mandarin to non-Mandarin speakers, there is not likely to be any real move in this direction for a long time to come.

The script not only gives the Chinese their linguistic unity and links them immediately to their whole ancient tradition. It also serves to mark off China from the rest of the world, perhaps more than any other single factor. It is probably responsible more than anything else for the seemingly invincible impression of exoticism which hangs over China in the eyes of the rest of the world. It is unique among the living scripts of the world in not being based on a simple phonetic principle. To the Chinese, trying to achieve mass literacy and modern education, it is a great burden (though not, it would seem, an impossible one in view of Japanese experience); but as long as they have it they are incomparably more bound up with their ancient and unique culture than are those who use alphabets. One must not fail to mention also the profound influence which the script has had on Chinese aesthetic sensibilities through the art of calligraphy.

So much for the formal and outward links with the Confucian past. What about the content? Here we are on more delicate ground, and one hesitates to speak in very positive terms. After all, for the past twenty years the rulers of China have been declared adherents of an ideology of Western origin which in many fundamental ways is totally alien to Chinese tradition. Not only has Confucius been dethroned but the basic principles of Confucian ethics have been subjected to frontal assault—particularly the principles of family loyalty and filial piety. The Red Guard enthusiasts of the Cultural Revolution have gone still further in denouncing lingering manifestations of the old order—everything that smacks of hierarchy and authority, even the prestige of learning itself. Though the occasional press reports of destruction of ancient cultural treasures seem to be grossly exaggerated, such an effort at root and branch remaking of men's minds can have few parallels in human history.

Nevertheless, I venture to suggest that even here we can see a greater continuity than one unfamiliar with traditional China could guess. Mao Tse-tung is supposed to be a Marxist, and no doubt the inspiration of Marxism as put into practice by Lenin has played an important part in his life. Still, Mao's roots in Chinese tradition run very deep, as those who have made a close study of him and his writings have recognized. Without undertaking a detailed exegesis of his work from this point of view, one or two points seem to stand out. Most striking, it seems to me, is the emphasis on man's ability to conquer adverse material circumstances by moral effort. I claim no profound knowledge of Marxism, and no doubt one can find texts in that vast corpus to justify almost anything. Nevertheless, to give first place to the human spirit in this way seems to be the very antithesis of the materialist dialectic, with its emphasis on the objective basis underlying the ideological superstructure.

Mao's successful revolutionary method, going to the country and the peasants rather than relying on the urban workers, from the outset flew in the face of Marxist orthodoxy. Since the Communist coming to power in 1948, the policies most closely associated with Mao personally have had this same romantic flavor. There was the Hundred Flowers movement, which was no doubt inspired at the outset by a genuine belief that communism had been so fully accepted that freer intellectual discussion was possible without undermining it. There was the Great Leap Forward, in which the Chinese peasantry, or at least its most energetic and active elements, were inspired to believe they could pull themselves up by their bootstraps, establish a communal utopia overnight, revolutionize agriculture, and at the same time make human effort substitute for lack of capital in establishing a decentralized industrial base in the countryside. The romantic disregard for material obstacles was shocking to orthodox Marxists in Russia. Most recently of all there has been the Cultural Revolution, in which even economic goals, even the achievement of technical expertise so necessary if China is to modernize herself, have been subordinated to the creation of a totally egalitarian society in which all that counts is selfless dedication and strength of purpose.

All this seems a far cry from Marx or Lenin or Stalin. The belief that all depends on man and that man depends on cultivating his inner moral strength and devoting it to the service of society is, however, of the essence of Confucianism. The Thought of Mao has replaced the classics as the source of inspiration, but if we look at the content of the aphorisms which are in the little red book and on everyone's lips, they mostly have the same message. It is true that Mao has allowed and even instigated the cult of personality that now surrounds him, but this seems to be much more directed toward raising still further the moral fervor of his followers and giving it a sharp focus than toward satisfying the brutal vanity of a tyrannical dictator, as was the case with Stalin.

One aspect of the Red Guard movement has seldom been mentioned by the Western press but strikes me very forcibly: the small degree of physical violence it has entailed. Despite tremendous rumors of gory battles, these have seldom, if ever, been confirmed and have often been totally discredited by eyewitness reports from returning travelers. Even attacks on foreign diplomats, for all the humiliation and discomfort they have caused, have not reached the point of doing serious bodily harm. The British Embassy was burned down, but only property was damaged. One has only to consider what happened to Chinese diplomats in New Delhi, where invading mobs beat them with iron bars, or to innocent Chinese in Indonesia and Burma, to see the contrast. Things have been different in Hong Kong, where there has been actual bomb terrorism, but even this has never reached the destructive scale of a minor race riot in the United States. Those Western observers (including the Russians and East Europeans) who have seen the Red Guards as juvenile delinquents, engaged in senseless rioting and destruction, have, it is clear, totally misconstrued them. However uncongenial their self-righteousness and intolerance may be to us, it is a far cry from teen-age vandalism and hooliganism as we know it in Europe and North America.

Most remarkable of all has been the way in which the long campaign against Liu Shao-ch'i has never been brought to a climax.* At the time of this writing, this "leading party person who has taken the capitalist road" is not only still alive but is still titular head of the Chinese state. It is all very mystifying, and I do not pretend to understand what the real situation is in terms of power. What one can say, so far, is that for a struggle that has been so violent in its

* A point well taken. Although Liu was deposed, he was not purged in a Stalinist manner.—ED.

*language,* the absence of physical violence is truly remarkable. It is certainly very different from Stalinist Russia.

If one can see in Mao's belief in man and in moral earnestness abiding elements from the Confucian side of Chinese tradition, this does not mean that he is not at the same time bringing about revolutionary changes in China that must seem very repugnant to many of those outside (and probably also inside) China, especially the better educated, those more deeply involved in the traditional value system. This is a source of alienation between the Two Chinas that will be hard to heal.

Yet one must also remember that the obverse of the hard, energetic, Confucian, *yang* side of Chinese civilization was the yielding, receptive, light-hearted, Taoist, *yin* side. The *yang* is very much in the ascendant at the moment. One cannot see much evidence of any saving grace of humor in China today—at least in her official pronouncements and the face she presents to the world. But as Lao-tzu and Chuang-tzu knew very well, an excess of *yang* inevitably gives rise to a movement toward its opposite. Sooner or later, if somebody else's *yang* doesn't blow everything up in one gigantic atomic fire, the *yin* cycle will manifest itself. I am sure that Mao, whose conception of dialectical process has much more to do with his traditional Chinese outlook than with anything he learned from Hegel or Marx, knows this. It is no doubt this knowledge, and the knowledge that outsiders expect it, that has been one of the main drives behind his last desperate efforts to complete his revolution as fully as possible before he dies. Yet the very frenzy of the effort will, we may be sure, make the ultimate reaction the more inevitable. Let us not be too absorbed in the immediate present. Let us have the patience to wait until the tempests that are now blowing have had a chance to subside.

What China will then be like, whether there will really be strong threads of continuity with a specifically Chinese past or whether industrial civilization, as it takes root, will turn China into just another replica of the advanced industrial nations of the rest of the world, only the future will reveal. It does seem to me that the distinctive character of Chinese civilization will not be extinguished and will make a very great contribution to the coming world civilization.

One of the threads of continuity that is most likely to survive is the acceptance of a single Chinese identity by all Chinese. How this will in fact work itself out is, of course, something that is difficult to foresee—there are so many complicated factors involved. What would happen, for instance, if the native Formosan majority were to gain control of their own destiny in the near future? My own guess is that in the long run the Chinese identity, which is being fostered among young Formosans as well as among the mainlanders on the island, will prevail, and that some basis for reunion with the mainland will be worked out. It is surely a matter which must be left to the Chinese themselves, and in which it is an impertinence for foreigners to interfere.

# Political Leadership and Modernization in Communist China

Henry G. Schwarz

O ver the past two years the Great Proletarian Cultural Revolution has dazzled the world with the specter of internal strife seemingly destroying the unity and authority of the Communist party. As spectacular as the violence and destruction have been, so has the very occurrence of the Cultural Revolution been unforeseen. Indeed, as recently as three years ago any prediction of a fight to the finish between Mao Tse-tung and Liu Shao-ch'i would have been met with scorn and incredulity by the world's China specialists.

This unanimous failure to reckon with the possibility of the breakup of Communist China's political leadership points up our collective failure to assess correctly the origin and nature of political leadership. It seems beyond dispute that the Chinese Communist party of the post-1949 period was viewed as monolithic and hierarchical, with Mao Tse-tung (the chairman) as sole, supreme decision-maker. This view was so thoroughly accepted by most China specialists that previous purges, like those of Kao Kang, Jao Shu-shih, P'eng Te-huai, and others, were interpreted as exceptions to the rule. In other words, they were seen as confirmations of a monolithic political leadership rather than as indications of a much looser leadership.

Literally tens of thousands of articles, speeches, broadcasts, wallposters, and leaflets since the summer of 1966 have portrayed a political leadership divided against itself since the formation of the Communist party. Many of the charges made in irregular media, such as wallposters and leaflets, are undoubtedly false, made for immediate tactical objectives by a local group. It is also clear that some accusations made by the Mao group against party leaders in the regular media are factually incorrect. But it is much too early to assert, as some China specialists have already done, that the Mao group has condemned past policies and actions of party leaders on an *ex post facto* basis. In short, actions which were consonant with the party's general line at the time they were taken have become, according to this view, "revisionist" by the present Mao group's reckoning. Such assertions may eventually be confirmed by a thorough investigation after the Cultural Revolution has run its course. But at present it seems prudent not to foreclose other interpretations.

The view that today's crimes were yesterday's virtues, reflecting the general line of that earlier time, is, after all, based on the old assumption of a monolithic and united political leadership before the Cultural Revolution. Because the Cultural Revolution has demonstrated conclusively that the leadership is not united now, we must at least consider the possibility that the post-1949 leadership has *always* been a rather loosely structured directorate with no single person in supreme command. In the essay to follow, this is my hypothesis, with a corollary: that the forces which have undermined the political leadership are largely the result of strains imposed by the modernization process.

"Modernization" involves, among many other things, trends toward industrialization and functional specialization in the economy; optimum education, universal values, and social as well as spatial mobility in society; comprehensive government authority;

and close bonds between leaders and led in politics. While differences in degree surely exist, modernization is a universal and perpetual process from which no state, not even those most advanced technologically, can graduate. The major trends of the modernization process appear to be universal, but their speed and configurations differ from state to state because each state contains a unique set of factors. The most relevant of these are human and natural resources, history, and the state's relations with other states.

I shall attempt to sketch, in a highly selective manner, (1) some key events in the early stages of China's modernization which may have influenced the nature and attitudes of the Communist leadership of a later day; (2) the nature of the Communist leadership before assuming state power; (3) problems of modernization since 1949 which may have weakened the leadership; and (4) a cautious glimpse into the future.

The beginning of modernization in China in the second half of the nineteenth century created conditions which allowed later political leaderships, including the Communists, to further the process of modernization.

Western military aggression and internal rebellions were the two most important factors determining change in the seventy years before the collapse of the dynastic system in China in 1911. The first armed clash between Great Britain and China around 1840 set the stage for the long and tragic record of China's external relations. Galling as it must have been for the rulers of a once-mighty empire to be forced by a mere seven thousand British troops to accept the Treaty of Nanking in 1842, the real tragedy was that the treaty settled nothing. In their world-views, the British (and other Westerners) and the Chinese talked past one another. The British, following the European tradition, adhered to the concept of the legal equality of all states. They also assumed that trade untrammeled by severe government restrictions was vital and beneficial for all states.

Europeans considered these ideas perfectly natural, but they were alien to East Asia, where instead of the egalitarian principle the concept of hierarchy dominated. Not only China but Japan and societies throughout Southeast Asia and the Pacific viewed all relations, personal and collective, domestic and international, in hierarchical terms. As late as the 1940's Japan sought to apply the hierarchical concept in her Greater East Asia Co-Prosperity Sphere, with herself at the center and the conquered states as her "younger brothers." In its theoretical formulation the idea was not the autocratic notion of a "master race" espoused by Nazi Germany. It presupposed a bond of obligations from which Japan was not exempt. It was not accepted by the peoples of conquered Southeast Asia nor, of course, by the Chinese. But the point is that they rejected a number of factors (for example, the identity of the claimant) and not necessarily the hierarchical form itself.

No matter how unnatural the Chinese may have considered the Western notion of equality, it was enforced in treaty after treaty until the Chinese seemed to accept the concept and sought to turn it to their advantage. Unfortunately, as the Chinese found out, the principle of equality in international affairs was but a thin veneer for a jungle in which the strongest dominated without the obligations demanded by a hierarchical world-view. Versailles provided the harshest lesson: on the one hand the peace conference proclaimed the principle of equality, including its constituent elements of self-determination and territorial integrity; but, on the other hand the former German holdings in the Chinese province of Shantung, taken by the Japanese during World War I, were not restored to China.

China experienced the negative influence of the outside world primarily through the treaty system. By 1900 there were nineteen treaty ports with some thirty-three concessions of land in China, the largest being the International Settlement in Shanghai. Small in territory as these concessions were, they did contain some valuable property which was placed beyond the jurisdiction of the Chinese government. Chinese sovereignty was also curtailed outside the treaty ports by the principle of extraterritoriality, whereby a foreigner could not be brought to trial by Chinese courts. Missionaries received special privileges; they were allowed, for example, to buy and lease property anywhere in China for whatever purposes they so desired.

On the other side of the ledger, the impact of the West brought with it several positive long-range influences. For the duration of the Ch'ing dynasty, the changes in the formal governmental structure were small. The foreigners insisted on the creation of a foreign office, and they themselves directed an entire branch of the Chinese government, the Maritime Customs Office, which was run according to modern methods of management and accounting. Foreigners also directly influenced the economy. After the first Sino-British war, foreign businessmen operated freely in the treaty ports under the protection of foreign garrisons and gunboats. Up to the end of the nineteenth century, they were engaged chiefly in trade and finance. The Treaty of Shimonoseki added manufacturing rights, and the treaty ports became the seedbeds of China's modern industry. Chinese merchants were attracted to the business atmosphere of Shanghai and soon competed with the foreign manufacturers.

At a slower pace, but no less significantly, Chinese society was also affected by foreign influences, through missionary schools and translations, and later indirectly by Chinese students returning from study overseas. One of the consequences of these influences was the establishment of government schools based on Western patterns, with curricula whose degrees were declared in 1904 equal to degrees obtained under the old examination system. Through their contacts with individual foreigners, many urban Chinese observed new social relations, particularly the equal status of women, and they began ever so slowly to adopt these new relations. Western ideas spread throughout Eastern China, and by the end of the dynasty tens of thousands of Chinese, mostly upper-class, had been introduced to the universalistic values of Western urban society.

To these various forces were added Western political ideas of representative government at home and legal equality in international relations, which directly challenged the dynastic principle of the emperor as sole supreme decision-maker and the Sinocentric view of the world. The Ch'ing court sought to take the initiative by using to China's advantage the Western principles of foreign relations. In 1868 it sent the Burlingame mission abroad to negotiate for treaty revisions on the basis of Western international law. The court may have viewed its seeming acquiescence in Western concepts as a tactical necessity which would not undermine the internal state structure, for it adamantly opposed its own transformation into a parliamentary democracy. But the court fought a losing battle. Provincial leaders whose powers grew rapidly during and after the T'aip'ing rebellion continued to support the overall structure and the ideology of the state, but were for various reasons more receptive than the court to reform. And then, there were the political leaders who rallied around Sun Yat-sen and from their exiles called for revolution.

Caught between these two forces, the Ch'ing dynasty reluctantly ordered in 1908–1909 the creation of representative assemblies in the provinces. At the national level, plans for an assembly were formulated and a cabinet of sorts was added to the court structure. To some these measures appeared to be last-minute attempts by the court to prolong its stay in power rather than a voluntary move in the direction of representative government.

Even if the court had been willing, it would remain a moot point whether it could have transformed itself into a modern representative institution, for it was abruptly removed from Chinese politics in early 1912. But one may speculate that the court's extreme reluctance was based on the feeling, best articulated by K'ang Yu-wei, that such political modernization could be successful only if it were slow and evolutionary. Events after 1912 seemed to vindicate this feeling. In the end, the old traditional political system had been held together by no more than the legitimacy of the court as the ruler of China. As long as the court existed, this aura of legitimacy prevented the centrifugal forces of provincialism from tearing apart the frail fabric of Chinese political unity.

The central leadership of nineteenth-century China was also weakened by several major rebellions, of which the T'aip'ing (1850–1864) was the most momentous. Although it was eventually crushed, the T'aip'ing rebellion had a tremendous impact upon the surviving Chinese political system. First, it resulted in enormous bloodletting in the heavily populated provinces of the lower Yangtze valley, which left its mark for almost a century.[1] Second, the devastation all but eliminated the land tax as the major source of government income. The central government came to rely more on maritime customs collected on its behalf by foreigners, and on sharply increased sales of official ranks. Government posts had been filled primarily through competitive examinations. Now that more merchants than ever could buy their way into office, the once rigid prestige ladder, which had placed the scholar several rungs above the merchant, began to crumble.

Third, the T'aip'ing rebellion resulted in the decentralization of political power. In order to crush the rebellion, the court granted provincial leaders like Tseng Kuo-fan and Li Hung-chang permission to raise their own armies. After the rebellion some of these new armies, built upon personal loyalty to provincial leaders, never wholly integrated with the rest of the imperial army, and they later formed the nucleus of warlordism. Provincial leadership was greatly strengthened by the introduction during the T'aip'ing rebellion of a transit fee on goods, called *likin*. Created initially by provincial leaders because the central treasury was insufficient to underwrite the war and subsequent reconstruction, *likin* became such an ample source of revenue that many provinces remained beyond the reach of the central government's "power of the purse" long after the fall of the dynasty.

When the Ch'ing dynasty was removed, the two main forces mentioned earlier, internal discord and foreign influence, grew sharply. In tangible matters, Japan quickly became the most important foreign power in China. Her capital, enterprises, and manufactured goods dominated the Chinese market and became the targets of boycotts and strikes. But, on the negative side, Japan's greatest impact on China's modernization was by force of arms. The first incursions into Chinese territory after the fall of the Ch'ing dynasty were made in 1915 when Japan took over the German possessions in Shantung. Japanese military expansionism, after a decade of relative quiescence, reawakened in 1931 with the conquest of the entire Northeast and the establishment of a puppet regime, Manchukuo. The next five years saw a gradual expansion of Japanese military and political control over parts of Northern China and Inner Mongolia, culminating in the Sino-Japanese War of 1937–1945.

Intangible and more diffuse foreign influences contributed even more to China's modernization in the four decades between the dynasty's demise and the Communist conquest. Banking, trade, commerce, industry, communications, and transportation all advanced, particularly during the nine years of Kuomintang rule before the outbreak of the Sino-Japanese War. Western education

spread rapidly, with the greatest progress recorded in higher education, where by the early 1940's 143 universities, colleges, and
technical schools had been established.[2] A great literacy movement
sought to bring minimal education to the vast illiterate majority.
The increase in commercial and industrial activities in the cities
created a degree of spatial mobility rarely known before except in
times of war and natural disasters. While many thousands of mi-
grants to the cities found little but misery, the process contributed
to modernization. It instilled in many a wider awareness which
helped to shape values more attuned to the nation than to the
native locale and province. Unfortunately, it also created an ever-
increasing pool of human exasperation which could be and eventually was exploited by political organizers.

But economic and social modernization could not progress much
further without political modernization as well. Essential to successful sustained modernization in China were (1) an end to the in-
terminable fighting among warlords, (2) a government in actual
control over the entire state, (3) a government having close and
direct links with the people, and (4) a truly united political leadership. Tragically for China, none of these four conditions was wholly
fulfilled until the Communist rise to power. The Northern Expedition of 1926–1928, in which the troops of the Kuomintang under
Chiang Kai-shek drove from Canton to Peking, eliminated some
warlords, and it decreased but did not eliminate entirely clashes
among them. But China continued to be rent by warfare after the
expedition. Chiang thus decided to apply military pressure against
provincial strongmen while throwing more military power against
the Communists, who, after the establishment of territorial bases in
Kiangsi in 1928, became the principal challengers to the newly
established central government.

The central government appeared stronger than it actually was.
Many regions of China had not been touched by the Northern
Expedition and thus remained outside effective central control.
China's entire western half, in fact, including Tibet, Sinkiang,
Ch'inghai, and parts of Kansu, remained autonomous throughout
the period of Kuomintang rule on the mainland. Even in the eastern
half, which was directly affected by the Northern Expedition, the
central government was more suzerain than sovereign because its

leadership was not united. The victory of the expedition had been purchased for a political price which turned out to be one of the major reasons for the Kuomintang's ineffective modernization and national defense programs during the subsequent twenty years. Warlords had joined the Kuomintang campaign to oust the warlord government in Peking. In exchange for their services, they were appointed to branch political councils of the Kuomintang. These appointments helped to keep their provinces relatively independent. Warlords were also appointed to the State Council in Nanking, thereby giving them an opportunity not only to make national policy but to check attempts to undercut their regional authority.

In its disunity the Kuomintang leadership strongly resembled Sun Yat-sen's revolutionary movement in 1911. In both cases the movement broke up shortly after attaining its principal goal of ousting the existing central government. Both Sun Yat-sen's movement before 1911 and the Kuomintang during the Northern Expedition were united on one essentially negative goal rather than for reasons of organizational discipline or a commonly shared commitment to an ideology. Moreover, neither group's victory was so complete as to bind the movement together after the attainment of the principal goal. Thus both Sun Yat-sen's revolutionaries and Chiang Kai-shek's Kuomintang differed in this respect markedly from the Communists on the eve of their victory about twenty years later.

Despite their patently superior organization and what seemed to be their solidly united leadership, the Communists had their own problems throughout the insurrectionary period, which persisted after the assumption of state power in 1949 and have played an important role in China's modernization.

The unity of the Communist leadership on the eve of its rise to power was not only not solid but also of relatively recent origin. Their spectacular defeats in 1927 at the hands of the Kuomintang had severely shaken the party's early leadership. An added divisive force was the growing struggle between Stalin and Trotsky over the "correct" strategy for the Communist international movement. The shock waves reaching China resulted in bitter recriminations among leaders and, at one time, in the coexistence of two central committees, one in Shanghai and the other in the newly established base area in Kiangsi. Despite latter-day claims to the contrary, Mao was far from being the undisputed leader of the party at the time. It was not until 1938 in Yenan that he was able to overcome the last major overt opposition to his rule.

By then the fortunes of the party had also improved considerably. Its military strength and membership were at an all-time high. The most important reason for the Communist resurgence was the Japanese invasion. In response to this national emergency, the two main political forces in China temporarily reconciled their differences and formed the second United Front. This enabled the Communists to move out of their isolated enclave around Yenan and to set up other base areas in Northern and Eastern China. These bases not only survived but prospered during the war primarily because the Communists perfected a set of correct policies aimed at extending their authority down to the villages.[3] This was a clear step toward political modernization. Traditionally, direct government control had stopped at the county level, leaving the villagers uninvolved in national affairs.

The war also imposed its stamp on the nature of the top party leadership with consequences that have lasted until the current Cultural Revolution and that will probably influence the future course of China after Mao and Chiang. As soon as Mao had won out over his last major rival, Wang Ming, in 1938, supreme control over party activities eluded Mao's hands not because of overt rivalry but because of the exigencies of war. While Mao and a few other high-ranking leaders remained in the headquarters at Yenan, many other leaders established bases elsewhere in China. As the various base areas became increasingly isolated from one another, much decision-making power devolved upon local party leaders. As a result, continuous experimentation with new institutions and functions of politico-social control in the outer base areas determined general policy directives from Yenan rather than the other way around.[4]

The predominantly military character of the outer base area made matters potentially worse for the future of a truly united Communist leadership. Many of the bases were less secure than the Yenan headquarters area, so that military affairs predominated.

Their leaders, besides being party officials, were also military commanders. The potential danger, however, lay not in a challenge to party supremacy by a united military command, or in a Communist version of warlordism, any more than these dangers exist today. As long-time party members the politico-military base leaders were too firmly committed to the principle of party supremacy; and they were not graduates of conventional military academies where they may have been subjected to the idea of military elitism. What developed during the war was less dramatic and less tangible but definitely a factor in the modernization of Communist China. Small cohesive groups changing little in membership, a long period of time (eight years), and extraordinary hardships were the ingredients for clusters of friendship, trust, and loyalty that developed in the base areas and were to persist long after 1949—in fact until now. But considerable changes in composition *have* taken place. Other similar groups emerged after 1949 which were not based primarily on commonly shared commands during the war, and, except for the Cultural Revolution and possibly a few prior instances, these groups did not overtly disrupt the unity of the leadership.

In short, the war produced a coalition leadership in the Communist party which was clearly reflected in the seventh Party Congress in 1945. Mao was elected chairman, but his office had no explicit supreme powers. He was at best first among equals. Both the thirteen-man political bureau and the five-man inner circle, the central secretariat, were almost evenly balanced between Mao and his Yenan comrades, and outer base leaders and others who had spent considerable time away from Yenan. The leader of the "non-Yenan" group was Liu Shao-ch'i. His election to the second highest position clearly reflected the immense influence Liu had built among leading party officials in the outer bases and behind enemy lines. Many delegates to the 7th Congress who owed their appointments to Liu repaid their debt in this manner.

In the broadest sense the formal lineup of the leadership in 1945 was a strategic preparation for the forthcoming struggle against the Kuomintang government. It was an alliance between Mao and the politico-military leaders headed by Liu Shao-ch'i. Both possessed attributes considered vital for success in the subsequent civil war. Leaders of the outer base areas, and especially Liu Shao-ch'i, knew intimately the vast arena of Eastern and Northern China, still under Japanese control and soon to revert to the Kuomintang government. This knowledge, plus their military forces, were needed to overcome the numerically vastly superior armies of Chiang Kai-shek. Mao Tse-tung, on the other hand, was the symbol of a purposeful, united, and invincible party.[5] In the relative tranquility of Yenan, Mao had written several essays on policy and Marxist theory which helped to support the claim made by the party constitution adopted in 1945 that "the Chinese Communist Party takes the theories of Marxism-Leninism and the unified thought of the practice of the Chinese revolution, the thought of Mao Tse-tung, as the guideline for all of its actions."[6] This bold statement, which put Mao on a par with Marx and Lenin, did not so much grow from the leaders' acknowledgement of Mao as a great theoretician[7] as from their belief that the elevation of Mao would help the Communist cause in the impending struggle against the Kuomintang.

In short, toward the end of World War II an alliance was forged between Mao, the symbol of the "wave of the future," and the several leaders of personal groups who, with their military forces and politico-organizational know-how, were to make this "wave" a reality. Their smashing success in the ensuing civil war confirmed in the minds of the Communist leaders the correctness of their collective efforts. This conviction was strong enough to carry over into the post-1949 period. The collective nature of the top leadership has remained until today; at no time has any one leader held a supreme position comparable to Stalin's in the thirties and forties.

Of course, it was not common strategy alone that helped to keep the leadership together during the insurrectionary period. Ideology was undoubtedly a binding factor. But it is difficult to determine exactly how and to what extent Marxism-Leninism helped the Communist victory. One can readily see various needs that may have been satisfied by ideology. The Communists were underdogs in practically all respects and needed assurance that in the end victory would be theirs. Ideology may have given this assurance. It spoke of linear progress in life and, in periodizing history, predestined the Communist stage to be the highest. Its concept of the dialectic, or perpetual struggle, seemed to be reflected in the chaotic conditions of the pre-1949 period. At the same time, Marxism's class analysis appeared to help the Communists to derive strength from chaos, and to relate themselves not only to all facets of Chinese society but to the world at large. Perhaps most importantly, this body of doctrine of foreign origin was adapted by a Chinese to Chinese conditions. Herein lies the importance of Mao to the Communist movement. Despite his weakness as a Marxist theoretician, and perhaps because of it, Mao made the ideology's assurances of final victory relevant to China and hence credible to his fellow Communists.

In 1949 the Communists' major objective shifted from the seizure of power to modernization in all fields. Because of this fundamental change in their objectives, ideology seemed to lose much of its *raison d'être* at the moment of victory on the battlefield. Actually, the Communists did not wish to de-emphasize ideology as much as to expand its relevance. Like all ideologies, the Marxism-Leninism of the insurrectionaries contained two elements: doctrine and action program. As we have seen, the doctrinal element had given the Communists certain crucial advantages for almost thirty years since the party's formation. Considering the tremendous tasks they set for themselves, and their small numerical strength among a population of several hundred millions, the Communists had every reason in 1949 to retain the doctrinal component of their ideology in essentially unaltered form. But the action program grew in size and complexity as the regime moved ahead rapidly with ambitious projects to reshape the state, society, the economy, and culture.

Some tasks, particularly in the restructuring of society and culture, seemed partially amenable to doctrinal guidance because they required, in David Apter's words, the redefinition of roles according to explicit moral principles.[8] But the link between theory and practice, or between doctrine and action program, became tenuous in tasks related primarily to management and technology. The problem of this link, present in all Communist states, could be ameliorated if not wholly solved by applying a mixture of two leadership styles. One subordinates action programs to unaltered doctrine with its emphasis on class conflict and revolutionary methods, and thereby jeopardizes progress in management, technology, and similar fields. The other style places a premium on modernization and de-emphasizes or ignores those facets of doctrine that conflict with particular action programs; or it makes formal changes in the doctrine. The latter leadership style, introduced into the Soviet political system by Stalin, has been termed by Robert Tucker "deradicalization" to indicate the submergence and partial metamorphosis of an originally revolutionary doctrinal element. Chinese Communist leaders, and the Maoist group in particular, have called it "revisionism."

Since the establishment of the Chinese Communist political system, leadership styles have varied in their mixture of doctrine and action program. In two periods, the Great Leap Forward of 1958–1960 and still more so during the Great Proletarian Cultural Revolution which began in August 1966, the overwhelming emphasis was on revolutionary methods and on the pre-eminence of doctrine. It is no coincidence that these two periods were also the only two occasions when Mao Tse-tung was clearly in command. At other times revolutionary methods were less conspicuous than more routinized methods, and doctrine was de-emphasized especially during the early sixties.

Several kinds of revolutionary methods have been employed. During the early fifties, terror was used against large numbers of people including landlords, a few rich peasants, and people who had had some connection with the old regime. A second method has been mass mobilization for such diverse purposes as eradicating sparrows, demonstrating against some foreign state, and afforestation. One such campaign, the water-work brigade movement of 1957–1958, precipitated the Great Leap Forward. A third method has been the purge, in two forms. One has been the dismissal from office practiced in all political systems. The other has been the elimination of unorthodox ideas among party and government members. Both forms of purge originated in the insurrectionary period.

The more routinized methods of modernization were most apparent in economic construction and education, except during the two periods already noted. The single most important event in this respect was the first Five-Year Plan of 1953–1957. Almost wholly an adaptation of Soviet experience, it allocated most state capital and material resources to industry, particularly to the heavy sector. The familiar comprehensive and detailed character of this Soviet-style economic plan resulted not only in very impressive gains, as in iron and steel production, but in an enormous government apparatus. The large and highly specialized ministries (by early 1965, eight for various kinds of machine-building alone) were at first in charge of all but the smallest construction projects. After the first Five-Year Plan much economic decision-making was shifted to the provincial governments. Like large hierarchical organizations the world over, they established routinized, impersonal chains of command, and they were effective enough to fulfill most production goals. But the government hierarchies also produced a blizzard of red tape. Judging by almost continuous condemnations of "bureaucratism" in the party press, red tape is as much a problem in China as it is on the other shore of the Pacific.

The growth of government also endangered the party's self-image as the state's supreme political authority. The preoccupation with heavy industry provoked a rapid expansion of formal education in science and technology which, like the Five-Year Plan, was largely Soviet in inspiration and importation. Education came to be geared to professional expertise, and admission criteria to high schools and colleges were almost wholly based on merit in competitive examinations. The party, whose members included few intellectuals and technicians, found it increasingly difficult to carry out its self-assigned role of supervision and guidance. Its discomfiture was roughly analogous to the United States Congress' feelings during budget time. Congress long ago lost its ability to appraise meaningfully the relative merits of budget requests, because it does not have as much technological manpower as the Executive branch. The Chinese Communist party was in a still more untenable position because it was supposed to be not merely a coequal branch of government but the master of government.

The party as the self-appointed tutor of China reflects a characteristic posture of political leaderships in other late-modernizing states. Monopoly of political power is explained in terms of the tutor principle by many military leaders, such as Suharto in Indonesia and Ayub Khan in Pakistan, and by other non-Communist revolutionary parties, of which the best known and most relevant example is the Kuomintang in China. Central to all is the elitist tenet that uniquely superior qualities legitimize the tutor's monopoly of political power.

The Chinese Communists' central claim to tutorship is their alleged exclusive ability to divine the "scientific truths" of Marxism-Leninism and, consequently, to lead China "correctly" along the road of modernization. Stripped of its ideological trappings, the party's claim contains a kernel of plausibility. It is relatively small, having fewer than 4.5 million members at the time of its rise to power in 1949. It is heavily indoctrinated with one comprehensive set of ideas, and its leaders had three decades of common experiences during the insurrectionary period. For these and other reasons, the party as a whole was probably more clearly aware of national problems than any other group and thus seemed to be in a superior position to give unified direction to political and social modernization.

But, as already noted, the party's experiences had not equipped it well for the task of economic modernization, ideological claims to the contrary notwithstanding. The stresses and strains among the top leaders, bursting into full view during the Cultural Revolution, had their beginnings in the first Five-Year Plan. The rapid growth of government as a result of the plan's emphasis on industry forced the party also to grow, possibly faster and larger than anticipated by the leaders. The party had to seed the myriads of government bureaus with its own men in order to keep a watchful eye on disliked officials. It also had to extend its own hierarchy downward into the provinces and eventually to the village level to parallel the nationwide tentacles of government. By the end of the first Five-Year Plan the party had grown to almost 13 million members.[9] The actual number of new party members was still larger than the threefold increase since 1949 suggests, because deaths and purges caused considerable turnover in membership.

The increasing emphasis of party purges on "bureaucratism" suggested that the party in its supervisory role not only failed to curb bureaucratic excesses in the government but became itself infected by them. The anti-official was in danger of becoming an official himself. The greatest danger in this trend was not so much the party losing its separate identity vis-à-vis the government but losing contact with the people. Popular attitudes toward officials since dynastic days had ranged from indifference in good times to hatred in times of stress. The most effective slogan of the T'aip'ing rebellion in the mid-nineteenth century had been *"ta kuan!"* (down with the officials!).[10] Mindful of popular attitudes and the close links with the people which helped it to power in 1949, the party leadership cracked down repeatedly on bureaucratic tendencies. The "fish-in-water" guerrilla principle (and many other facets of the pre-1949 period) was kept alive because, despite its rapid growth, the party remained a mere 2 per cent scattered among China's huge population. While government could remain aloof from the people and still carry out industrialization, the party's more delicate and complicated task of changing society's structure and orientations was wholly dependent on close links with the people.

The party's top leadership has remained united on this issue. Both Mao Tse-tung and Liu Shao-ch'i have always called for close ties between party members and the people and have denounced the "official." But divisions of opinion on many other issues of modernization later widened into hostile factions. The first, Soviet-style Five-Year Plan placed too great a burden on agriculture. In the Soviet Union, with its immense arable land and relatively sparse population, industrialization could be force-fed by exploiting agriculture. China did not have much agricultural fat to sustain the rapid pace in heavy industry. It became clear by 1955, midway through the first Five-Year Plan, that in order to retain the momentum of economic modernization only two viable alternatives were open. Either industrialization would have to be underwritten by vastly increased Soviet aid, or a much larger share of state capital would have to be devoted to raising agricultural production.

The first Five-Year Plan also complicated the party's role in education. First, as already noted, the highest premiums were placed on professional specialization and personal achievement. But, to a man, the top leaders instinctively disliked these values. In the almost thirty years of insurrection, far longer than that spent by the founders of the Soviet state, the Chinese Communists had developed the ideals of the *tomienshou,* or jack-of-all-trades, and of group effort.

Second, like Communists everywhere, the leaders disliked the trend toward specialization because it produced intellectuals in the broadest sense of the term. This antipathy and uneasiness toward intellectuals might seem odd in view of the fact that the Chinese party, more than any other major Communist party in the world, had been founded by intellectuals. But thirty years had passed, and the leaders were wary for several reasons. Intellectuals have the disconcerting quality of demolishing self-evident truths and other doctrinal verities. Given half a chance, as during the Hundred Flowers campaign of 1956–1957, they leave no stone unturned in their criticism. Recent persecutions of intellectuals in the Soviet Union seem to suggest that a rapprochement between ideologue and intellectual in a totalitarian society is at best a slow and painful process. The Chinese Communists were also uneasy because most higher intellectuals had received their advanced training in the United States and Western Europe. While their technical abilities were valuable and were soon harnessed, their political views remained suspect. The Communists who had been away from the cities since 1927 also remembered that when the Japanese invaded, hardly any older intellectuals and relatively few college students chose to go to the Communist base areas. Most of them went with Chiang Kai-shek's government.

Third, the rise of the intellectual in a predominantly rural society seemed to threaten another party role in education. Like other traditional societies, China had its sharp urban-rural dichotomy. As late as the thirties, mutual antipathies had still been so strong that appeals by the Kuomintang government to college students to make their careers as teachers in the villages were largely ignored. When the Japanese invasion forced the government to withdraw into the rural backwaters of the Southwest, the sudden meeting of peasant and intellectual was strained. While many students laid aside their feelings of superiority in the name of common national resistance, the peasants remained skeptical of the "city slickers."

The party sought to bridge this gap by giving preferential treatment to peasants (as well as to workers) in its ideology and in admission criteria for jobs, schools, and mass organizations. By doing so the party unwittingly widened rather than narrowed the gulf separating the city from the countryside. As long as agriculture was reduced to a holding operation under the first Five-Year Plan, glamour and prestige were bestowed upon the cities.[11] Millions flocked to the cities in search of industrial jobs and a college education, thereby disrupting rural production plans, overburdening urban facilities, and causing unemployment. Once they settled down in the cities, these people showed little inclination to return to their villages, despite incessant urgings by the party. Many of them, particularly college students, soon acquired the familiar disdain of the urban resident for farm life.

The Soviet-style educational system not only reinforced traditional antipathies against farm life but also fostered individualism, which was wholly contrary to the party's goals. An academically oriented curriculum with merit as the sole criterion for admission into colleges powerfully encouraged the drive toward personal achievement. The every-man-for-himself competition in the schools made assignment to the countryside after graduation a distasteful prospect, precisely because rural life was becoming increasingly collectivized.

Besides problems in the economy and in education raised by the first Five-Year Plan, China's external relations contributed to a sharpening of differences among party leaders. By 1955 it became publicly known that at least some party leaders, including Mao Tse-tung, were disappointed with and worried by China's close links with the Soviet Union. First, Stalin's death in 1953 and the slow trend toward liberalization in the Soviet Union undermined whatever teacher-pupil relationship might have been accepted by Chinese leaders in the early fifties. Stalin had been senior to Mao both as a Communist leader and as the head of a Communist state, but his successors were not.

Second, it became apparent that China's future industrialization drive would not be underwritten by vastly increased assistance from the Soviets. In February 1955 the Soviets concluded their first aid agreement with India, China's prime competitor as developmental model, by granting $120 million for the Bhilai steel center. While the Soviets explained to their Chinese comrades that Soviet diversification of economic aid was, in an age of nuclear stalemate, the optimum strategy for the common good of all Communist states, the Chinese were less than impressed by this argument.

Third, the growing disappointment with the Soviets was possibly strengthened by a reappraisal of Sino-Soviet relations. True, the Soviets had helped the Chinese Communists materially in the crucial early stages of the civil war by virtually handing over large stocks of Japanese arms in Manchuria. But the record during most of the years before 1949 was otherwise not so fruitful for the Chinese. Soviet strategic guidance, sometimes carried out by high-handed Comintern representatives, more than once imperiled the very existence of the Chinese Communist party. During the war against Japan, most Soviet military aid went to the Nationalist government. And after World War II the Soviets acted like the tsars in China. Russian imperial privileges in Manchuria were reappropriated by the Soviet Union and, after 1949, Soviet influence was widened through joint-stock companies in which Soviet managers had the upper hand.

Thus, only a scant six years after achieving state power in China, the Communists were faced with a whole set of problems which had been activated by the nature and direction of China's first massive attempt at modernization. These problems were generally similar to those which had existed, and still do, elsewhere in the world. Serious dislocations in the political, social, and economic spheres of a state appear to be unavoidable symptoms of modernization. At the same time, the problems raised in China after 1949 were in their particular aspects unique to that state, and they were growing in direct proportion to the speed of economic modernization dictated by the first Five-Year Plan.

Because a highly centralized leadership oversaw this modernization, the emerging problems had a direct and severe impact upon that leadership. Two broad policy lines seemed to form in the mid-fifties. One, represented by Ch'en Yün and P'eng Te-huai, favored continued modernization along the lines of the first Five-Year Plan: massive investment in heavy industry, relative neglect of agriculture, specialization of manpower, routinization of government, and close links with the Soviet Union. The other line, represented by Mao Tse-tung, did not reject outright any of these specific goals but sought to strike a balance between city and village, intellectual and peasant, specialist and all-round handyman, and domestic resources and foreign aid. This balance, soon made famous by the slogan "walking on two legs," was predicated on Mao's judgment that China could best be modernized by relying on domestic resources.

The two approaches were not mutually antagonistic; their differences were due largely to personality factors. Mao seemed to have a deep-seated antipathy toward all foreign influences, perhaps because he was sensitive to their negative effects upon China since 1840. He also felt that the first Five-Year Plan had not made full use of China's greatest asset, unskilled labor, and had also threatened to undermine the still fragile bonds of national unity. Above all, Mao seemed to hanker for the relatively idyllic and less complicated days of Yenan.

While difficult to prove conclusively, this hypothesis is highly plausible. After all, Mao, unlike Liu Shao-ch'i and many other leaders whom he would later attack, had little experience with the cities, intellectuals, foreign travel, and administrative responsibilities. It might be argued that these relative "blind spots" enabled him to see better than his co-leaders could that economic and social modernization was being achieved to an alarming extent at the expense of agriculture and China's rural majority. But this presumed advantage was wholly negated by Mao's relative inexperience in and even disdain for administration. The party leaders who since 1949 had actually been running Communist China may well have agreed with Mao's analysis, but they had their reservations about his suggestions for bringing about a more balanced and a more broadly based modernization.

Mao's recipe was revolutionary, a resort to doctrine. He argued for labor-intensive programs not as an engineer or government official might, with slide-rule in hand and efficiency in mind. He advocated multipurpose mass campaigns not only to reach certain production goals but to inculcate new value orientations. When he finally had a chance to implement his policy line in the Great Leap Forward, it became evident that Mao did not want a mere union of professional expertise and political reliability. As a revolutionary, he scorned such a union as static. As a Communist, he perceived through his dialectic prisms the inevitable struggle between these two goals and feared that, with the tremendous impetus imparted by the first Five-Year Plan, professional expertise would win out. To counteract this trend, which he later was to denounce as "revisionism," Mao gave primary consideration to political reliability and therefore sought to politicize all facets of modernization. His key slogan of the Great Leap Forward became *"chengchih kuashuai"* ("politics takes command").

The Great Leap Forward marked the great divide in the existence of Communist China. It led China downhill economically and set back economic production, except in defense technology, a full decade while other Asian states made slow but steady progress.[12] It sowed discord with the Soviet Union and hence greater isolation from the rest of the world. It undermined the efforts of previous years to forge a national consciousness and helped restore particularistic value orientations among the people.

Most important, the Great Leap Forward raised disagreements within the top leadership to the point of bitter conflict. The conflict may well have broken out later anyway, but it was certainly precipitated by the economic and social costs of the Great Leap Forward and by Mao's call for total politicization.

Early in 1958 the regime created communes to speed collectivization, but four months later they were practically dismantled in all but their governmental functions. Other facets of the Great Leap Forward, such as the backyard furnaces and the mass militia, soon followed suit. Mao not only resigned from (or, as he claimed nine years later, was pushed out of) the state presidency but assumed a relatively passive role in decision-making. Liu Shao-ch'i, who replaced Mao as state president, resumed his role as the party's chief executive. But it was much more than a return to the *status quo ante*. Bitterness now divided the top leadership. At the Lushan conference of the central committee in August 1959, two clearly distinguishable factions joined in battle. Mao was able to retain the party chairmanship and to have the opposition's chief spokesman at the conference, P'eng Te-huai, ousted from his post as defense minister. But it was a hollow victory. The majority under Liu Shao-ch'i had already ratified depoliticization and a return to a more routinized administration.

These changes succeeded in keeping Communist China physically intact and allowed it to turn the corner in economic production by 1962. But both major factions were preparing for the final showdown. With Liu's tacit permission, Mao was subjected to a systematic campaign of ridicule. In hundreds of newspaper articles written between 1959 and 1964, many of them distributed in book form throughout China, Mao was called, among other epithets, a charlatan who in the end could only emerge "with a bleeding nose under the impact of facts."[13]

While he was being derided and his programs obliterated, Mao, with the help of P'eng's replacement, Lin Piao, sought to make the army personally loyal to himself. Only a few days after he assumed command, Lin Piao ordered the study of Mao's works, and the army was believed sufficiently indoctrinated by 1962 for Mao to start his long, slow comeback. With the tenth central committee plenum in September of that year, the Mao minority and the Liu majority actively resumed their struggle in two major campaigns, the socialist education campaign and, since August 1966, the Great Proletarian Cultural Revolution.

The struggle has become harsh and brutal. During the Cultural Revolution Mao has repaid the insults hurled at him in the early sixties by unleashing a campaign of vilification against Liu Shao-ch'i and many other party leaders in which "ogres" and "monsters" are among the milder epithets.[14] The major reason for this growing bitterness is undoubtedly Mao's advanced age. For the past four years he has stressed the need for "revolutionary heirs." He seems to feel that he has little time left in which to ensure the survival of his vision of modernization.

The setting also has changed drastically. Compared with the situation in the mid-fifties, China now has few friendly ties with the outside world. The same foul language which the Mao faction uses against its internal opponents is hurled at practically all foreign states, Communist and non-Communist alike. Chou En-lai had generated at the Bandung Conference of 1955 and for several years thereafter good will, and in some cases even a vague sense of solidarity, among leaders of Asia, Africa, and Latin America. Today, Mao calls upon "revolutionary people" everywhere to overthrow their governments.

At home, the crucial relationship between party and people has greatly changed. Fifteen years ago everyone, except young children, still vividly remembered the agonies and hardships of the years before 1949. Although their living standards may not have been raised much by then, the first Five-Year Plan seemed to promise uninterrupted improvement, peace, and stability. Today, living standards do not appear much higher—and in the early sixties they sank perilously low. Not only living standards but the party's policies toward property, education, family planning, and many other problems have vacillated. As a likely result, hopes for steady and orderly progress have been dampened. At the same time, despite the ups and downs, improved formal education, communications, and transportation have given more Chinese a greater national awareness. Without necessarily shifting their primary value orientation from their families and localities, more people are better informed about domestic and foreign affairs than they were fifteen years ago.

It appears, therefore, that the aspirations of most people today are closer to the policy line of the temporarily muted Liu Shao-ch'i faction than to that of Mao. The recent attempts by the Mao faction to restore order, to make peace with most party leaders, and to rebuild the party may be partly a recognition that, for the time being at least, a clear-cut victory for Mao's vision of modernization cannot be won.

Turning to the final task of predicting the future course of the present leadership crisis and of the modernization process to which it is so closely linked, we must above all remember that both are still in their early stages and are developing in a state to which we have no access. This is the crux of the problem facing every student of contemporary China.

The petrified ritual of hostility between the United States and Communist China has prevented Americans from entering China, but the kind of access needed for appraising modernization is denied to all foreigners. The carefully circumscribed itineraries for all visitors make it impossible to gauge the extent to which, for example, traditional value orientations have been changed during the past eighteen years. Nor do interviews of refugees, however intensive, help us answer this question. On the contrary, given the highly unrepresentative nature of such samples, the impressions gained through such interviews may well have resulted in false appraisals. These particularly vexing limitations make interpretations of post-1949 trends, as discussed in the preceding section, more speculative than one cares for. And, of course, any prediction based upon such interpretations is necessarily more hazardous than forecasts about more accessible states.

One can fairly safely say at this time that the Great Proletarian Cultural Revolution has gone beyond the point where the leadership, as currently constituted, could once again unite in purpose and be flexibly responsive in its policies. But it does not follow from this that the Cultural Revolution will spread its divisive influence throughout the Chinese state and thus bring to a halt centrally directed modernization. The struggle, after all, has taken on the character of a personal feud between Mao and Liu and their closest supporters. Their departure from leadership is imminent, and there is every reason to anticipate that the new leadership will be collective and united in purpose. This unity will be based not so much on commonly shared hardships as on current factors, of which the most powerful will be internal pressures for professionalization and rapidly rising living standards. These pressures are being fed by two sources. One is the majority of party and government officials, technicians, and managers who have a vested interest in a return to the routinized leadership style that prevailed before the Cultural Revolution. This source is sustained and reinforced by the second source, the continuing increase in man's knowledge and particularly by the resultant growth in communications and transportation which will draw China closer to the rest of the world. Those within China who prefer a less radical political system to the current Maoist leadership style can take comfort from the knowledge that in virtually all other major states, Communist and non-Communist alike, ideological fervor is ebbing and the pace of modernization is accelerating.

NOTES

1. See Ping-ti Ho, *Studies on the Population of China, 1368–1953* (Cambridge, Mass., 1959), pp. 258, 283.

2. *China Handbook, 1937–1944,* cited in Leo A. Orleans, *Professional Manpower and Education in Communist China* (Washington, D.C., 1961), p. 10.

3. Perhaps the most authoritative account of measures taken to link the Communist leaders to the people during the war is the hitherto unavailable report by Liu

Shao-ch'i, *Huapei chan-ch'ü kungtso ti chingyan (Work Experience in the North China War Zone)*, translated and analyzed in my forthcoming *Liu Shao-ch'i and "People's War"* (East Asian Research Publications, University of Kansas).

4. An excellent illustration is found in Liu Shao-ch'i's report mentioned above.

5. The use of the word "symbol" is by no means meant to imply that Mao was powerless. He did not have his "own" military units as other Communist leaders had, but he did enjoy unrivaled prestige in the Yenan areas.

6. Conrad Brandt, Benjamin Schwartz, and John K. Fairbank, *A Documentary History of Chinese Communism* (Cambridge, Mass., 1952), p. 422.

7. In fact, there are indications that top party leaders had not been greatly impressed with Mao's powers as a theoretician. See Karl A. Wittfogel, "Some Remarks on Mao's Handling of Concepts and Problems of Dialectics," *Studies in Soviet Thought*, III, No. 4 (December 1963), 251–266, and Liu Shao-ch'i's report cited above.

8. David E. Apter, *The Politics of Modernization* (Chicago, 1965), the section on "The Uses of Political Religion," pp. 365–366.

9. Figures on party strength are from Franz Schurmann, *Ideology and Organization in Communist China* (Berkeley, 1966), p. 129.

10. *Ibid.*, p. xxxi.

11. The step-by-step expropriation of livestock, implements, and land reinforced the attraction of the cities.

12. For some production figures, see Robert F. Emery, "Economic Developments in China," *Asian Survey*, June 1966, p. 307; Wu Yüan-li, *The Economy of Communist China: An Introduction* (New York, 1965), pp. 138–139; and *An Economic Profile of Mainland China* (Washington, D.C., 1967), pp. x–xi, 93, 145, 265.

13. "Liangtzu waikuo yüyen" ("Two Foreign Fables"), in Teng T'o, *Yenshan yehhua (Evening Chats at Yenshan)* (Hong Kong, 1966), p. 144.

14. For a brief description of some of these terms, see H. C. Chuang, *The Great Proletarian Cultural Revolution: A Terminological Study* (Berkeley, 1967).

# Economics, Ideology, and the Cultural Revolution

Yuan-li Wu

The course of economic development in Communist China passed through several distinct phases from 1949 to 1967. Each of these phases reflected the predominance of a particular "development strategy," and each of the "development strategies" was predicated upon certain basic ideological and political decisions.

Before the first Five-Year Plan was initiated in 1953, the main concern of Peking's economic policy was to rehabilitate production, restore price stability, and adopt those economic measures that would help to consolidate power in the hands of the Chinese Communist party. This initial phase of economic recovery was therefore characterized by an economic pragmatism designed not to repeat

This article was written before the author entered federal government service in June 1969. The observations and views expressed herein are the author's own and do not reflect in any manner the views of any agency of the U.S. government.

the mistakes which the Soviet Union had made during her own experience with war communism. Nevertheless, for purposes of political consolidation, radical institutional changes such as the redistribution of land ownership and the curbing of urban private capital were carried out relentlessly and at great human cost.

The second phase of Chinese economic development corresponded with the period of the first Five-Year Plan (1953–1957). A "Stalinist development strategy" was adopted in its entirety. The task of economic development was to build modern industry at an increasingly rapid pace in a heavily populated agricultural society. The heavy investment required was to be financed by domestic savings, while the equipment and producers' goods needed by the development program were to be paid for primarily by current export. Thus consumption had first to be curtailed and then maintained at a minimal level, a policy which in turn called for low wages, rationing of essential products, and controlled allocation of materials and distribution of finished goods. The high priority accorded to industry led to the virtual neglect of the agricultural sector which, as a source of the supply of food, raw materials for industry, and exports, was to be exploited in order to maintain necessary levels of capital accumulation and export.

The economic policy of 1953–1957 was based upon a conscious decision to emulate the Soviet model. While Soviet technical and material aid was sought and received, there was a political and ideological decision to forgo the benefits of foreign capital from non-Communist sources. The increasing, breakneck speed with which industrialization was pursued reflected an attitude that equated industrialization with economic progress; it also revealed a burning desire on the part of Peking's leaders to gain great-power status. The new heavy industry was to confer this on China, virtually at any cost.

Nationalization and the development of an administrative structure for central planning and control went ahead during this period. By the end of 1956 agriculture had become collectivized, and non-agricultural sectors had been either nationalized or converted largely into cooperatives. An apparatus of economic planning had fully emerged. The desire to accelerate capital accumulation and industrialization had made these developments necessary. For without them China's limited resources would not have been voluntarily allocated to promote rapid industrialization under autarky. The same measures were also an inevitable outcome of the Communist ideology, which can envisage economic development only within a planned and socialist system.

The second phase of Communist China's economic development met with considerable success. The record shows a 5.2 per cent annual increase in total output in 1952–1957. During the same five-year period, gross industrial production rose by 123 per cent. Agriculture, on the other hand, showed only slight progress; even official reports, which were exaggerated for various statistical reasons, could not prove otherwise. Soviet assistance played a major role. The fact that nationalization and central control were extended only gradually was perhaps an even more important contributing factor. As long as private sectors existed to some degree and personal consumption had not yet fallen to the bare minimum, the shocks generated by haste and planning errors could still be absorbed.

The third phase of Communist China's economic development began in 1958, when two major deviations from the Stalinist model were introduced. The first was the establishment of the commune; the second was the start of a mass movement to install numerous small industrial production units using primitive technologies. The economic justification for this policy lay in the apparently large number of underemployed workers (including women and children) in rural areas whose employment with relatively little capital was expected to increase output significantly. The ideological basis of this policy was found in Mao Tse-tung's desire to establish a Communist society which would rely on normative rather than material incentives and which, through the many industrial production units in the countryside, would eventually merge the industrial and agricultural communities into a homogeneous unit of Communist men.

This third phase, commonly known as the period of the Great Leap, met with total failure. The principal reasons were: too great a reduction in personal consumption, undue sacrifice of material incentives, overconcentration of managerial functions in the ill-prepared and technically incompetent party cadres, and, last but not least, the sheer inadequacy of traditional methods in certain areas of production. The displeasure of the Soviet Union, which led to the peremptory withdrawal of technical assistance from Peking in mid-1960, compounded these internal difficulties. Both the Soviet withdrawal and the *raison d'être* of the Great Leap were again dictated by ideology, in this case primarily that of Mao Tse-tung.

Economically, the failure of the Great Leap ushered in a great depression. The decline began in the latter part of 1960 and reached its low point in mid-1962. Politically, this period coincided with the temporary eclipse of Mao from his previous position of unquestioned power. In the place of Mao's Great Leap policy, a new approach was substituted. The commune was downgraded as a mode of life and a way of organizing production and distribution. More individual initiative was allowed in agriculture, and private plots were restored. Many investment projects were discontinued so as to reduce the rate of capital accumulation. Greater emphasis was given to agriculture to increase food production and domestic consumption. A technological drive was initiated which would enable China to free herself gradually from total dependence upon foreign assistance. This new economic policy was adopted out of necessity: the survival of the Chinese Communist state itself was at stake.

Yet, even as the economy recovered the same institutional problems and choice of "development strategies" had to be faced again. The policy of economic recovery espoused by Liu Shao-ch'i had by now become "revisionist" in the eyes of certain Chinese Communists.[1] The principal issues were collectivism versus individual initiative, normative versus material incentives, and the relative priorities of industry and agriculture. It was at this juncture that the Great Proletarian Cultural Revolution made its debut. What constitutes the best economic institutions and policies for China at this state of her development looms large in the ideological "rectification" which the Cultural Revolution attempts to perpetrate.

Economics, however, is not simply a topic on which serious differences in attitude and policy are registered. It will exert a decisive influence on China's future in several ways: by influencing the tactics employed by the contending factions in the Cultural Revolution, by affecting the outcome of the struggle in terms of the identity of the victorious faction(s), and by defining the economic institutions and policies that will be pursued afterward, not to mention the obvious relationship of economic performance to the growth of military potential. Since Communist China's external policy is, to a large degree, necessarily a function of her military capability, the indirect consequences of China's economic development will be no less important to the rest of the world than its direct consequences will be to China.

## THE TIMING OF THE CULTURAL REVOLUTION AND THE THIRD FIVE-YEAR PLAN

We can only speculate on the many reasons for the decision to launch the Cultural Revolution in the winter of 1965–1966. It might have been imprudent to attack the party apparatus earlier, because time was needed for the reindoctrination of the People's Liberation Army under Lin Piao after the dismissal of Peng Te-huai in 1959, and in view of the demoralizing effect of the hard times in 1961 and most of 1962.[2] The exact timing of certain specific events, such as the dismissal of Peng Chen, may also have been dictated by tactical considerations. The condition of Mao's health was doubtless another factor. Perhaps it was even thought by Mao that the earlier Socialist Education Movement might prove sufficient as a periodically administered purge to the party cadres and the populace at large. In general, however, one is tempted to argue that a decisive influence on timing may have been Mao's belief that the consequences of not launching such a radical movement then would have been too horrible to contemplate—horrible for the future of communism in China if not for himself, although the same may not be said for some of his followers. The long-delayed third Five-Year Plan (originally scheduled for 1963) was to begin in 1966, according to Chou En-lai's announcement[3] at the end of 1964, and this timetable may have played a key role.

Although the contents of the third Five-Year Plan have never been officially disclosed, it is not difficult to imagine what must have been some of the issues on which definite decisions had to be made if orderly economic development was to take place. First, the peremptory withdrawal of Soviet technical assistance in mid-1960 caused serious disruptions of current production, as well as of investment undertakings and scientific research and development projects under way. There were certain commonsense measures that had to be taken in the face of such a crisis—for example, selective completion of the most important projects, reorientation of trade toward Japan and Western Europe and away from the Soviet Union,[4] accelerated development of a domestic technological capability,[5] and resuscitation of the civilian economy, especially with respect to the depressed sectors (notably agriculture) and personal consumption.

But once recovery had progressed beyond a certain point, the anti-crisis policy of 1961–1964 was no longer enough. New investment criteria and priorities had to be established, and the enthusiasm of workers and peasants had to be assured. Yet in order to do so it would be necessary to (1) re-examine priorities in pursuit of the regime's political goals; (2) decide on an incentive system for managers, peasants, and workers; (3) determine the proper place for the market and price mechanism in ordering the country's economic affairs; and, as a corollary, (4) define the relative roles of individual initiative versus administrative controls in planning production and distribution. Externally, relations with the Soviet Union, and perhaps even with the United States, would have to be reviewed; they could not but have a significant effect on domestic political priorities, not to mention considerations of economic and technological needs that might be met from abroad. The question whether the Soviet Union might not again be regarded as a source of supply and assistance, even though not in the same exclusive manner as before 1959, must have occurred to some of the leaders in Peking.

There is little hard evidence on what Liu Shao-ch'i intended to do in the third Five-Year Plan, other than the "revisionist" and "Khrushchevist" policies that have since been attributed to him by his detractors. Circumstantial evidence suggests that in some respects at least his accusers are quite correct in their claim of what he advocated, though, one would suppose, not in their assertion about his motivation. During the period of economic recovery there was active discussion about the use of profitability as an index of efficiency for management.[6] In the agricultural sector in 1961–1962, the progressive downgrading of the commune as a production planning organ and as the arbiter in distributing output were important features of the prevailing policy line, which was described as one of "consolidation and adjustment." To the extent that agricultural production rose during the recovery period, the improvement was far more notable in the production of meat, poultry, vegetables, and so forth than in that of staple grain, which continued to lag behind, at least until 1967.[7] This improvement would seem to reflect the restoration of private plots and the "little freedoms" granted the peasants. But the social manifestations of these liberalizing measures may well have offended the doctrinaire Communist.[8] Those planners whose policy had rescued the Chinese economy from disaster, thanks actually to the resilience and versatility of the long-suffering Chinese worker and peasant, would naturally have hesitated to see the policy of the recovery period abandoned at one stroke. In the circumstances it is reasonable to assume that the third Five-Year Plan incorporated some of these "revisionist" characteristics and that Mao, fearing their implications, would not allow the plan to proceed unchallenged.

## "MAOIST ECONOMICS"

As we shall explain later, the "revisionist" economic policy attributed to Liu Shao-ch'i by his accusers is not the only alternative to that advocated by Mao. While Liu may have done some of the things for which he has been attacked, he may have done them for different reasons, and his own preferences could be quite different. But from the attacks on Liu we can discern some of the ideological and theoretical underpinnings of "Maoist economics."

Liu was accused of emphasizing production to the exclusion of politics and of ignoring the need for a continuing class struggle.[9] In Maoist economics, on the other hand, "politics must take command" and priority must be given to the "revolutionization of people's ideology." Mao also has faith in the "revolutionary initiative of the broad masses," a mythical innate wisdom, as it were, that should and could be exploited on a massive scale. All these ideas can be definitely related to the institutional framework and the development strategy advocated by Mao.

Institutionally, Communist—and Maoist—ideology requires the abolition of private ownership of the means of production. Consequently, if politics were to take command, private plots and private ownership on the farm, which had been partly restored after 1961, would have to go. In the nonagricultural sector the 5 per cent "annual dividend"[10] to expropriated owners of some former large private enterprises would have to be stopped, although little else would appear to be necessary at present since private ownership was not restored outside the farm during the recovery period.

Maoist "politics" and ideology also require that the material incentive be shunned. As the *People's Daily* stated approvingly, quoting the joint editorial of several other publications:

> In capitalist fashion, China's Khrushchev said: "Give him a good reward if he works honestly. . . . If you don't give him more money, there'll be no incentive and he'll not do a good job for you." He attempted to corrupt the masses by bourgeois egoism, divert people's attention from politics, enlarge the income gap, and create a privileged stratum.[11]

Implicit in this statement is the doctrine of egalitarianism and a warning against the rise of new classes, which provides the justification for a continuing class struggle. The pragmatic approach of the recovery period, including its private plots, free markets, and material incentives for workers and management alike, necessarily led to uneven improvement in economic well-being and to new "class divisions." In Maoist economics, material incentives are to be replaced by ideological incentives. This will be possible when the "socialist man" has been created, and to keep him from straying from the correct path he must be "purified" continually through "struggle," "criticism," and "self-criticism." Ideologically, the Cultural Revolution provides one of these periodic regimens.

The Maoists' preoccupation with ideological correctness does not mean they are ready to ignore production. Rather, production is supposed to be taken care of automatically once the "proper" social conditions have been created. The latter will set free "tremendous productive forces" and make possible the "phenomenal development of industry and agriculture."[12] But how is such a large increase in productivity to be brought about in practice? What is the "development strategy" inherent in Maoist ideology, beyond the hard work and fanatic dedication which the thought of Mao Tse-tung might inspire in some of Mao's followers?

The following economic policies, as distinct from the institutional parameters described above, may be traced to their ideological roots. First, since the selfless "socialist man" should desire egalitarianism and an ascetic life, and since the poor tend to be more revolutionary—an asset from the point of view of the continuing revolution—a policy to maintain a universally low standard of personal consumption would be ideologically sound. It would also provide a high rate of capital formation. Second, production would be augmented not only through investment in modern enterprises, which is never denied by the Maoists, but also as a result of the employment of labor-intensive methods in a large number of smaller, even miniscule, production units established by the masses themselves. This concept of "industrialization by mass movement," which would not be so farfetched if it were limited to industries where labor and capital are highly substitutable for each other and where economy of scale is insignificant, is also a reflection of Mao's peculiar notion of "grassroots democracy." "Walking on two legs," or the simultaneous development of a dual economy, is therefore an essential part of Maoist economics. Third, since the advantage of a mass movement in economic development lies in the impetus of a massive assault on a limited number of objectives (e.g., iron production, small fertilizer plants, and so forth), it follows that Maoist economic strategy implies the "big push" approach and, with it, "unbalanced growth." If growth is not "proportional," it cannot be even in tempo. Hence the Maoist strategy envisages the growth process as a wavelike motion—a series of great forward leaps succeeded by periods of "consolidation and adjustment."[13]

If the preceding analysis is correct, it follows that Maoist economic principles were most faithfully reflected in the policies of the Great Leap period (from 1958 to the first part of 1960) which immediately preceded the disastrous two-year economic decline beginning in the last part of 1960. If the Cultural Revolution should result in an *undisputed* Maoist leadership, one could expect an economic policy such as we have just described. The crucial qualifier here is the term "undisputed," to which we shall return later.

## ALTERNATIVE TO MAOIST ECONOMICS

Mao's Cultural Revolution Group in the Central Committee has cast its foes in a "revisionist" mold. "Revisionist" economic policy is characterized by (1) sole emphasis on the machine and on modern technology, (2) lack of faith in the wisdom of the masses, (3) preference to direct both the government and the economy by administrative decree rather than through spontaneous grassroots initiative, (4) sole reliance on material incentive, and (5) oblivion to the need for continuing revolution and class struggle. As we have pointed out, allowing for exaggerations, the above bill of particulars is in general applicable to the policies of the recovery period. But to pose the conflict as one between these two extreme positions is to oversimplify the issue. Reluctance to abandon certain policies of the recovery period may not be the same as advocating them as a permanent part of the economic system.

Before the Great Leap of 1958–1960, the Chinese economy went through two distinct phases—the initial regime of the Common Program and the subsequent first Five-Year Plan. While the policies and institutional framework of the first Five-Year Plan did not fully take shape until 1956, by then a planned system resembling the pre-Khrushchev (or, more precisely, pre-Liberman) Soviet model had been established. Central planning, bureaucratic control, emphasis on modern technology, and an expanding state sector were accompanied by the employment of mass movements and a mixed system of ideological and, to a lesser extent, material incentives. The policies under the Common Program, on the other hand, resembled in many respects those of the later recovery period. The main difference is that while the Common Program marked the transition to more socialism and more planning in order to minimize chaos and restore production from the ravages of hyper-inflation and war, the recovery program was a transition to less planning and less extreme forms of socialism in order to salvage the economy from the effects of doctrinaire excesses. Thus, opposed to the Maoist economics described above are at least two alternatives, if the experience of the recent past offers any guide at all to evaluating available options. These alternatives are (1) a form of orthodox, "non-revisionist," Soviet-style planning characteristic of the first Five-Year Plan, and (2) the policies of the recovery period.

One conclusion to be drawn from this analysis is that if opponents of Mao's Cultural Revolution Group were to win complete ascendancy, there would be as much a chance for China to become truly "revisionist," as the Maoists have warned, going even beyond the degree of economic "liberalization" permitted during the recovery period, as there would be for her to revert, possibly gradually, to an orthodox, Soviet-type, bureaucratically planned and administered system in which private ownership and individual initiative would be strictly limited. This being the case, why has the difference between these two alternatives been purposely glossed over? Surely the Maoists must be fully aware of the evolution of Communist Chinese policy since the Common Program.

Although the attacks on Liu have attempted to pin on him the "crime" of having obstructed agricultural collectivization in 1955–1956, and of having cooperated with capitalists at the time of the Communist victory in China, there is no denying the fact that Mao Tse-tung was in full control at least up to sometime in 1959. If the Common Program resembled what later has become "revisionism," and if the first Five-Year Plan did not establish socialism in China fast enough, the institutions and policies of both periods nevertheless unquestionably bore the imprint of Mao. For the Maoists now to claim that serious deviations and transgressions on Liu's part were somehow responsible for the difficulties encountered in bringing socialism to China, they would in effect have to deny the prescience of Mao himself.

One could rationalize by saying that while Mao had been content to proceed slowly in 1949 and again during the first Five-Year Plan, before 1956, as time passed he became increasingly disillusioned and impatient with a "go-slow" policy. This, it can then be argued, led to his initiation of the Great Leap in 1958. The same might be said of the Cultural Revolution in 1965–1966. But if some such shift in Mao's thinking has actually occurred, it cannot *fully* explain the vehemence of the attacks on Liu, Mao's heir apparent until the Cultural Revolution. Furthermore, this line of argument would suggest that in view of unfortunate past experiences, the Cultural Revolution should be continued until all traces of "revisionism" have been eradicated. The tactical flexibility exhibited in the Cultural Revolution in 1966–1967 would seem to refute such a thesis as the sole explanation of the conduct of Mao's Cultural Revolution Group. Hsieh Fu-chih's statement on August 27, 1967,[14] that the

Cultural Revolution would enter its third and final phase by June 1968, and that it would end in June 1969, offers further evidence that the struggle is no longer expected to root out all revisionist influences.

As a second explanation of the nature of the attack on Liu, which does not rule out the evolution of Mao's own thinking suggested above, one may point to the political aspect of the Cultural Revolution. While the ideological conflict is real enough, there is no escaping the fact that Liu was Mao's heir apparent. If the succession is to be contested, both Liu and his supporters would have to be removed. It would also be a good tactic to have such "surgery" performed by Mao himself and in his name. This theory would emphasize the twists and turns of the Cultural Revolution as it has unfolded. It would point a finger at certain figures in the People's Liberation Army (for example, Lin Piao), the security police (K'ang Sheng and Hsieh Fu-chih), and Mao's inner entourage (Chiang Ch'ing and Ch'en Po-ta) as sources of the contest for political power. The ingredients of a dynastic[15] change in a totalitarian regime are thus fully present.

## INTERACTIONS BETWEEN ECONOMIC DEVELOPMENTS AND THE CULTURAL REVOLUTION

The future of China's economic system and its development cannot therefore be discussed solely in terms of the ideological differences between the Maoists and their opponents. Attention must be paid to the manner in which the Cultural Revolution has developed during the past two years. The struggle against the party and administrative apparatus headed by Liu has had certain effects on the economy and has evoked certain responses from those under attack. New maneuvers have had to be carried out. These in turn have produced further effects. And so the struggle goes on. In short, the Cultural Revolution has produced its own dynamic, and speculation on its outcome must be predicated upon an understanding of this process.

In spite of our lack of full information about the Cultural Revolution, certain events stand out quite clearly and may be described in broad strokes. First, the initial targets of the Cultural Revolution were the party leaders and cadres at different levels, including members of the Peking Committee and the staff of the

*Peking Daily.* They included especially those who were employed in the propaganda, "cultural," and communications departments. The attack was spearheaded by student Red Guards and other rebel groups, apparently with the logistic support of army units for feeding and transportation. During the summer and fall of 1966 large numbers of Red Guards traveled to Peking and throughout the country to demonstrate, to pressure party and administrative officials, and to "exchange revolutionary experiences."

Second, by the winter of 1966–1967 the attack was widened to include factories and enterprises, and "poor" and "lower-middle" peasants were instructed to carry on similar "revolutionary activities" on the farms. Third, this broadening of the objects of attack was followed at the time of spring sowing in 1967 by the dispatch of the army to the countryside. Ostensibly to help with the pressing farm work, the army was soon given a rapidly expanding role in maintaining order and safeguarding production. Through the summer and fall of 1967 there were reports of active fighting, disruptions of transportation and industrial production, and clashes between peasants and the revolutionary groups. A few major outbreaks involving the army were also reported, including the notorious incident of Wuhan.[16] Lastly, by September 1967 and in the following months, the role of the army was strengthened still further. Its new assignment was to help organize throughout the country the three-way alliances which had been proposed at the beginning of the year, and to engage in criticism, refutation of "revisionism," and rehabilitation of those who had erred, in an all-embracing movement of revolutionary alliance. On the one hand, the people were told that they should love the army. On the other hand, the army was now instructed to put the house in order. This résumé of events permits us to reconstruct the following interpretation of economic developments.

ECONOMIC DEVELOPMENTS IN 1966

Viewed with the benefit of hindsight, the concentration of the initial attack on the party committees and secretariats at different levels, especially the propaganda departments, is easily understandable. These organizations were the depositories of political power in China and provided immediate support for those members of the

Central Committee who had been singled out for replacement. Furthermore, for the Cultural Revolution to succeed it was tactically necessary to control the communications media.

The targets selected and the means employed in the attack had two economic consequences. On the one hand, most of the party members under attack had held positions of authority for a considerable time; it was only natural that they would have their own underlings and allies, and that the latter would be found among the many administrators and managers of government enterprises and agencies. Both for self-protection and as a tactical riposte, this group could therefore be expected to try to confound their attackers through confusion and infiltration. Thus the *People's Daily*[17] was moved to accuse these opponents of fanning opposition to the Cultural Revolution among the country's workers. They had also been charged with having deliberately organized their own Red Guards, led demonstrations, and encouraged travels to Peking. As a matter of fact, it was quite clear that the rampaging Red Guards were clogging rail transport. With their clashes with workers, this created work stoppages in a number of cities, though the disruptions were not prolonged.

In general, therefore, agricultural production apparently was not seriously affected by the Cultural Revolution during 1966, even though little increase was registered during the year. Industrial production and transportation suffered, but only during the latter half of the year and perhaps not in very many places or for protracted periods. Foreign trade, a mirror of production, actually attained a record level of $4.2 billion for total exports and imports. Thus the Cultural Revolution did not noticeably affect the level of aggregate economic activities.

ECONOMIC DEVELOPMENTS IN 1967

The Maoists' response in the winter of 1966–1967 to what they felt were the opposition's tactics had a far greater effect on production than before. The extension of the activities of the Cultural Revolution to the industrial sector and the intensification of similar activities on the farms were in themselves disruptive. When the army was brought in, ostensibly to safeguard production but in effect also to restore order and impose unity, the struggle began to take on greater proportions of violence. While reports in the spring and summer of 1967 were confused, clashes involving the army and both peasants and workers definitely increased. For instance, while official claims in late September 1967[18] referred to overfulfillment at certain steel mills, coal mines, and power plants, as well as other factories and individual areas, for parts of the year, claims of *overall* increases in industrial production, or of increases for major industries on a national scale, were conspicuously absent. Other sources, including some hostile to the Maoists,[19] reported declines of production in coal, oil, steel, and machine tools not to mention transportation. These reports have been indirectly confirmed by official sources. For instance, provinces in Central and Southern China found it necessary to conserve oil consumption at about the time petroleum production—and transportation—in Manchuria and Northwest China were reportedly encountering difficulty.[20] Similarly, curtailment of coal consumption was also reported. And reports from Hong Kong at the end of August[21] contained a number of accounts of work stoppages during the first half of 1967 at such widespread centers as Shanghai, Fushun, Tsingtao, Taching, Anshan, Shenyang, Harbin, Kirin, Lanchow, Chungking, and Canton.

But the reported disruptions and claims of overfulfillment were not necessarily mutually exclusive: they could have applied to different places and times. It is a real possibility that both were true. In other words, the record of industrial production was a spotty one. While there were no outstanding successes in single industries, any decline of output may not have been large except in some areas, such as Wuhan. According to some estimates from Hong Kong, for industry as a whole, output in 1967 may have fallen by as much as 10 to 15 per cent. But there were few reports of serious plant destructions as distinct from loss of current production.

The estimate of agricultural production in 1967 was equally puzzling. At the end of September 1967 the summer harvest was said to be 10 per cent above the corresponding figure for 1966.[22] The same was claimed for the early autumn harvest. On the whole, 1967 appeared to be a bumper year for food grain, due particularly to good weather. This favorable development, contrary to the decline in industry, was not carried over into 1968. Besides, the increase in production, if any, lagged behind that of government collection, and the latter may have served to alienate the peasants from the army. Thus, economically, 1967 was probably a much worse year than 1966. On the other hand, there is no evidence that these were permanent declines.

The Maoists' response to the difficulties encountered by the army was to give the latter even greater responsibility. On October 17, 1967, the Central Committee, the State Council, the Military Affairs Committee, and the Cultural Revolution Group of the Central Committee instructed all factories, schools, and department and enterprise units to follow the principles of revolution and to form revolutionary great alliances.[23] The next day the Military Affairs Committee further instructed all army members to "help the left, help industry and agriculture, exercise military control, and give political and military training in the factories, countryside and schools."[24] The army's new role was to be that of the unifying force, to enforce conformity and provide the organizing focus for a country in disarray. This was apparently one of the decisions reached by Mao after his inspection tour of North and East China, as well as the Central-South, earlier in the year.

## THE POST–CULTURAL REVOLUTION LEADERSHIP, THE ARMY, AND ECONOMIC POLICY

The twists and turns of the Cultural Revolution have brought the People's Liberation Army to the forefront. Several consequences are apparent. First, it is unlikely that the Maoists (or the anti-Maoists) can achieve complete ascendancy without the active support of the army. Second, where the army's support is divided, or where the faction that momentarily dominates is unable or unwilling to use the army ruthlessly, an uneasy balance may have to be maintained for some time. Third, the army may take over completely. Last, the country may become fragmented if the army is fragmented. The likelihood of the last two alternatives will be enhanced if Mao Tse-tung passes from the scene, inasmuch as none of the Cultural Revolution Group, including perhaps even Chou En-lai, would seem to possess the same unchallengeable image of authority that Mao still retains.

Regardless of the outcome of the struggle—and the situation may be clarified before very long—China's economic prospects for the next few years will most likely be affected by the army's approach to economics. While there has never been a study of this particular facet of the army, two significant points may be noted. In the first place, the army more likely than not will stress the development of weapons systems and war industries. Even Lin Piao and those who extoll the virtue of the "people's war" would not neglect the development of more sophisticated weapons. Second, the tradition of the army has always been to emphasize the power of numbers, forced marches and other physical exertions, and concentrated assaults on a few enemy positions. By analogy, this is the same approach described earlier as "Maoist economics." Consequently, the trend would seem to favor a strategy of unbalanced growth, although this may be modified if a nonmilitary leadership remains in control after the Cultural Revolution and if it is "anti-Maoist" in outlook. Furthermore, the Great Leap of 1958 was made possible by a large corps of disciplined party cadres who were fanatic followers of instructions, whether the latter made sense or not. Has the Cultural Revolution undermined cadre discipline and dedication to a degree that such a mass movement can no longer be effectively carried out? If so, errors may actually be minimized for this unusual reason.

Short of fragmentation, therefore, one would expect the Chinese economy to resume economic expansion once the Cultural Revolution ends or wanes. One would also expect the military to expand. In this connection, there is no convincing proof that military technology will be pushed beyond China's economic capability. Only the emergence of specific shortages or accidents could slow down China's current drive toward a moderate nuclear capability in the near future. Even during the worst period of economic retrenchment and chaos in 1961–1962, Communist China was able to insulate the nuclear weapons program from the rest of the economy, and the same has happened so far during the Cultural Revolution. There is no reason to expect specific bottlenecks in the present context of international relations.

On the matter of China's foreign relations, it may be well to quote the *People's Daily* of October 16, 1967. While refuting a statement, attributed to Liu Shao-ch'i, to the effect that China could develop friendly relations with the United States if the latter would withdraw its support from Taiwan, the Maoist organ declared: "But we are opposed not only to U.S. imperialist aggression against China but to its aggression against people of all other countries." In other words, Liu's position would be "national egoism" and a betrayal of "proletarian internationalism."

Since even Liu would not halt the development of nuclear weapons—it was during his regime in the early sixties that the program was accelerated—one must expect that Maoist ideology will succeed in the long run. We must look elsewhere for conditions which might reduce the long-term Communist Chinese threat.

NOTES

1. *New China News Agency* (hereafter, *NCNA*), Peking, September 5, 1967, quoting an article originally published by the *Capital Red Guard* and reprinted in the *People's Daily*.

2. Data on this point can be found in abundance in J. Chester Cheng, ed., *The Politics of the Chinese Red Army* (Stanford, 1966).

3. See *People's Daily*, Peking, December 31, 1964.

4. An export surplus in trade with the Soviet Union was created, probably at considerable cost to the Chinese economy, in order to repay the outstanding balance of past Soviet loans. One wonders if the effort to repay was taken on Chinese initiative or under pressure from the Soviet Union.

5. This subject has been treated fully in a study of the Surveys and Research Corporation, Washington, D.C., entitled *Organization and Support of Scientific Research and Development in Mainland China*.

6. There were many articles in *Ching-chi Yen-chiu (Economic Research)* in the early 1960's which dealt with this problem. See, in particular, the writings of Sun Yeh-fang, former director of the Economic Research Institute, who was purged during the early phase of the Cultural Revolution.

7. Such improvements have generally been reported by foreign travelers to China. See, for instance, a report by Branko Bogunvic, Yugoslav correspondent for *Tanjug*, who was interviewed by the Associated Press in November 1967.

8. Many reports of "abuses" of "small freedoms" are contained in a series of documents obtained from the Lian-chiang county of Fukien Province, which will be made available in a forthcoming Hoover Institution publication.

9. *NCNA*, Peking, August 25, 1967, quoting the *People's Daily* and an article which appeared jointly in *Wen Hui Pao*, the *Liberation Daily*, and the *Party Branch Life*.

10. These payments reportedly have ceased since the end of 1965.

11. See n. 9.

12. See an article from the *Capital Red Guard*, reprinted in the *People's Daily*, September 5, 1967.

13. The consolidation periods are not, however, supposed to be phases of absolute decline, as was the case in 1961–1962.

14. Reported by *Tokyo Sankei*, September 5, 1967.

15. See L. La Dany, "Mao's China: The Decline of a Dynasty," *Foreign Affairs* (July 1967).

16. First reported in June 1967, the Wuhan incident involved armed clashes since April after mass arrests of alleged "counterrevolutionaries" in Hupeh between February and mid-April. The incident became full-blown in July 1967, when Wang Li and Hsieh Fu-chih, emissaries from Peking, were manhandled by rebellious workers and army units. For a full summary based on wall posters and the official press, see Minoru Shi-bata's report in *Tokyo Sankei,* September 29, 1967.

17. Editorial in *People's Daily,* Peking, December 26, 1966.

18. *NCNA,* September 29, 1967.

19. Radio Moscow, domestic service in Russian, October 29, 1967.

20. Radio Peking, November 2, 1967.

21. *Far Eastern Economic Review,* Hong Kong, August 31, 1967, p. 402.

22. *NCNA,* Peking, September 26, 1967.

23. *NCNA,* Peking, October 17, 1967.

24. *Ibid.,* October 18, 1967.

# The Style of Politics and Foreign Policy in Communist China

Melvin Gurtov

Foreign policy consists not only of the principles and practices governing one nation's relations with others; in certain respects it reflects the way a leadership guides, motivates, and controls its own society. To the extent that this is so, an integrated analysis of domestic and foreign policy can help us better understand a nation. Ideally, such an analysis should include a detailed study of these policies at specific times (for example, in periods of stress and relaxation); the ideological framework in which the leadership operates; and the psychological and historical roots from which its "national purpose" derives. This essay is not a coordinated "model" of politics and foreign policy. But, by looking at China under Mao,

Any views expressed in this paper are those of the author. They should not be interpreted as reflecting the views of governmental or private research sponsors, or of the RAND corporation.

I hope to explain an interesting interrelationship between domestic politics and foreign policy that seems grounded in similarities of what I call style.

For some years the discipline of political science has been wrestling with various ways to describe the motivations of states, their peoples, and especially their leaderships. From those methods I have adapted the notion of style to indicate some characteristics of one leadership's way of dealing with its society and the world. Style, whether in politics or foreign policy, differs from the concepts of "political culture"[1] and "operational code."[2] Whereas political culture seeks to define the boundaries of a society's political behavior by analyzing its value system, history, and psychology, and whereas an operational code looks specifically at a leadership's "general belief system about the nature of history and politics" to develop insights into the decision-making process,[3] style concentrates on the underlying principles that account for a leadership's political action and conduct of foreign policy.

For a country like China, still deeply enmeshed in political, economic, and social transition, style is a product of the leadership's interpretation of national needs and goals during the critical process we loosely call "modernization." The Great Proletarian Cultural Revolution now taking place on the mainland and certain to have lasting impact on the course of Chinese communism well illustrates the relationship between style and modernization, specifically the confused and confusing changes in policy wrought by the stresses of dissimilar (though not necessarily diametrically opposed) modernizing ideologies. In view of that significant relationship, and to try to clarify some of the major consequences of the upheaval in China, I shall focus on style primarily in the context of the Cultural Revolution.

## THE SENSE OF "CHINESENESS" AND CHINA'S DESTINY

Have the men who have ruled China since 1949 been more Communist than Chinese, or more Confucian than Marxist? The question has been debated often in academic and other circles. By its very nature the debate probably can never be satisfactorily resolved, but in terms of style the present leadership has pursued policies domestically and internationally that justify considering its members as much Communist Chinese as Chinese Communists. It was primarily as Chinese that those who would form the top echelon in Peking experienced, in the first half of this century, the futility of China's attempts to unite the nation; to coalesce social forces; to combat economic chaos; to fend off and simultaneously adapt from the West amid world war, invasion, and economic depression; to establish efficient government and fiscal responsibility; to instill momentum into a stagnating resource base; to bring the rural areas into the modernizing process; and to stop the trend toward educational exclusivism and backwardness. These experiences were shared with all other politically conscious Chinese, and were, for most of the later leaders of the Communist party, compounded by a lack of interaction with non-Chinese environments. As nearly all specialists on China would agree, the end product was and remains an acute historical consciousness which has influenced the ruling elite to magnify past humiliations, has reinforced their feelings of isolation and hostility toward the outer world, and has convinced them that China must "go it alone" if necessary to restore her rightful place in the world community.

These components of the sense of "Chineseness" and China's destiny have been translated into political action. First, the determination to eliminate the disturbing cycle of dismemberment and short-lived unity has undoubtedly been the driving force behind the leadership's insistence upon strong central control over national resources. In practice, recent studies have shown that central control has, as in the pre-Communist period, ebbed and flowed in response to local circumstances. While the quest for unity therefore does not indicate the present government's capacity to command all that it surveys, the fact remains that China under communism has achieved unparalleled national unity. Apparently it has been sufficiently resilient to weather the massive party purge and local outbreaks of dissidence that have marked the Cultural Revolution.

In a second sense, political style has also included a movement for China's "self-reliance" (*tzu-li keng-sheng*). The phrase appeared at least as early as 1942,[4] but has been especially prominent since 1964 in response to the heating up of the Sino-Soviet debate. No doubt the leadership in Peking has always aimed at making China as self-contained as possible; but the rift with Moscow compelled them, perhaps as much out of pride as economic necessity, to propagate the idea that China can survive and prosper without foreign assistance. As Mao phrased it in alluding to his Olympian feat of swimming the Yangtse, China must "learn to swim while swimming."

The experience of civil war (against the Kuomintang) and resistance to invasion (against Japan) has, of course, profoundly influenced the leadership's style. Domestically, it has meant the application of Mao's guerrilla tactics to social organization. Having come to power in large part through the "correct" application of creative military thinking to China's unique circumstances, Mao has never strayed from the view that China, even in the transition to socialism, must "attack" its problems and see them through to final victory in much the same way that an army advances and conquers. The vocabulary of guerrillaism has thus worked its way into the nation's organization: mass movements are conducted as "campaigns"; the general party line consists of red flags; communes, at least in their heyday, were manned by teams and brigades of peasants toting "a rifle in one hand and a hoe in the other"; the People's Liberation Army must take part in construction as well as defense; the army must maintain close relations with the masses (just as, during the War of Resistance, soldiers were told to adhere strictly to the "eight rules of conduct" in dealing with peasants). The Cultural Revolution, in this respect, is a gigantic effort initiated by Mao to ensure that the guerrilla mentality survives him. He may even enjoy a certain pleasure in doing battle in his waning years, for he is most comfortable when waging the kind of protracted struggle that is clearly necessary against opposition forces who would, he is certain, return China to her pre-"liberation" days of lethargy and capitalism.

The style of politics in China has also incorporated a pronounced element of hate.[5] Arousing hatred has been a common organizational device, particularly useful in channeling frustration and anger away from the regime and toward the "responsible" parties, i.e., the class enemies. In the early 1950's (during the *san-fan* and *wu-fan*, or "three-anti" and "five-anti" movements) no less than in the course of the Cultural Revolution, the leadership has found the controlled release of pent-up mass hostility against enemies of the people much more useful than the suppressive measures practiced by other totalitarian regimes.

A final element in the theme of "Chineseness" and political style concerns a dilemma common to most developing societies: breaking with the past without expunging it. In China, of course, this has meant the ongoing process of eliminating "bourgeois" thinking and creating the new Communist man. The Cultural Revolution has sharpened the inherent conflict between traditional and modern cultures, and Mao has come to identify tradition with the larger, always latent threat of a "capitalist restoration." The Red Guards' attack on the "four olds" (old culture, old tradition, old values, and old thinking) was a desperate measure to eradicate a competing culture. To extend the metaphor of Joseph R. Levenson,[6] Mao did not simply relegate the traditional culture to the museum, where it might be harmlessly preserved; he was prepared to destroy the museum itself.

In foreign relations as well as domestic policy, "Chineseness" and China's destiny form a major component of the style of the People's Republic. Peking's obsessive concern for the security of her frontiers, and her desire to restore those border lands considered to have been illegally acquired or aggrandized by the imperialist powers at a time of China's weakness, are well-known principles of foreign outlook common to the Nationalists and Communists alike. Peking's passion for security has been a major factor in China's negotiation of border agreements with her neighbors (Burma, Nepal, Afghanistan, and Pakistan), conclusion of mutual nonaggression treaties (Cambodia, Afghanistan, and Burma), and resort to force to settle disputed border areas or threats to their security (India, Tibet, and Korea). Those areas "rightfully" Chinese which cannot be claimed because the risks are too high (portions of the Sino-Soviet border and Taiwan) are problems for future resolution. In these various ways the leadership has sought to assert a predominant Chinese influence or, at the least, keep alive its continuing interest in lands within China's proper "sphere of influence."

The idea of self-reliance also has a direct parallel in China's foreign policy. Peking has not only stressed the desirability of economic self-sufficiency for itself but, in its aid program to Asian,

African, and Middle East states, has sought to convince them that only self-reliance (promoted by China's type of assistance) can prevent their economies from becoming hopelessly tied to those of the Soviet Union and the United States.

As Defense Minister Lin Piao's famous article of September 3, 1965, made clear, self-reliance is also the approved style of conduct for China in dealing with "national liberation movements." Despite the attention given to those portions of the article that seemed to declare China's open-ended support of such movements, the key portion may have been Lin's insistence that they develop on their own. While China has the duty to assist them, Lin wrote, she cannot initiate revolutions that do not already have the essential ingredients for independent growth. Nor, for that matter, is China's revolutionary model meant to be emulated exactly once insurgency begins. Peking has long recognized—indeed, here is the rationale for the creativity of "the thought of Mao Tse-tung"—that Mao's Chinese model has general validity for budding revolutionaries, but that they must adapt its principles to their own circumstances.[7] The "China model" is a framework, not a blueprint, for revolutionary success.

Self-reliance, the guerrilla mentality, and strong central control are parts of a search to give China national expression as a strong, viable, progressing society. These same organizational devices are also intended, it seems, to assert China's international standing. As Chinese, the leaders of China, whomever they may be, have no doubt that China, *qua* China, is entitled to consideration as a world power having the right of access to all important international councils. Ethnocentricity—the "Middle Kingdom complex"—is a real policy dynamic: China's historic greatness requires pre-eminence in world affairs today. In contrast, for example, to Thailand and Cambodia, which look back upon their once-great empires and region-wide power with fond memories but few misguided notions about the realities of the present, China believes it has the resources, power, and influence to command recognition and respect no less now than before. There can be no aspiring to that which is inevitable.

AUTHORITY AND UNANIMITY
One of the central concerns of the Communist Chinese leadership

has been to maintain orderly relationships within society, so that lines of authority are clear to party cadres, workers, and intellectuals alike. Party, state government, commune, and family are not simply organizational (or functional) units but components of a broad hierarchical structure which provides a slot in life. Within this structure participation in the political system can be controlled. Thus the so-called "mass line" to promote closeness between the proletariat and the party is, of course, mainly intended to assure greater control over the society at large. Authority, in the style of the leadership, has consequently meant the imposition of centralism in such a manner as to assure "democracy"—democracy understood not as the individual's freedom to act but as his duty to participate and to develop a commitment to the regime through collective education.[8]

Democratic centralism implies not only the imposition of authority but equally an insistence upon unanimity, whether among the masses or within the party. As Edgar Schein has observed, ordinary citizens and party members in China share a common psychological burden: the leader's demand for their approval of ideology and the policy of the moment. The Chinese in Communist society, whether cadre or worker,

> must be committed sincerely to an ideology, but he must not think through the consequences of this ideology for himself; instead he must be prepared ritually to affirm what his leaders dictate and must be able to rationalize his leaders' conclusions in terms of the ideology.[9]

There is no better illustration of this demand for ritualistic approval than the Cultural Revolution, during which the Maoist leadership has constantly called for the establishment of "revolutionary great alliances," opposition to factionalism, unity against the enemy, and elimination of the "small-group mentality." An article in the *People's Daily,* the official party organ, defined the Cultural Revolution as nothing less than the fullest effort to restore unity in all its dimensions to the Chinese polity:

> The Great Proletarian Cultural Revolution is a movement of mass democracy in which hundreds of millions of the revolutionary masses educate and liberate themselves. It is a revolutionary mass movement guided by a highly cen-

tralized, unified leadership. The unifying factors are Mao Tse-tung's thought, Chairman Mao's proletarian revolutionary line, and his great strategic plan. If we earnestly study, correctly understand, and really implement Chairman Mao's latest instructions, we shall have unified thinking, a unified will, a unified direction, and unified action.[10]

The tactic of relying primarily on army-backed and in many instances army-controlled "great alliances" is a distinguishing characteristic of the Cultural Revolution's drive for unanimity. A more typical and somewhat related device, one that has been employed by the party since the early 1930's, is the united front. Although the united front has passed through many functional changes—from a tactic in the party's struggle for power against the Kuomintang and Japan, to a strategy in the period of the New Democracy and the transition to socialism, and, finally, since 1954, to an ideological proposition offered to foreign revolutionary movements[11]—its purpose has remained fairly consistent: to differentiate friends and enemies in the class struggle so as to ensure the kind of social action the party "line" demands. When unanimity was required during China's "liberation struggle," the united front embraced the urban petty bourgeoisie and the "national bourgeoisie" as well as peasants and workers. After the seizure of power, rich and middle-class peasants were temporarily included for unanimous backing of the drive against landlords. The examples could be multiplied, but the point is that the regime's desire to *legitimize* its authority has led it to *ensure* authority through the creation, where necessary, of majority support.[12]

As the united front has given way during the Cultural Revolution to "great alliances," so has the party line yielded to "the thought of Mao Tse-tung" as the supreme source of authority. The remarks of Jen Li-hsin quoted above are indicative of this development; so too are the attacks on Liu Shao-ch'i, once the party's leading theoretician and now "China's Khrushchev," "the leading person in authority in the party taking the capitalist road." Perhaps the single most concentrated assault on Liu has been directed toward his *How to Be a Good Communist*,[13] which until recently was the accepted standard work on the training of party members. Put briefly, Liu is said to have spread the doctrine of the "docile tool" governing relations between the party and the masses. For many years, so the indictment runs, Liu has advocated that *all* party leaders are subject to criticism and ultimate control by the masses but that, once the party line has been determined, absolute obedience to it is required whether or not the line is "correct."[14] In view of the many inconsistencies in the charges and the question of how Liu's theory went unchallenged for so long, it is likely that Liu's guilt is not at all related to his revisionist party line. Rather, it is probably due to his having failed in recent years to follow unquestioningly *Mao's* prescriptions for China's development and the necessity and methodology of a cultural revolution. As John W. Lewis has noted, the party approved the "docile tool" theory as far back as 1960;[15] once Liu began to waver in his support of Mao, the past was manipulated so that advocacy of his theory could be construed as opposition to Mao himself. Liu's case demonstrates clearly that the "correct line" in China today is not necessarily the party line but the line espoused personally by Chairman Mao.

In Communist China's style of foreign relations, the quest for authority and unanimity proceeds, as in domestic affairs, from a determination to order relationships. Peking is the fountainhead of authority for true Marxism-Leninism throughout the world, just as it is, or must be, for Chinese society. As a consequence, enemies and friends must be selected with care, sometimes in defiance of previous relationships. The Sino-Soviet rift is the obvious example. China's stated belief that all-out support of the Communist effort in Vietnam is the touchstone of genuine proletarian internationalism is only the most glaring instance of China's willingness to sacrifice united action in order to maintain theoretical consistency and a leading role in support of revolutionary movements. As Foreign Minister Ch'en I said in 1965: "All common and concerted action [in Vietnam] must be founded on a common understanding of the aggressors and on the common determination to combat them. If this basis were laid, common action would be possible. Otherwise it would be impossible."[16] Since the Soviets still practice peaceful coexistence with the imperialists and do not render Hanoi the fullest support, a "common understanding" and a "common determination" obviously are nonexistent so far as the Chinese are concerned.

The Sino-Soviet imbroglio over Vietnam is, of course, not the only example of disharmony. Inasmuch as the Chinese Communists formulate foreign policy in the same terms as domestic policy—constantly reassessing "the general situation and our tasks"—today's friends can easily become tomorrow's enemies, as witness the mercurial drop from favor of Indonesia and Burma, and the near-crisis in relations with Cambodia. Under the impact of the Cultural Revolution, priorities have dramatically changed abroad so that, as on the domestic front, cadres must be attuned to the new line. Peking's world-wide recall of its ambassadors during late 1966 and early 1967 was, in this light, clearly necessary if members of China's foreign service were to remain true representatives of the new spirit of Chinese politics.

In suddenly shifting gears in its conduct of foreign relations, the Peking regime is only continuing a practice begun when it was still a struggling party. The united front tactic, which we have already mentioned in the domestic context, proved extremely useful for the party when it confronted the Japanese invaders in 1937 at the same time it was fighting the Kuomintang. The party then, as today, held that there is always one principal enemy, thus making possible unity with a secondary enemy for as long as necessary to defeat the primary one. Between 1937 and 1945 the party line was "cooperation with and struggle against" the Kuomintang; once the Japanese were defeated, the Kuomintang again became the principal enemy. Now the Soviet Union apparently has replaced the Japanese, while the United States seems to have become something less than the principal enemy—though certainly not a temporary ally.

As has been true domestically, too, the united front admits the existence of a middle group of "wavering elements" whose allegiance, while far less certain than that of Marxist-Leninist states or parties, is nonetheless desirable for China's long-term interests. Until the Cultural Revolution Peking had proven willing and able to live under the "five principles" of peaceful coexistence first proclaimed in the spring of 1954 and subsequently confirmed at the April 1955 Afro-Asian Conference in Bandung. Border agreements were signed, potentially dangerous overseas Chinese communities were instructed against political involvement by Peking, and mutual noninterference in internal affairs was assiduously practiced. In

general, "people's diplomacy" rather than support of armed revolution was the rule in China's relations with all those states that
would accept her legitimacy and power, cut ties to the American
defense system, and pursue foreign policies of genuine nonalignment or "pro-Peking" neutrality. Thus, such "wavering elements"
as Cambodia's monarch, Burma's Revolutionary Council, and Pakistan's SEATO-tied parliamentary democracy were over the years
brought within China's friendly camp; many newly independent
African states were wooed by Peking's diplomatic offensive in the
hope they would remain free of American or Soviet political and
economic programs; and West European capitalist industries were
encouraged to trade with and assist China—despite the emphasis
on "self-reliance."

   Obviously, much changed once the Cultural Revolution began.
The united front was used, in some ways similar to the early period
of China's foreign relations (1949–1952), not to harmonize different social systems abroad for the sake of China's long-term struggle
against the United States, but to line up only those nations and
parties absolutely faithful to Maoist doctrine. Consequently, in
Asia, aside from North Vietnam and Pakistan, and with the very
shaky exception of Cambodia, not a single state can today be said
to have friendly (i.e., stable as well as "correct") relations with
Peking. Difficulties ranging from ideological differences to outright
interference in internal affairs by fanatical Chinese embassy personnel arose with Ceylon, Nepal, Burma, Indonesia, and the Communist parties of North Korea, Japan, India, and Mongolia. Much
the same could be said of Western Europe, Eastern Europe (Al-
bania excepted), and Africa—a general deterioration of relations
that took several years to build. And with this seeming radicaliza-
tion of foreign policy came a return to the early theme of the united
front as a tactic to be applied by Communist revolutionary movements wishing to make the best use of Maoist methods. For
instance, Peking frequently broadcast during 1967 to the Thai and
Burmese Communists, in tones that could not be mistaken for
anything other than instructions, that they must build an army close
to the people, a revolutionary Communist party, and a united front
of "democratic elements" led by the party if they expected to gain
final victory. For a time it appeared that Peking had taken a long

step backward to the early years of Communist rule, when it was the central authority for Asian revolution and when unanimity in the face of the imperialist enemy meant "leaning to one side."

## STABILITY AND INSTABILITY: CONTRADICTIONS AND STRUGGLE

The goal of unity embraces, but is also separate from, that of stability. In the political style of the Peking leadership one senses a peculiar relationship between the desire for stability and the willingness to produce instability to attain it. This style, which might appear on the surface to be dysfunctional, is actually in perfect accord with the Maoist notion of "contradictions" in all societies, socialist and otherwise. Mao's concept of contradictions is central to his theory and practice of politics and foreign policy, and it is to that concept that we turn now.

We need not repeat the excellent dissections of the theory of contradictions made by other analysts.[17] What is relevant for our purposes is to understand the theory as a dynamic, motivating element of political style and of the conduct of foreign policy. The theory of contradictions, first enunciated in Mao's "On Contradiction" (1937),[18] codifies a universal, immutable struggle of opposites which Mao sees as the fundamental explanation for every development in the history of man. In the manner of the Hegelian dialectic, struggle between opposite forces is essential for change; upon resolution of the struggle, a unity is produced, only to be unsettled by a new struggle between the changed force and its opposite. Since, however, the nature of the contradictions in things is bound to be different, the forms of struggle will likewise differ. "Some contradictions," Mao has written,

> are characterized by open antagonism, some are not. Based on the concrete development of things, some contradictions, originally non-antagonistic, develop and become antagonistic, while some contradictions, originally antagonistic, develop and become non-antagonistic.[19]

This last phrase has particular contemporary relevance, for it goes a long way toward explaining the theoretical basis for Mao's view of the need for struggle against the Soviet Union externally and against the possibility of a "capitalist restoration" internally.

Mao's political style demands a constant reassessment of changing forces in society, for new contradictions may appear among the masses and even within the party. Indeed, Mao has stated explicitly that struggle to resolve contradictions is necessary for the party's very survival.[20] A corollary point is that a certain amount of stress, strain, and flux is desirable for China's political development. Even though, in socialist societies such as China's, contradictions are supposedly nonantagonistic, the fact of their existence, and of the party's need for them, means that the social "pot" must be kept simmering without bringing it to a boil. Thus, for example, when Liu Shao-ch'i announced the general line for 1958 of socialist construction, he "explained that tension 'is simply normal revolutionary activity to which we should give our heartiest approval. This kind of "tension" is nothing to be afraid of.' "[21] A dash of instability keeps party members on their toes, creates psychological pressure on the masses to participate in the political-ideological process and to produce, and generally compels the entire society to "gain new victories" and make temporary sacrifices for the sake of a brighter future. Without struggle, in short, contradictions will go unresolved, the party's mission will be negated, and the transformation of China into a socialist and eventually Communist society will never be completed.

In practice the contradictory impulses to stabilize and destabilize take many forms. Since I am dealing with political style primarily in the context of the Cultural Revolution, I shall refer in particular to the use of mass campaigns, coercive persuasion, and efforts to resolve the educational dilemma of rearing youths to be loyal successors to Mao.

Campaigns in Communist China have sought to focus the resentments, power, or productive capacity of the masses on a single goal, whether that be to curb landlordism, to "learn from the People's Liberation Army," to "counter revisionism," or, as in the Hundred Flowers movement, to release tensions in intellectual circles by permitting unprecedented freedom to criticize the regime. In all these cases the ultimate purpose has been to unify the society behind the party's current line. Yet while the strategy is unity, the tactics are often those of momentary fragmentation. The campaigns aim at some deficiency in the political or economic system, so a certain amount of disruption of the status quo is necessary before the desired new status quo (a resolution of "contradictions") can be achieved. In this light, the Cultural Revolution is a campaign on the broadest scale to reverse what Mao evidently believes is a disastrous trend toward bureaucratization, one that will lead to the kind of capitalist restoration he already sees in the Soviet Union. In his view the enormity of the task—measured by the fact that the society for the first time is said to be riven with "antagonistic" contradictions[22]—demands extraordinary measures. Mao apparently concluded that it was essential to upset the society, and particularly the Communist party, in a violent way—by purging less fanatical elements in the party, the universities, and cultural circles, by openly denouncing the "four olds," and by relying on army rather than party leadership in establishing a new, more trustworthy political order.

The political style of Mao and his group in implementing the Cultural Revolution has been strikingly similar to that employed during earlier rectification campaigns. When Mao launched the first rectification of party deficiencies between 1942 and 1944, he made clear that he intended to induce members with shortcomings to understand and correct their errors, not to identify them for the purpose of liquidation.[23] Similarly, in the course of the Cultural Revolution, despite a widespread, unprecedented purge at the start, Mao has gradually moved (or been persuaded to move) in the direction of using the party's more traditional rectification methods. With phrases first used in 1942, Mao has called for "punishing the past to warn the future" and for "saving men by curing their ills," which has in practice meant retaining middle- and low-level cadres and non-party functionaries whose skills are too sorely needed to make them dispensable.[24] As in the past, coercive persuasion has become the pre-eminent device for ideological purification, with the result that group discussion of Mao's thoughts, criticism and self-criticism, and ultimate purgation of sins are again being carried out extensively on the mainland.

One of the important destabilizing agents in the course of the "revolution" has been the Red Guards, whose employment by Mao and Lin Piao also marks a step unparalleled in ideological rectification movements.[25] The resort to the Red Guards has, however, deeper significance; it goes to the heart of Mao's concern about the next generation of leaders. It has long been Mao's style, as already noted, to maintain situations in flux, even in the party. Yet he has also made clear that just as party leaders and cadres are vulnerable to mistakes because of their pre-revolutionary class backgrounds (such is assertedly the case with Liu Shao-ch'i and the former General Secretary of the Party, Teng Hsiao-p'ing), so are the youth, despite the fact they have been schooled solely in a communized environment. There seems little doubt that Mao, as revealed in his speech of September 1962 before the party Central Committee's Tenth Plenum, was anxious lest the ideological backsliding he perceived in cultural and intellectual circles affect the "redness" of the young.[26] His concern was again evident in the summer of 1964, when a flurry of articles appeared in the official press analyzing the problem of youth and succession, and attacking revisionist philosophy allegedly being advocated in the universities.[27] The thrust of these articles was that the minds of youth were by no means unalterably Communist-oriented, that a struggle for control of them was taking place between true proletarian and bourgeois elements, and that, in the largest sense, the danger existed that youth would be poisoned by "revisionist" thinking unless new attitudes were adopted toward education and intellectuals.[28]

We have already spoken of the Cultural Revolution in terms of an effort to resuscitate the guerrilla mentality and of a major ideological rectification campaign. To these themes might be added another—that the revolution is also part of Mao's desperate and continuing effort to mold a new Communist man who will nevertheless have the spirit of struggle and sacrifice that Mao and his "close comrade-in-arms," Lin Piao, developed during the War of Liberation. As in other countries, such as Taiwan, where a revolutionary leadership must compete against the fact that its revolution is history, Mao's regime realizes that unless a revolutionary situation can be re-created, the total revolution is endangered. Before the Red Guards became so fanatical as to be virtually unmanageable, they served an important purpose: through their creation, apparently under army supervision, they were shown how revolutionary fervor can be manufactured when the educational system becomes stifled with revisionist thinking, and how youth have the power to rebel (as Mao did) against distasteful authority. The cross-country "long marches" of some Red Guard groups, and reference to the Red Guards as "back-ups" for the army illustrated plainly that the youth were intended by Mao and Lin to make China's revolutionary history a contemporary reality. Once that function had been served and the Red Guards ordered to return to their homes and schools, Mao's attention turned to revising school curricula and administration; again, the aim was. to ensure that "resolute successors to the proletarian revolutionary cause" would be raised to be loyal to the thoughts of Mao Tse-tung.[29]

The doctrine of contradiction and struggle applies to China's foreign relations as well as to its domestic politics. The antagonistic nature of contradictions in capitalist society and between capitalist and socialist states is, in a very real sense, self-enforcing and hence self-fulfilling. Since contradictions can only be resolved by struggle, any attempt by the object of struggle (the enemy) to resist simply reinforces the leadership's initial certainty about the inevitability of the struggle. A kind of vicious circle is produced, illustrated below with respect to China, the Soviet Union, and the United States:

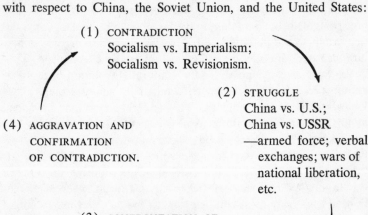

(1) CONTRADICTION
Socialism vs. Imperialism;
Socialism vs. Revisionism.

(2) STRUGGLE
China vs. U.S.;
China vs. USSR
—armed force; verbal
exchanges; wars of
national liberation,
etc.

(4) AGGRAVATION AND
CONFIRMATION
OF CONTRADICTION.

(3) CONFRONTATION OF
STRUGGLING PARTIES
Imperialist (U.S.) intervention,
aggression, oppression;
Revisionist (USSR) adventurism,
capitulationism, collusion with
imperialism.

The notion of external contradictions and struggle is not only reinforcing but, as Richard H. Solomon has observed,[30] satisfying to China's revolutionary leadership. Just as Mao believes the absence of domestic struggle leads inevitably to the party's decay, so the absence of an external enemy depresses China's revolutionary fervor. "Wanton U.S. imperialist aggression and intimidation can further raise our political consciousness, strengthen our unity and enhance our combat readiness," wrote Peking's *Observer* in early 1966.[31]

The present leadership's conviction of the need for struggle and for an enemy should not obscure the important distinction between struggle in theory and struggle in practice. Ideology in China, after all, functions on two planes: on the theoretical level the good Communist should be able to perceive that contradictions abound; on the practical level he must know how to resolve them in accordance not only with theory but also with the reality of the moment.[32] Thus we return to a point expressed earlier, that China's self-perceived role as the leading revolutionary power in the world has not led it into unrealistic decision-making. Although some features of China's foreign relations in the summer of 1967 were reminiscent of the crude diplomacy that characterized the 1949–1952 period, her foreign policy then as before was to calculate carefully risks and costs, to refrain from overt actions that would not be in keeping with good sense, and to sustain an image of revolutionary backbone without undertaking commitments that would defy China's own interests. The carryover of the Cultural Revolution into Burma and the primarily political support being given the Thai Communist party must not be overlooked; but it should also be recognized that the Chinese have become increasingly cautious rather than reckless in the course of American escalation in Vietnam, and that hostile Chinese statements have not been supported by action with regard to developments in Cambodia, Malaysia, and Indonesia. China's encouragement of revolutionary movements beyond her borders has more often been designed to focus domestic resentment on an external scapegoat (as in the "Resist America" movements during the Korean and Vietnam wars); to exploit China's revolutionary posture vis-à-vis the Soviet Union; to demonstrate China's continuing interest in and, where physically possible, material support for, national liberation struggles; and to warn the "imperialist" camp of China's capacity to resist when directly threatened. Lucian W. Pye has written of the gap between emotions and actions among Chinese living under communism;[33] if the statement is accurate, China's political culture has revealed an important psychological basis for her relatively cautious actions abroad. As Mao would likely argue, while unremitting struggle must be waged against forces with which China is in antagonistic contradiction, there are many different kinds of struggles, not all of which require China's direct participation or assistance.

While China's trumpeting of revolution is in many instances ritualistic, the style of foreign policy, notably in the Cultural Revolution phase, unquestionably accepts limited types of involvement to destabilize points of conflict with her main enemies. China would, I imagine, prefer to consolidate her national interests either by direct control over areas considered historically Chinese (such as Taiwan and certain disputed border regions) or by recognition of predominant Chinese influence in adjacent countries (through the elimination of American aid programs, bases, and alliances). Until that situation comes to pass, and given the makeup of the present leadership, China will not likely accept a stabilization of circumstances under which the United States is dominant in South Vietnam, has a large military complex in Thailand, and maintains a strategic arc of bases from Japan to Taiwan and the Philippines. In order to achieve the kind of stability she wants, therefore, China must promote the principle of destabilization abroad as well as at home: supporting, where circumstances permit, political and military action against unfriendly regimes while minimizing the risk of complete loss of control. Thus the crucial question seems to be not simply how to contain China, but rather how, without sacrificing a reasonable security framework for those nations desiring it, to avoid feeding the theory of contradictions and giving Peking cause to promote destabilizing actions abroad.

## "STYLE" AND CHINA'S MODERNIZATION: SOME IMPLICATIONS

If the style of the leadership tells us something about Chinese Communist political action and foreign-policy conduct, it also reveals a good deal about the problems faced by a radical regime seeking to sustain China's revolutionary pace at home and abroad. Like other developing countries that are searching for the appropriate tools of political and economic growth after post-independence enthusiasm has dissipated, China must eventually confront the bald fact that continued "revolutionization" (*ke-ming-hua*) is not the most productive means of harnessing the nation's power or of projecting its influence.

The strong sense of humiliation and the resultant desire to re-establish China's past greatness, two forces which were earlier identified as components of political and foreign-policy style, act also as obstacles to the very kind of progress her leaders wish to achieve. By downgrading the traditional culture and by attempting to bury some of the more positive aspects of the Western intrusions of the last two centuries, Mao has only made it more difficult for China to attract sorely needed foreign (including overseas Chinese) assistance and to compete abroad for trade markets. "Self-reliance" and Maoist dogma may be temporary rallying cries to unite the masses; but they also weaken the country's overall attractiveness both as a place of business and as a model of independent development.[34] At the same time, as the sordid episodes in Macao and Hong Kong demonstrated, China's capacity to vindicate the past is limited—in those instances, by the fact that British and Portuguese control of traditionally Chinese territories is the only alternative to losing one of the few remaining sources of "imperialist" dollars. Unfortunately, the present leadership's feelings of weakness and humiliation seem only to be intensified by the inability to retaliate effectively and to reciprocate alleged injustices.

The leadership's insistence on authoritarian lines of control and unanimous sanction for its actions likewise hinders the goal of fully mobilizing the nation's human and material resources. While the regime seeks to maintain strict lines of command in all spheres of life, whether military, social, or political, the inevitable growing complexity of the Chinese society—seen, for instance, in the dispute over professionalism and the place of ideological training in the army that led to the ouster of Lo Jui-ch'ing, chief of the General Staff; the apparent persistence of the profit motive in agriculture and industry; and the development of factionalism and bureaucracy in the party—tends to blur those lines. As a consequence, the Cultural Revolution has revealed sharp differences of opinion over a wide range of social and economic issues. All beg the question how a society enveloped and supposedly guided by ideology can efficiently divide its labor without sacrificing practical achievement or purity of theory. The prolonged and as yet unresolved debate in China over the appropriate roles of theoreticians ("reds") and practitioners ("experts") is only one part of this fundamental problem that faces all developing countries. It is particularly excruciating in a highly ideologicized environment such as China, where political and economic modernization often pull in different directions.

Closely related to these hindrances are those produced by the theoretical foundation of Mao's style—the doctrine of contradictions and struggle. If progress is determined by contradictions and measured by struggle, a tight chain of command is clearly essential to prevent anarchy. Yet, as has been suggested, the command center in Peking has also found it politic to destabilize for the sake of order —to manufacture, if you will, synthetic contradictions so as to induce "orderly struggle." In practical terms, this approach requires not one but many cultural revolutions, not a single stage of class struggle but ongoing struggles in the transition to socialism and communism.[35] This frenetic cycle will never completely succeed in channeling China's vast, unexploited energies in a single direction. Indeed, the latest cultural revolution has evidently already prompted considerable rethinking among previously unimpeachable party and intellectual leaders regarding the appropriateness of Mao's style for solving China's pressing problems.

As for the future, this brief analysis of style in Communist China raises important questions about the extent to which change can be induced from the outside. The trend of events in China since the Eleventh Central Committee Plenum of August 1966 would seem to indicate that departures from past theories and practices by the Mao-Lin "group" cannot be readily prompted by long-standing party comrades, let alone by foreign powers. Meddling in or otherwise seeking to influence the course of events in China during this tumultuous period—on the assumption, for example, that this is the long-awaited rise of a pragmatic leadership which will deal Maoism a crushing blow—might well prove counterproductive. Mao's determination would be more likely to harden under the impact of foreign "intervention"; and there is little evidence that his opponents are more amenable to compromise.

No one expects the revolutionary course of Chinese politics and foreign policy to remain rigidly reactionary indefinitely. But it does seem that so long as Mao is an active political force, we cannot expect harmonious relations between his followers and the various groups or individuals he has identified as objects for struggle. Mao's style is to regard struggle as inevitable, to interpret resistance to struggle as the signal for its intensification, and to reject reconciliation by compromise with those who have been identified as the principal enemies. My own feeling is that Mao is fighting a losing battle against a slow-moving tide of change—change not induced by hostility to Maoist ideology, by a desire to sweep Mao out of power, or by the victory of pragmatism on the mainland, but rather by a belief shared in widely separate quarters that Maoism, with its emphasis on revolutionization, must be modified if it is to remain relevant to China's needs and national interests.

NOTES

1. For definitions, see Gabriel A. Almond's essay in Almond and Sidney Verba, eds., *The Civic Culture: Political Attitudes and Democracy in Five Nations* (Princeton, 1963), and Lucian W. Pye's introductory essay to Pye and Verba, eds., *Political Culture and Political Development* (Princeton, 1963).

2. This concept was developed by Nathan Leites in his groundbreaking *A Study of Bolshevism* (Glencoe, Ill., 1953).

3. The definition is from Alexander L. George's restructuring of Leites' study, *The "Operational Code": A Neglected Approach to the Study of Political Leaders and Decision-Making,* RAND Corporation, RM 5427–PR, September 1967, p. v.

4. Donald Klein has informed the author that a Communist political officer used the phrase at that time in describing the Red Army's activities in Shansi province.

5. The importance of hate in modern China is dealt with in Lucian W. Pye, *The Dynamics of Hostility and Hate in Chinese Political Culture* (Cambridge, Mass., 1964).

6. Joseph R. Levenson, *Confucian China and Its Modern Fate,* Vol. III, *The Problem of Historical Significance* (Berkeley, 1965), pp. 113–114.

7. For an excellent analysis of Mao's thought which separates out his truly unique contributions to the "treasurehouse" of Marxism-Leninism—the theories of guerrilla war being one—see Arthur A. Cohen, *The Communism of Mao Tse-tung* (Chicago, 1964).

8. On the ramifications of "democracy" as it is practiced in Communist China, see H. F. Schurmann, "Organisational Principles of the Chinese Communists," *China Quarterly,* No. 2 (April–June 1960), p. 56.

9. Edgar H. Schein, *et al., Coercive Persuasion: A Socio-psychological Analysis of the "Brainwashing" of American Civilian Prisoners by the Chinese Communists* (New York, 1961), p. 72.

10. See the article by Jen Li-hsin in *People's Daily,* Peking, January 4, 1968, p. 1.

11. For a comprehensive treatment of the united front, see Lyman P. Van Slyke, *Enemies and Friends: The United Front in Chinese Communist History* (Stanford, 1967).

12. *Ibid.,* pp. 209, 224, 226, 235.

13. The original title, *Lun Kung-ch'an-tang yüan ti hsiu-yang (On the Cultivation of Communist Party Members),* was a 1939 lecture by Liu. The lecture was revised three times subsequently, most recently in 1962 (Peking, 1964), and it is this latest revision that is usually singled out for attack.

14. For the fullest critique of Liu Shao-ch'i's theory, see *People's Daily,* April 10, 1967, p. 2, the reprint of an editorial originally published in *Pei-ching jih-pao (Peking Daily),* April 7, 1967.

15. John W. Lewis, *Leadership in Communist China* (Ithaca, 1963), p. 64.

16. The statement was made in an interview with K. S. Karol and was published in the *New Statesman* (London) on May 28, 1965. See Karol, *China: The Other Communism,* translated from the French by Tom Baistow (New York, 1967), p. 456.

17. See, in particular, Lewis, *Leadership in Communist China,* pp. 47–60, and Franz Schurmann, *Ideology and Organization in Communist China* (Berkeley, 1966), Chap. 1.

18. Mao, "On Contradiction," August 1937 (as revised), in *Selected Works,* II (New York, 1954). A spokesman for Mao's Cultural Revolution Group has commented that the Chairman's theory of contradictions is his single greatest contribution to Marxist-Leninist theory. He argues that Marx, Engels, Lenin, and Stalin were all for varying reasons unable to grapple with the problem of a restoration of capitalism during the period of proletarian dictatorship, and that only Mao, foreseeing such a possibility, sought to prevent a restoration by taking it into account in his analysis of the class struggle in China. See Jen Li-hsin, "Never Forget the Dictatorship of the Proletariat: A Study of the CCP Central Committee 'Circular' and 'A Great Historical Document,' " *People's Daily,* May 21, 1967, p. 2.

19. "On Contradiction," p. 50.

20. In "On Contradiction": "If in the party there were no contradictions and no ideological struggles to solve them, the life of the party would come to an end." Quoted in Lewis, *Leadership in Communist China,* p. 57.

21. *Ibid.,* p. 60.

22. In his speech "On the Correct Handling of Contradictions Among the People" (February 27, 1957), Mao admitted that contradictions in Chinese society still existed, but he said these were "non-antagonistic." In an important article by Commentator in the authoritative ideological organ *Hung-ch'i (Red Flag)* during 1967, however, the Cultural Revolution was said to be undertaking the resolution of "antagonistic" *(tui-k'ang-hsing ti)* contradictions "between the proletariat and the handful of party people in authority taking the capitalist road." Commentator, "Take Hold of the Principal Contradiction, Keep to the General Direction of the Struggle," *Red Flag,* No. 7, May 1967.

23. In an important statement on February 1, 1942, Mao told party workers: "Past errors must be exposed with no thought of personal feelings or face. We must use a scientific attitude to analyze and criticize what has been undesirable in the past so that more care will be taken in later work, and so this work will be better performed. This is the meaning of 'Punish the past to warn the future.' But our object in exposing errors and criticizing shortcomings is like that of a doctor in curing a disease. The entire purpose is to save the person, not to cure him to death." Mao,

"Correcting Unorthodox Tendencies in Learning, the Party, and Literature and Art," in Conrad Brandt, Benjamin Schwartz, and John K. Fairbank, *A Documentary History of Chinese Communism* (Cambridge, Mass., 1952), p. 392.

24. Alluding to the party's earlier experience, Mao is quoted as having said: "The key to forming the revolutionary great alliance and making a success of struggle-criticism-transformation in each unit is the correct attitude in dealing with cadres, and this question must be solved properly. Through the rectification campaign in Yenan [1942], our party educated the masses of cadres and united the whole party, thus ensuring the victory of the War of Resistance Against Japan and the War of Liberation. We must carry forward this tradition." See the editorial published January 1, 1968 by *People's Daily, Red Flag,* and the army newspaper *Chieh-fang chün pao (Liberation Army Daily),* reprinted in *Peking Review,* No. 1 (January 3, 1968), p. 11.

25. This is not to say that the mobilization of youth for political purposes in China is without precedent. See John Israel, "The Red Guards in Historical Perspective: Continuity and Change in the Chinese Youth Movement," *China Quarterly,* No. 30 (April–June 1967), pp. 1–32.

26. For insights into the impact of the Eighth Plenum on the Cultural Revolution, see Harry Gelman, "Mao and the Permanent Purge," *Problems of Communism,* XV, No. 6 (November–December 1966), 506.

27. The revisionist philosophy was said to be the particular work of Yang Hsien-chen, a member of the Central Committee and a former president of the Higher Party School. His doctrine that "two combine into one" *(ho erh erh i)* was condemned as an expression of peaceful coexistence in violation of the "correct" formula of contradictions, namely, that "one divides into two" *(i fen wei erh).* See, e.g., *Peking Review,* No. 37 (September 11, 1964), pp. 9–12.

28. One example is this statement from a report of Hu Yao-pang, First Secretary of the Chinese Communist Youth League Central Committee, on June 11, 1964, to the League's 9th Congress:

> . . . we must also bear in mind that young people, coming from different classes and strata of society, still bear the impress of various class ideologies. Since they have been brought up under conditions of peace and stability, it is easy for them to lapse into a false sense of peace and tranquility and to look for a life of ease and security. Because they have not been through the severe test of revolutionary struggle, they lack a thorough understanding of the complexity and exacting demands of revolution. . . . It is wrong and dangerous to think that youth, "born in the new society and brought up under the red flag," is "born red" and can automatically be heirs to the revolutionary cause without revolutionary Marxist-Leninist education, steeling in practical revolutionary struggle, and conscious ideological remoulding.

The full report, entitled "For the Revolutionization of Our Youth!" is in *Peking Review,* No. 28 (July 10, 1964), pp. 8–22.

29. The "bourgeois" line in educational policy, which has been attacked as anti-Maoist, is said not to give proper attention to ideological training, and instead to give priority to professional skills and academic subjects. The chief target has been Lu Ting-i, formerly an alternate member of the Central Committee Politburo, head of the Central Committee's Propaganda Department, and a vice-premier in the government. A complete critique of Lu's position is in a *People's Daily* article by

the revolutionary alliance, general headquarters of the Central Research Institute of Educational Science, December 6, 1967, p. 4.

30. Richard H. Solomon, "Parochialism and Paradox in Sino-American Relations," *Asian Survey*, VII, No. 12 (December 1967), 831–850. China's "need" of an enemy is not unusual; many African leaders have, for instance, sought to implicate the former colonial regime for economic and political failures in the post-independence period.

31. "A Retort to Bundy," *People's Daily*, February 20, 1966, p. 6, cited in *ibid.*, p. 842. ("Observer" is widely assumed to be a very high-ranking party member, perhaps Mao himself.)

32. The importance of and distinction between theoretical and practical soundness are best emphasized in Liu Shao-ch'i's *How to Be a Good Communist*, pp. 16–34.

33. Pye, *Dynamics of Hostility and Hate*, pp. 49–50.

34. Some examples of the adverse impact of Mao's style in this regard are the rejection of China's revolutionary approach by a number of African nations, their enthusiasm (shown by political support) for the foreign aid rendered by the Republic of China (Taiwan), and the movement of capital of overseas Chinese, especially in Hong Kong, into investment on Taiwan.

35. See Schein, *et al.*, *Coercive Persuasion*, p. 37.

# The Taiwanese in Taiwan

Stephen Uhalley, Jr.

mericans are normally frustrated and otherwise discomfited
in their study of China because of their lack of access to that
country. They would like to be able to make their own observations
and judgments as to what is going on. But access does not necessarily dispel frustration, nor does directly perceived limited evidence
resolve basic questions. We know this well enough from the experience of our more fortunate foreign colleagues who have visited
Communist China and who return with conflicting impressionistic
accounts.

We know this even better from our own experience in Taiwan,
where certain subjects cannot be explored satisfactorily. One of the
most intriguing and fascinating and most fundamentally important
of these is the Taiwanese themselves. Few topics are more elusive,
more difficult to research properly to a confident conclusion. In

Taiwan it is neither politic nor prudent to inquire extensively into the subject of Taiwanese-mainlander relationships. Surveys are out of the question, except perhaps for the most discreet and limited types which may reveal unrepresentative information. Accurate and honest information in any case depends ultimately on the degree of confidence that can be established between researcher and respondent, and only a naive inquirer can believe that this is easily done. The problem, therefore, is not only that it is a topic forbidden to researchers by the authorities, but that it requires special care in the handling of the few respondents who may be willing to discuss the issue.

At bottom, one does not find among the Taiwanese a widely held, well-articulated, and unitary attitude toward the Chinese mainlanders or about the most desirable political settlement for their island. Some of the reasons for reticence and lack of thoughtful opinion are obvious, but some reasons are less so. Certainly the Chinese army, the secret police, and the many past examples of punishment for those who dared to exploit the issue are self-evident reminders of why people hesitate to speak out. But Taiwanese really are divided on the subject; what is good for the Taiwanese intellectual or businessman may not appeal at all to the farmer. And partly because it has been a closed subject for so long, and because of the ineluctable processes of acculturation and absorption, many Taiwanese probably do not think much about the problem at all.

The problem is also generally ignored by Americans, or is often oversimplified. Taiwan, after all, is at the heart of the conflict between the United States and China. Here the United States has decided to intervene in the Chinese civil war to protect one last province from Communist victory. If we learn more about Taiwan we may be in a better position to fit that important island into a proper perspective vis-à-vis our relations with China. It can be one of the keys toward an understanding of China as a whole.

Taiwan's legal and national status is a good starting point, for if Taiwan is beyond question legitimately the territory of Nationalist China, then there is little point in discussing the issue further. No matter what Taiwanese feelings or aspirations might be, they would not really matter except as a Chinese domestic problem of little international significance.

It is difficult to argue that Taiwan does not seem properly to be a part of China, even though some Taiwanese and others make this claim. Their arguments are forceful if not entirely persuasive. Taiwan's geographical position and history do seem to lend some support to the separatist contention. The island is large and rich in resources. The channel that separates it from the Chinese mainland is much wider than that which divides the United Kingdom from Europe. Being so well endowed and physically situated, it *could* be an independent country, and one that would compare favorably—in terms of wealth and prospects for development—with a good many sovereign nations today.

Before 1945 Taiwan had known rulers of different nationalities, and it had known independence as well.[1] The Spanish, the Dutch, and the Japanese figure in the island's politics during the early seventeenth century, but it was the Dutch who first gave the island a sound government. Their administration created the inviting environment that led to Chinese immigration, which in turn was stimulated by the turmoil that accompanied the end of the Ming dynasty in China, and the subsequent conquest by the Manchus. At this juncture China, which had been an organized political entity for many centuries, made no claim on Taiwan, nor had she shown any interest in the island. Though the Chinese drove out the Dutch in 1662, it was evident that they represented no government in China itself, despite pretensions of loyalty to the Ming and vows to liberate the mainland. The regime they established was politically independent. Under it the island seems to have flourished, with both population and production increases, during its twenty years of existence.

In 1683 the Taiwanese regime succumbed in the face of a threatened Manchu invasion. Its third and last ruler was given a title and retired in luxurious comfort in Peking. The Manchus dispatched military and civil officials to the island, which would now be under the formal control of China for the next two hundred years. For most of this period Taiwan was formally part of the province of Fukien on the mainland. The rule seems to have been primarily passive and largely ineffectual, for the island was well known on the mainland as an unstable, rebellious area. In the nineteenth century alone it experienced more than thirty bloody outbursts. In many cases these were undoubtedly the result of resentment generated by rapacious mandarins. On the other hand, the picture is not entirely a black and white one. We hear of good officials as well. One prominent example is the perhaps mythical Chinese official, Wu Feng, whose wise, humane, and self-sacrificing policy toward the island's aborigines persuaded even the Japanese to pay tribute to his memory.[2] Another is the capable Liu Ming-chuan, the first governor after Taiwan was declared a province in 1887. This event signaled Peking's sudden realization of the economic and political importance of the island, another result of pressures from the West. Liu was a good administrator and an avid reformer who sought to make real improvements. With the help of foreign advisers he tried to reform the island's military establishment, develop a viable transport and communications system, reform and modernize the educational system, and make an extensive land survey, which succeeded in greatly increasing tax revenues to the government. But this temporary bonanza was soon absorbed by the lower and middle reaches of the Chinese bureaucracy, and the additional tax collections themselves provoked uprisings. In 1892 Liu was transferred elsewhere and the reform program ended. Only three years later, after the Sino-Japanese War of 1895, the Manchu government, which had been the first to extend mainland control over Taiwan, now ceded the island "in perpetuity" to the Japanese in the Treaty of Shimonoseki.

This concession was made grudgingly. The Manchu authorities tried to avoid making it at all, but the Japanese were adamant. Even after the formal cession there was real resistance on Taiwan itself. A combination of Chinese officials and literati, refusing to accept the transfer, founded the "independent" Republic of Taiwan, the first republic in Asia. This political entity resisted the Japanese for a short while in northern Taiwan, and much more determinedly and for a longer time in the south. The short-lived republic was apparently a connivance of mainland authorities, but it undoubtedly enjoyed some local support in Taiwan as well. It is an interesting historical interlude, but it hardly seems to be a truly solid instance of Taiwanese assertion of autonomy for, aside from the connivance of mainlanders, its first act was to announce the recognition of China's sovereignty over Taiwan. Of course, one might say equally that it was an episode that does not argue strongly for China's claim over the island either. As a matter of fact, we can see from a review of history that really responsible Chinese government from the mainland had been limited to a period of only about five years out of the entire historical period before Japan's takeover. During this whole period the mainlanders actually did very little in the way of reducing Taiwanese provincialism, of effacing the distinction between themselves and the islanders.

This distinction between Chinese mainlanders and Taiwanese, natural as it is in many respects, was greatly sharpened by the half-century of Japanese rule in Taiwan. Although the Japanese ruled Taiwan as a colony, exploiting it and strictly subordinating the Taiwanese in the process, the island registered marvelous economic gains that redounded to the benefit of the local population as well as to the Japanese. Indeed, by 1945, regardless of heavy American bombing of the island during the war, it was far better situated economically than the mainland. When the Nationalist Chinese took control of Taiwan in 1945 they gained possession of China's richest province.

But the Japanese contribution to Taiwan, and to the distinction between Taiwanese and Chinese mainlanders, is not to be measured in economic terms alone. Thanks to the Japanese, Taiwan emerged also as China's most literate province. Indeed, its 80 per cent literacy rate was probably the reverse of what obtained in China.[3] This is a significant distinction, but it is perhaps less crucial than the psychological gulf that had developed. This gap was caused primarily by Taiwan's isolation from the momentous development of Chinese nationalism which was occurring on the mainland in the twentieth century. This is not to say that racially Chinese residents in Taiwan did not respond to China's modern awakening. But such response was minimal and went unarticulated and unpublicized in Taiwan. There was therefore no real excitement on the island over the May 4th Movement[4] that swept China and helped jolt the country into a modern attitude. There was no equivalent vibration to the May 30th Incident,[5] nor to the Northern Expedition[6] which brought nominal unity to the divided nation. Taiwan was protected from a headier appreciation of these positive psychological developments by its Japanese colonial rulers. Of course, the

Taiwanese were also spared the tortured travail of China—the chaos and confusion of the warlords, the civil war, the worst of the war of resistance, and the results of the stagnation and corruption of the once revolutionary Nationalist government that lost its élan, vigor, and purpose in World War II. Thus, even though Taiwan may have been more advanced economically and in terms of literacy than the mainland, it was decidedly less nationalistic, at least as far as a significant portion of the population was concerned. A few politically conscious Taiwanese did chafe under Japanese authority, but the vast majority learned to be apolitical, even consciously unconcerned about politics. This would prove to be a practiced quality of mind that would be required long after the Japanese left the island.

Interestingly enough, the psychological gap was intensified in another way. The Japanese were able to engineer great improvements in Taiwan's economy, and in the education and health of its population without seriously disturbing the basic Chinese social structure.[7] Aside from having important ramifications for the increase in population on the island, this policy also helped to perpetuate among the Taiwanese much of the traditional Chinese social order and its beliefs and practices. This has led to some curious paradoxes: the Taiwanese, despite their literacy and technologically advanced environment, are often more "traditional" than the mainlanders, despite the latter's conservative ideology.

This dip into history in search of perspective on Taiwan's legal status is illuminating but not exactly conclusive. Until 1945 it would seem that China had established a certain legitimate claim on the island, however tenuous. This was lost to the Japanese rather decisively, even if under questionable circumstances. But Japanese occupation and its influences did not entirely rule out the Chinese claim; they merely served to make Taiwan's status somewhat less than clear.

The precise status is *still* unclear. China's position was strengthened by the Cairo Declaration of December 1, 1943, which inaccurately stated that "All territories Japan has stolen from the Chinese, such as Manchuria, Formosa, and the Pescadores, shall be restored to the Republic of China." This was a declaration of intent, and was not legally binding. Yet nothing has ever been done since to make it legal in terms of international law. The Potsdam Proclamation of July 26, 1945, confirmed that the terms of the Cairo Declaration would be implemented. The occasion on which the problem should have been settled was the signing of the Japanese Peace Treaty at San Francisco in 1951. But neither Communist nor Nationalist China signed this treaty. In any case, the treaty did not specifically transfer title of the island to China. It merely renounced Japanese sovereignty over Taiwan.

The attitude of the United States is of the most crucial importance on the issue. The United States is primarily responsible for the Cairo and Potsdam statements on Taiwan, but its policy overall has been ambiguous. After the Communists won on the mainland and the Nationalists had fled to Taiwan, the United States declared a "hands-off" policy toward the island. The Korean War changed this attitude abruptly; still, President Truman, as he ordered the Seventh Fleet to safeguard the Straits of Taiwan, reaffirmed that "the determination of the future status of Formosa must await the restoration of security in the Pacific, a peace settlement with Japan, or consideration by the United Nations."[8] American policy, however, continued to harden, and by May 18, 1951, Dean Rusk, then Assistant Secretary of State for Far Eastern Affairs, declared:

> We recognize the National Government of the Republic of China even though the territory under its control is severely restricted. We believe it more authentically represents the views of the great body of the people of China, particularly their historic demand for independence from foreign control. That government will continue to receive important aid and assistance from the United States.[9]

This statement was considered unqualified support for the Nationalist government on Taiwan. But, however much this support has crystallized—and indeed it is now considerable in moral and financial terms[10]—the question of status for Taiwan remains unresolved. As a matter of fact, four months after Rusk's statement, John Foster Dulles explained that the recently signed San Francisco Treaty (the Japanese peace treaty) "merely takes Japan formally out of the Formosa picture, leaving the position otherwise unchanged."[11] This interpretation was reiterated by Secretary Dulles on December

1, 1954.[12] The significance of this review of some of the fundamental elements of the issue is quite clear: the Nationalist government's position on Taiwan rests decisively on the support of the
United States. This support has been forthcoming, and handsomely.
But this has not affected the basic legal question. It would appear
that the door is still open for legal maneuvering in the future; the
status quo is not necessarily binding.

While there certainly is a question regarding the legitimacy of the
present Nationalist government's claim to Taiwan, there is good
reason to suspect that many Taiwanese, as Chinese, desire to be a
part of a larger Chinese national or political entity. This nationalistic impulse, despite the differences among Chinese, is the ultimate
argument against the separatists who seek an independent Taiwan,
or, as these Taiwanese Nationalists prefer, Formosa.

The basic desire of Taiwanese to be integrated into China, albeit
with some degree of self-rule on a democratic basis, was seen clearly
enough at the end of World War II. There were no strong voices
for independence, whatever real differences had developed between
Taiwanese and mainlanders. In fact, the islanders looked forward
to Chinese rule after so many years of colonial subjugation. The
story of what the Taiwanese were subjected to, in spite of this positive attitude, is nothing short of shocking. It is an incredible record,
and one that must be understood if one is to gain any appreciation
of Taiwanese psychology, even today. Instead of treating the Taiwanese as liberated brethren who were also potential contributors
to the entire Chinese nation's efforts to rebuild, the Nationalists
treated them contemptuously as conquered subjects.

Ironically, the affluent province was refused equal status with the
mainland; a military government with arbitrary powers was imposed. Chiang Kai-shek chose as Administrator-General Chen Yi,
an old colleague who had already become notorious as governor of
Fukien. Under this man, with the help of "carpetbagging" mainlanders and unkempt and ill-disciplined Nationalist soldiers, an
official system of monopolies was instituted to control and systematically exploit all important commercial and industrial enterprises. Movable capital assets were confiscated, to be sent to the
mainland or sold for the profit of corrupt officials.

These and other measures exacerbated the results of earlier
American bombings. Soon the corrupt rule incited profound resent-

ment and increasing protests from among Taiwanese the length and breadth of the island. Characteristically, the government underestimated the situation, ironically attributing it to a "psychic phenomenon" that causes people "to look with disfavor on the present and idealize the past," rather than to economic chaos and political repression.[13]

On February 28, 1947, the Taiwanese revolted—not against Chinese authority but against the misrule of the local Nationalist administration. They demanded reform of the Taiwan administration, not independence. The text of their "Thirty-two Demands" may still be consulted for verification of this point.[14] Chen Yi, suddenly aware of the gravity of the situation and realizing the inadequacy of his troops, resorted to duplicity. He allowed the formation of a committee composed of Taiwanese leaders to negotiate a settlement. But while he provided the committee with time to present their grievances in the form of a Draft Reform Program, he also won time for reinforcements to arrive from the mainland. It is reliably reported that the Taiwan committee acted with responsibility and restraint, even though the regime was helpless. There was no ultimatum involved; not even the threat of a declaration of independence should the demands not be met. But on March 8, 1947, some fifty thousand Nationalist troops arrived—two days before the date set by Chen Yi for submission of the Draft Reform Program.

Chen Yi now turned on the Taiwanese with a vengeance, launching a reign of terror that lasted for almost a month. The primary targets were members of the committee which had been authorized by Chen Yi and all who had cooperated with it, especially students. The obvious motive was to exterminate most of the natural leadership of the island. But the slaughter became indiscriminate. It was witnessed by foreigners, whose outraged accounts are undeniable evidence. Even many mainland Chinese were shocked. One, who had also witnessed the Japanese "Rape of Nanking" in 1937, conceded that this barbarous act was worse. Yet this was not the explosion of passion in the midst of war, as noted by George Kerr, an American vice-consul in Taiwan at the time, but an act of vengeance conducted by the Chinese government on its own people, who had not revolted but merely agitated for necessary reforms.[15] We might note in passing that the Communists played no significant role in this entire affair. Accounts of the uprising, of its suppression, and of the Taiwanese position throughout were of course sadly distorted in the controlled and contrived press releases that emanated from Taipei.

In the end, an estimated ten thousand Taiwanese were murdered in the bloodbath. Some Taiwanese sources claim a figure as high as twenty thousand. Later, even more would be arrested and executed for alleged involvement in the 1947 movement. Even today arrest on these grounds is quite possible in Taiwan. The Nationalists continue to do their part in keeping alive the notorious symbol, expressed simply as *"erh-erh pa"* or "February 28," that is burned into the minds of almost all adult Taiwanese.

It took tactful American representations to Chiang Kai-shek to bring about the recall of Chen Yi, who was then compensated with the governorship of Chekiang Province. Taiwan was made a province, and Wei Tao-ming, recently ambassador to the United States, was made governor. His administration was not efficient; although he made an honest effort to institute reforms, his key officials were uncooperative. Arrests and executions continued. But these events were overshadowed by the collapse on the mainland of the Nationalist government itself.

As the mainland debacle neared its end, Chiang Kai-shek prepared to move to his island refuge. He sent ahead trusted General Chen Cheng to replace Governor Wei. Once again martial law was instituted and the purge of persons charged with being pro-Communist intensified. The Taiwanese were forcefully subdued, a measure that was hardly necessary even though their Chinese ardor had noticeably cooled. When the Nationalist government made its move to Taiwan, Chen Cheng was elevated to the presidency of the Executive Yuan. The Nationalist government itself was streamlined somewhat. The Taiwan governorship was given to Dr. K. C. Wu, who had established a fine reputation as mayor of Shanghai. Although strictly limited in its power, the provincial government under Wu made great strides irrespective of its exceptional burdens —a huge military establishment, the large bureaucratic superstructure of the central government, and the more than a million refugees.

The case of Dr. K. C. Wu is particularly instructive for anyone wishing to understand Taiwan. A mainland Chinese, he did an outstanding job and in the process won the support of many Taiwanese. He was a man obviously concerned for the welfare of the people. He knew what their feelings were and what troubled them most deeply. Among their fears were the activities of Chiang Kai-shek's son and heir-apparent, Chiang Ching-kuo, who had capitalized on his twelve years of experience in the worst of Stalin's Russia in the 1920's and 1930's. He ran the dreaded secret police apparatus and was extremely unpopular. Governor Wu reportedly made the mistake of calling this fact of life to the attention of the Generalissimo. As a result, Wu was engineered out of office and narrowly missed assassination. He was permitted to leave Taiwan in April 1953 but had to leave his son behind as hostage. Fortunately, influential Americans interceded, and the boy too left about a year later. Dr. K. C. Wu was free to speak.

By means of a series of open letters to the Nationalist Chinese National Assembly, Dr. Wu presented his indictment of the regime. This included criticism of: (1) one-party rule, (2) the influence of political agents within the army, (3) the secret police apparatus, (4) the lack of guaranteed individual rights, (5) the absence of press freedom, and (6) the Youth Corps, whose organization pervaded the educational system and served as a thought-control mechanism. These letters were suppressed, and Wu was suddenly accused of dereliction of duty, corruption, and treason dating over a number of years. Wu replied that if the charges were true, why had he not been dismissed for them, and why had he had to resign repeatedly before his resignation had been accepted? He also expressed willingness to stand trial in any impartial court. Wu then published a series of questions focusing further on the unsavory features of the regime, from among which the following few are selected as examples:

> How many secret police organizations are there in our country?
> What are the limitations on their powers?
> . . . the actual number of people who have been arrested and put into custody by the secret police?
> Are there, or not, secret jails and detention houses in Formosa?[16]

Dr. Wu was not merely a disgruntled politician but a respected gentleman with an excellent reputation, a man who had accomplished much when he had been asked to shoulder responsibility. His word has particular authority. Nevertheless, his experience has received minimal publicity in the United States.

The Wu episode is a revealing one, for it tells us two very important things. First, we are reminded of the necessity to distinguish between mainland Chinese in Taiwan as individuals and the Nationalist regime, which is, of course, identified almost exclusively with the mainlanders. In other words, mainlanders obviously can govern well when the responsibility for doing so is in capable hands. Second, Dr. Wu reveals much about the nature of the Nationalist regime which we should never allow ourselves to forget, although Americans seem to have a strange facility for doing so. The regime is clearly a one-party, authoritarian state (remember that the Kuomintang party was modeled after the Soviet Communist party),[17] in which the power concentrated in one man's hands is being readied for transfer, in dynastic fashion, into the hands of his son. There is little room for democratic values or practices anywhere in this political-military machine, except at times as a façade for the purpose of deceiving its chief benefactor, the United States. The opportunity of the Taiwanese people for meaningful political self-expression, much less self-determination, is effectively stymied in such a dictatorial framework. There is little prospect that the future will see any appreciable liberalization. It is not only the poor governmental record to date, which gives little cause for those in power to believe they have won the support of the Taiwanese people. It is primarily that with the passage of time the regime's very justification for existence inexorably depreciates. Realizing this, the regime holds onto its power all the more tightly.

The question of justification is important, though it is not often raised. Whatever injustices the Nationalists perpetrated upon the Taiwanese people, because they were Chinese and anti-Communist it might be argued that they were obligated to provide a refuge for their fleeing Nationalist brethren. That these Chinese brethren were not simply scattered refugees but an entire superstructure of government which the Taiwanese would be expected to support, changed the picture somewhat. But the obligation remained, so it might be argued, for the Taiwanese to afford their central government with a base for fighting back, or, at the very least, with an opportunity to justify itself as the government of all China, whatever the dreadful mistakes of the past. For its part, the Nationalist government had an obligation to return to the Chinese mainland as quickly as possible. In fact, the assumption that the Nationalists would return to the mainland is the only real justification for the maintenance of their central government organization. Now, with each passing year the prospect of the return to the mainland has become less likely. Even so, they might have maintained the viability of this assumption—perhaps through greater creative response to opportunities presented inadvertently by the Chinese Communists. Failing any such hope of return or real responsiveness, the least the regime could have done was to transform itself into a political expression that more closely reflected the reality of its environment and the needs of the people of Taiwan. But neither development has taken place, nor is it likely to on a voluntary basis.

The Taiwanese then, as anti-Communist Chinese, might have been expected to overlook the past, and to endure much while the Nationalists made their decision. It has now been almost two decades since that government based itself on this single province of China. The Taiwanese have endured much, namely the burden of the unwieldy central government with its authoritarian characteristics that have been aimed particularly at keeping the Taiwanese in place. In this regard, appearances should not be allowed to deceive. Many Taiwanese occupy administrative and political positions on the island. In 1965 they held more than half of the provincial and nearly two-thirds of the municipal offices.[18] But these men work within limits prescribed by mainlander officials in the central government superstructure. None have any real power; few are in office without the sanction of the Kuomintang party or the secret police. There is surprisingly little participation in the Nationalist or central government itself. Out of the 3,045 members of the National Assembly, only ten are Taiwanese. In the 473-member Legislative Yuan there are only six Taiwanese.[19]

Much of the wealth of the island resides in the hands of the Taiwanese. This is only natural since it is their home, and their families are well established on most of the property of the island.

They also represent a vigorous portion of the business community; about 80 per cent of the private enterprise is in their hands.[20] This has produced considerable resentment from mainlander bureaucrats, an attitude born both of a lingering Confucian bias against commercialism and downright envy. Professor Allan B. Cole, in a penetrating study, has pointed out that there has as yet been little fusion between mainlander and Taiwanese business groups.[21] The mainlander businessmen are strong in the public sector of the economy, which is government controlled, and seem hesitant to take aboard too many Taiwanese for fear of their solidary family and clan associations and other types of in-group preferences and obligations. The Taiwanese managements, on the other hand, may retain a mainlander for liaison purposes with the mainlander-controlled central bureaucracy in order to expedite the processing of applications and licenses and to seek government contracts. They shy away from too many mainlanders, however, because of their in-group preference and because this practice might result in eventual mainlander takeover, or to the levying of more exactions by officials and by the Kuomintang, evils which plague the mainlander-run government corporations. The mainlanders enviously eye the close and profitable relationships enjoyed by the Taiwanese businessmen with Japan. Some of this trade has reached considerable proportions. For example, the Taiwanese control about one-third of the distribution system for bananas in Japan. This advantage is shored up by family connections in Japan, where most of the 45,000 Chinese residents are Taiwanese. The mainlander bureaucrats compensate themselves for the Taiwanese businessmen's prosperity by engaging in extensive squeeze practices. It has been said that this form of corruption would exist in Taiwan even if official salaries were tripled.[22] The Taiwanese seem resigned to the practice and indeed are not above indulging in it themselves (as an almost venerable Chinese tradition) when opportunity allows.

For the most part, Taiwanese businessmen abjure politics. They profess cooperation with the government but undoubtedly are basically suspicious of it. Despite this, they have learned and are learning how to use political contacts, at least opportunistically. These men certainly display little interest in opposition politics, perhaps because they understand so well the realities of their situation. Thus in 1960 only one prominent Taiwan businessman became associated with the ill-fated attempt of Lei Chen, whom we shall discuss in a moment, and others to found an opposition party which sought to appeal particularly, although not exclusively, to the Taiwanese population. As a matter of fact, as long as the economy remains buoyant and business prospers, these men are not likely to become politically restive. In a way this is unfortunate, because many among them are potential leaders. But few of them are concerned with true democratic political forms, undoubtedly because they have experienced so few meaningful influences of this kind.

Taiwan businessmen are resigned to the imposition of the mainlanders as long as things are at least as tolerable as they are now. This says much about the situation in Taiwan: it bespeaks a certain minimal accomplishment by the Nationalists, i.e., to have achieved such tolerance, although there have been other contributing factors. The economy is one area in which gains have been made, though the current economic prosperity is a tenuous one. In general the current picture does not seem too bad; therefore the Taiwanese are not restive.

This all-important economic dimension is worth elaborating. It is often said that the land reform program has been a great success and should be a model for other countries. The Sino-American Joint Commission on Rural Reconstruction (JCRR), an exemplary organization, sponsored the program. On Taiwan, the JCRR for the first time had an opportunity to make significant changes in land tenure which did not affect influential landlords within the Kuomintang or the government. Taiwanese landlords were the targets—precisely the class that had produced the leadership so troublesome to the government in the late forties. The program was in two parts. The first was a rent reduction program in 1951, in which rentals were limited to 37.5 per cent of the crop value. This was fine, except that some sources maintain that the Chinese initiated exorbitant rents in the first place, after 1945. The Japanese had controlled rents and had held land courts before the war. The second part of the land reform was the Land-to-the-Tiller program in 1953, which limited land holding to about seven and a half acres of middle-grade paddy field. Land owned in excess of this amount had to be sold to the government for land bonds and stock in government-owned industries. This step benefited thousands of poor farmers, but it also reduced considerably the modest standard of living of thousands of others.

Nevertheless, Taiwan's overall economy had boomed sufficiently by 1965 so that American economic aid was ended that year. With industrial production running about 20 per cent and agricultural output 6 per cent above the previous year, and with foreign exchange reserves at about $300 million, Taiwan had reached the status of a semi-developed country, as measured against other nations of the world.[23] Prospects for continued development without direct U.S. economic aid were good. But it should be kept in mind that Taiwan already had an excellent economic base as one of the legacies of Japanese rule. One of Taiwan's advantages in the competitive world market is its cheap labor, which will remain so because of the sizable unemployment rate, expected huge accessions from a young population, and the unlikelihood of independent or militant labor unions developing amidst Taiwan's authoritarian politics. Since 1965, too, agencies of the United Nations have substantially increased their aid to Taiwan. The Vietnam War has contributed to Taiwan's prosperity.

There are also economic shortcomings. While the economy has finally reached the levels established under Japanese rule and then surpassed them, the population of the island has doubled. This continued growth threatens to negate temporary economic achievements. And the regime has allowed serious gaps to develop in the economic institutions and policies necessary for future progress. Effective investment, banking, and capital market institutions are needed to channel public savings into industrial investment. Consumer credit financing facilities are lacking. The public accounting and management-consulting professions are grossly inadequate and lacking in necessary prestige. In terms of economic policy there is an urgent need for continued liberalization of restrictions on imports and for encouragement of foreign investment. This possibility is handicapped by a fear of Japanese penetration and influence—a fear the Taiwanese do not share.

The government must also develop a wise strategy of development. New fiscal and monetary policies are needed. The educational system as a whole needs overhauling in order to produce trained people for an industrializing society.[24] Progressive income taxation is urgently needed as inequalities of income continue to grow. Desperately required are sanitary sewerage facilities and better transportation and traffic controls, as well as a number of other provisions for the social needs of the island.[25] Whether all of these problems can be met soon is questionable, for despite the vigorous activity of a handful of capable officials, there loom in the background the conservative bureaucracy and the equally conservative wielders of power. Of course, always to be calculated are the economic consequences of a large, unproductive bureaucratic superstructure and an oversized army.

As long as the economy remains reasonably viable, the Taiwanese seem to have great capacity for remaining politically quiescent. Perhaps most of them never seriously think about their plight. Some see nothing oppressive about it at all, and these would include such diverse representatives of the population as those who are willing tools of the government, those whose ambitions are satisfied (even if in limited fashion by the opportunities available), and even many of the small farmers who gained in the land reform. Even service in the army is viewed as no real burden by many Taiwanese, although some students may resent it. The peasant lad from the rural villages and towns may actually regard two years of military service as a welcome break in his routine. It may afford opportunities to serve in the large cosmopolitan cities such as Taipei and perhaps even on the offshore islands where extra pay and savings for the future might be earned. The army, after all, is well-clothed, equipped, and provided for, thanks to U.S. aid, so that life in it is not too dreary an experience. Of course, this all presupposes that the army will never go to war or be used for serious domestic suppression. In such an eventuality, it is not likely that the army would be able to keep the Taiwanese under full control.

The relatively few politically conscious Taiwanese have long since learned to speak circumspectly. The secret police are aimed primarily at them. Occasionally there are cases of ruthless suppression which come to the public's attention, such as the Lei Chen case in 1960, when this doughty, but perhaps imprudent, editor was sentenced to ten years by a drumhead court, an extremely harsh punishment for a man already advanced in years. His major crime was probably less that his opposition party was a real threat than that he used unkind expressions in castigating Chiang Kai-shek personally. This case received international publicity, for Lei Chen and his periodical, the *Free China Fortnightly,* were well known. But there are other cases involving persons who, because they are unknown abroad, are done away with quietly. The execution of Su Tung-ch'i and his two associates in 1962, and the arrest of dozens more allegedly connected with them is a case in point.[26] There are other such arrests of which we hear nothing at all. In Taiwan, for a person to be well known or at least known to Americans is considered a valuable "lifeline," for it is calculated that the regime will deal less arbitrarily with one who might tarnish the façade that is painfully maintained to please the United States.

Many of those who are potentially politically conscious leave the island regularly. They are the students (both Taiwanese and mainlanders) whom the island has sent abroad each year for many years. Of utmost significance is that about 95 per cent of these young men and women never return. Thus the quotient of intelligent, critical minds that might prove troublesome is kept under closer control. Of course, this fantastically high brain-drain also has implications for both the economic and the administrative development of the island.

The regime has not been seriously challenged, despite its authoritarian practices, for a combination of calculated and fortuitous reasons. The economy is viable and growing, almost in spite of the regime, and there are a number of reasons why political or social agitation is kept to a minimum. There is also the inescapable fact that time itself has lessened, and will continue to reduce, tension between the Taiwanese and the mainlanders. The forces of assimilation and acculturation have already been at work for almost a quarter of a century. Young Taiwanese in many ways share more in common with young mainlanders than with their own older generation. Likewise, young mainlanders are, up to the age of eighteen at least, actually Taiwanese themselves in that they were born on the island and this is the only home they have known. The young people have not coalesced by any means, but clearly there is no substantial animosity between the two groups. Significantly, both consider themselves Chinese first and Taiwanese second. This may be due to the educational curricula and other forms of incessant propaganda, but it also has something to do with racial and national pride.

If both groups share the feeling of being primarily Chinese, many of the politically conscious among them share common misgivings about their government as well. It is not only Taiwanese students who hesitate to return to Taiwan; mainlander Chinese are equally reluctant. The Taiwanese are orphans at home, to the extent that they have been short-changed by their government. But many mainlanders, too, feel alienated to the point of orphanhood, at least spiritually, from their inadequate government for which they feel more embarrassment than pride or loyalty.

There are many Taiwanese *and* mainlanders, therefore, who are deeply dissatisfied with the present political framework. Both groups feel that justification for the continued existence of the Nationalist government in its present form is slipping. This rapidly diminishing respect was signaled especially forcefully in the incredibly weak response by the Nationalist government to the Cultural Revolution in Communist China. The turmoil and political uncertainties engendered by this upheaval would seem to have presented an opportunity for an imaginative and creative response by Taiwan which would have captured the interest of Chinese everywhere, and perhaps induced many to return to a regenerated proud standard. Of course, nothing of the kind happened. As if to emphasize, with the poorest timing possible, its reactionary character, the government launched a "Cultural Renaissance." This patently political gesture was not even properly defined so that it might possess even a modicum of meaning, or be used as a mass movement in order to accomplish some positive end. The Cultural Renaissance is a joke, and although it is not without deleterious consequences, it is being laughed down in Taiwan and ignored without.[27]

The Taiwanese and many of the mainlanders are orphans at home in Taiwan. They are governed by a regime that has outlived its legitimacy, that no longer has the charisma for a successful return to the mainland, and that is unable even to represent an attractive alternative for the Chinese people. The plight of the people of Taiwan should be relieved whenever the international situation permits. The recommendation of the Conlon Report, written by Professor Robert Scalapino for the Senate Foreign Relations Committee in 1959, still deserves serious consideration. This proposed the establishment of a Republic of Taiwan. The United States would guarantee its defense and would assist all the mainlanders who wished to return to China or go elsewhere. Perhaps as a means of lessening objections to the Two Chinas concept which so upsets both China and Taiwan, a formula might be worked out to express the ultimate desire of the new republic to rejoin China "at whatever time in the future that this becomes a practical possibility." A premature re-union with the mainland would hardly be better than a continuation of the present unsatisfactory situation. But some such formula would serve the Chinese, and Taiwanese, aspiration to be part of a single, larger Chinese political entity, and would actually leave the way open for eventual implementation. In the meantime, the mainlanders who choose to remain in Taiwan could stay and participate in its destiny. Their talents would undoubtedly be welcomed. With a democratic government more closely and realistically attuned to the immediate needs and future hopes of the island's population, the chances for Taiwan to become a "bastion of democracy" in Asia and a "showpiece province" for all of China would be improved immeasurably.

NOTES

1. The reader is referred to the following selected historical works: James W. Davidson, *The Island of Formosa: Past and Present* (Shanghai, 1903); William Campbell, *Formosa Under the Dutch* (London, 1903); Yosaburo Takekoshi, *Japanese Rule in Formosa* (London, 1907). See also the two excellent articles: Shinkichi Eto, "An Outline of Formosan History," pp. 43–58, and Maurice Meisner, "The Development of Formosan Nationalism," pp. 147–162, in Mark Mancall, ed., *Formosa Today* (New York, 1963). This excellent work, with its incisive introduction by the editor, remains one of the best general works on Taiwan.

2. The non-Chinese aborigines were the original inhabitants of the island. As Chinese populated Taiwan the aborigines were pushed into the remoter and less hospitable areas. They were often exploited by the Chinese so that a tradition of hostility developed between the two ethnic groups. Thus a Chinese official who treated the aborigines justly was apparently so unique a phenomenon that he became a legend. Today the aborigines, still a small minority, live for the most part in the mountains and along the rugged east coast. Their feeling toward the Chinese, whether mainlander or Taiwanese, remains something less than affectionate.

3. General Albert Wedemeyer's report to the Secretary of State of August 17, 1947, U.S. Department of State, *United States Relations with China* (Washington, D.C., 1949), p. 257.

4. The May 4th Movement is the designation given to the wave of national indignation in China when the Versailles Treaty in 1919 awarded erstwhile German interests in Shantung Province to the Japanese. The term usually applies more broadly as well to the wave of enthusiasm for political and cultural change in China in the year or two preceding and following May 4, 1919.

5. On May 30, 1925, British-led Chinese police fired into a crowd of demonstrating strikers in Shanghai, killing several of them. The reaction throughout China signaled a new stage in the development of Chinese nationalism.

6. The Northern Expedition of 1926–1927 was the sweep northward from Canton of the Nationalist Army under the leadership of Chiang Kai-shek in cooperation with the Chinese Communist party. The objective was to unify China under Nationalist rule and eliminate the warlords.

7. George W. Barclay, *Colonial Development and Population in Taiwan* (Princeton, 1954), p. 257.

8. U.S. Department of State *Bulletin*, XXIII, No. 574 (July 3, 1950), 5.

9. *Ibid.*, XXIV, No. 620 (May 21, 1951), 847.

10. U.S. aid to Taiwan reached by mid-1967 a total of almost $4 billion. By 1965, when U.S. economic assistance ended, economic aid amounted to almost $1.4 billion. By mid-1967 U.S. military aid reached $2.5 billion. U.S. Bureau of the Census, *Statistical Abstract of the United States 1967* (88th ed., Washington, D.C., 1967), pp. 258, 824.

11. U.S. Department of State *Bulletin*, XXV, No. 638 (September 17, 1951), 462.

12. *Ibid.*, XXXI, No. 807 (December 13, 1954), 896.

13. Meisner, "Development of Formosan Nationalism," p. 154.

14. George H. Kerr, *Formosa Betrayed* (Boston, 1965), pp. 475–479. This book gives an excellent fuller description of the Nationalist takeover in Taiwan and of the 1947 uprising. Its author is an exceptionally well-informed Taiwan specialist.

15. *Ibid.*, p. 300.

16. *Ibid.*, pp. 480–486.

17. Sun Yat-sen agreed to the refashioning of his Kuomintang party by Russian Communists in the early 1920's in order to make it a more effective revolutionary instrument. Soviet advisers were dispatched to China for this purpose. The new Kuomintang party included in its ranks Chinese Communists who, curiously enough, were allowed membership and office.

18. Allan B. Cole, "Political Roles of Taiwanese Enterprisers," *Asian Survey*, VII (September 1967), 648.

19. Peter P. C. Cheng, "The Formosa Tangle: A Formosan's View," *Asian Survey*, VII (November 1967), 800.

20. Cole, "Political Roles," p. 645.

21. *Ibid.*, p. 646. Professor Cole was a Fulbright Scholar in Taiwan during 1964–1965.

22. *Ibid.*, p. 649.

23. Neil H. Jacoby, *U.S. Aid to Taiwan: A Study of Foreign Aid, Self-Help and Development* (New York, 1966), p. 231.

24. Education in Taiwan is severely handicapped. For an industrializing society there is far too little concern for technical arts curricula. An archaic examination system stresses rote memorization rather than problem-solving capabilities, and its pervasive influence is extremely deleterious. Finally, teaching is an underpaid and overburdened profession whose depressed condition reflects well the inadequate attention given to education by the government.

25. Jacoby, *U.S. Aid to Taiwan*, pp. 234–236.

26. John Israel, "Politics on Formosa," in Mancall, ed., *Formosa Today*, pp. 64–65.

27. Stephen Uhalley, Jr., "Taiwan's Response to the Cultural Revolution," *Asian Survey*, VII (November 1967), 824–829.

# Chinese in Southeast Asia

Claude A. Buss

As a young graduate student in the twenties I was first attracted to the problem of the overseas Chinese by the fascinating story of Wellington Koo, whom I had the pleasure of watching in action at the Washington Armaments Conference. His attractive wife came from a distinguished Chinese family in the Netherlands East Indies, as it was then called. Subsequently, as a foreign service officer in China, I was responsible for studying the role of Chinese abroad in the unfolding of the Nationalist revolution. On the eve of World War II it was both my pleasure and my obligation to deal with the Chinese components of the population of the Philippines. Since the war I have traveled among the Chinese in every one of the new states of Southeast Asia. I cannot speak for all of them, but many have shared their thoughts with me.

These people are individuals: real flesh-and-blood human beings and much more than pawns in a game of domestic and international politics. Their views of the future are not theoretical, but they are very vital and very personal.

At the outset of my remarks I shall suggest that the overseas Chinese will have no more influence on the future of China than Boston policemen will have on the future of Ireland, or Milwaukee bankers on the reunification of Germany. But the status of the overseas Chinese will be of continuing interest to any Chinese government, whether in Peking, Taipei, or anywhere else. Their protection, and the possibility of attracting their sympathy and support, will always rank high as a Chinese national interest. Perhaps the most significant key to understanding Chinese policies in Southeast Asia will be their anticipated effect on the welfare of those Chinese who retain their cultural bonds with the homeland, even though they have chosen to identify their political and economic futures with their adopted homes.

When we talk about the overseas Chinese in Southeast Asia, we mean about twelve million people out of 250 million, or about 5 per cent of the total population of the area. According to Lea E. Williams (in *Future of the Overseas Chinese in Southeast Asia*), they are distributed as follows:

|  | Total No. of Chinese | Total Population | Per Cent of Chinese in Total Population |
|---|---|---|---|
| Malaya | 2,920,000 | 8,090,000 | 36 |
| Sarawak | 275,000 | 830,000 | 32.5 |
| Sabah | 120,000 | 515,000 | 23.3 |
| *Total Malaysia* | 3,315,000 | 9,435,000 | 35.1 |
| Brunei | 25,000 | 95,000 | 26.3 |
| Singapore | 1,400,000 | 1,880,000 | 74.5 |
| Thailand | 2,600,000 | 30,500,000 | 8.5 |
| Burma | 400,000 | 25,000,000 | 1.6 |
| Indochina Peninsula |  |  |  |
| North Vietnam | 190,000 | 18,400,000 | 1 |
| South Vietnam | 860,000 | 16,300,000 | 5.3 |
| Cambodia | 435,000 | 6,250,000 | 7 |
| Laos | 45,000 | 2,100,000 | 2.1 |
| Philippines | 450,000 | 32,000,000 | 1.4 |
| Indonesia | 2,750,000 | 106,000,000 | 2.6 |

The overseas Chinese came from many villages and districts, but practically all came from the provinces of Kwangtung or Fukien or from the island of Hainan. They have their provincial guilds and their associations for welfare or social purposes, and they have tended to perpetuate innumerable secret societies. Some are very rich and some are very poor; some are highly sophisticated and cosmopolitan, others are little more than "country bumpkins." All have demonstrated a high degree of adaptability, whether they live in crowded cities or operate a "sari-sari" or tiny general store at the end of a jungle path.

Inescapable historical facts have a very important bearing on our subject. The Chinese who migrated to the South Seas did so for individual reasons and not because of state policy. The earliest travelers who chose to leave the Middle Kingdom did so in search of enlightenment and education in the Buddhist classics. Their intellectual discoveries have given us the best knowledge we have of life in the ancient Hinduized kingdoms of Southeast Asia. At a much later time Chinese merchants, without any real enthusiasm, decided to join the Parsees, the Arabs, and the Indians in pursuit of commerce. It was only with the age of European imperialism that the Chinese flocked to Southeast Asia in significant numbers. They came not only as traders but as settlers, and they contributed their skills to economic development. They became the miners and planters of Malaya, and they built the newly found cities of Singapore and Penang. They came with the idea that they would stay a while, prosper, and return home; therefore they lived to themselves, kept their own separate communities, and enjoyed the political protection of the European rulers. Chinese became the agents, *compradores,* bankers, and general associates of Europeans whose profits were often dependent on their local Chinese associates. The cooperation between the European and the Chinese heightened the native resentment against both.

The numbers of overseas Chinese swelled with the political chaos and economic deterioration of nineteenth-century China. The T'ai P'ing rebellion which ravaged mainland China from 1850 to 1864 forced thousands to leave, and a certain amount of revolutionary sentiment, or at least political awareness, was part of the intellectual equipment of the émigrés. They were in a sense ready at the turn of the century for the approach of Sun Yat-sen, the founder of the Kuomintang. In the countries of their new domiciles they worked hard, saved their money, and achieved positions of great economic power. They dominated the money-lending business and the retail trade, as well as the crafts and professions. Hard work and saving were the keys to their success. The native Southeast Asians loved the noonday siesta, but the Chinese worked from dawn until midnight. They stayed out of politics and felt more comfortable when the local government overlooked them or left them alone. As a matter of prudence they showed no concern for the politics of the Manchu empire, and the Manchus usually showed little interest in those who were so un-Chinese as to leave their ancestral home.

Gradually the nature of the Chinese occupation began to change as Chinese interests began to expand. Rice merchants and bankers became regional in their interests, and they began to deal in huge sums of money. Aw Boon Haw sold his Tiger Balm all over Southeast Asia, and K. C. Lee parlayed his rubber activities into an international financial empire. One Chinese broker in Burma might sell his wares to a brother who was the purchaser in Batavia, and other relatives would take care of the invisible aspects of the whole transaction. In modern times we see how Run Run Shaw has grown to affluence in the international movie market and how Adrian Zecha, the publisher of *Asia* magazine operating from Singapore, exercises tremendous influence on the thought processes of Chinese and non-Chinese throughout the entire Southeast Asian region.

Furthermore, the new breed of Chinese became permanent residents with no thought of returning to the mainland. They brought Chinese girls from home or they married native women, and in bringing up their families they gave more thought to eventual assimilation. They clung tenaciously to the cultural aspects of their Chinese heritage, but their attention shifted increasingly from the politics of China to the politics of their new homelands. And when they died they willed that they should be buried where they had lived. The Chinese cemetery in Manila is mute evidence of this readjustment in Chinese psychology.

Significant changes have become noticeable in the different generations of overseas Chinese. The first generation, the newcomers, were often shy, insecure, and poverty-stricken. Nowadays, because of immigration restrictions and the high price of bribes, fewer Chinese can get into Southeast Asia. Thailand once received ten thousand per year; now the quota is two hundred. These are carefully screened and usually get in because of their connections. They have language difficulties and will take almost any job and work for a pittance. Their main concern is to keep out of the clutches of the law, and so they are often victims of petty extortion. It is among these newcomers that Peking propagandists and party workers are presumably planted. Sometimes "innocent" refugees turn out to be newspaper writers or elementary schoolteachers who are exceedingly useful for subversive purposes.

As the first generation becomes the second generation, it is interesting how the profit motive intensifies. The older Chinese become conservative and want their children to preserve their Chinese cultural roots. They want their children to get an education and to study Chinese (as they think it should be), and they will often require their children to go for three or four hours to Chinese schools after a regular session in the local school. They want the youngsters to speak their native Chinese dialect, the local tongue, English, and Mandarin Chinese. This is a tall order, and some children naturally rebel. A Chinese merchant in Jesselton, Malaysia, lamented that he simply could not discipline his youngsters in this atomic age. But the young people learn things at school their fathers never taught them. It is in the civics classes of the higher schools that they hear about civil rights, political liberties, revolution, and Mao Tse-tung. Then they get the idea of involvement. The first thing the father knows, the generation gap has completely separated him from his children. Very often laziness infects the younger people, too, with the philosophy that father will take care of any difficulties. One finds in second-generation overseas Chinese society seeds which could easily sprout into delinquency.

Some second-generation Chinese, on the other hand, carry on and develop the opportunities which their parents have made possible. I had many students at the University of the Philippines who were training to carry on their fathers' businesses, and hoping to become better businessmen than their parents. Many Chinese enterprises are the product of the efforts of continuing generations. Often the children can get citizenship which was denied their parents and thus obtain a measure of very precious legal protection. In fact, prosperous second-generation Chinese often operate on a much larger scale than their elders. They rise above petty extortion and bribes to corner policemen and learn to deal with congressmen or cabinet ministers. They operate through huge banks, insurance companies, or chambers of commerce. They cannot remain aloof from politics, thus they try to play safe by contributing to almost any cause or campaign fund that solicits their contributions.

Not too many of these first- and second-generation Chinese whom I have known worry too much about their identity crisis. Whatever they are, they take in stride. It is only when some bright member of the family gets interested in philosophy or political science that he becomes interested in the nature of traditional Confucian concepts. Some overseas Chinese might find it expedient to attend a celebration or a party at the Chinese embassy or consulate, but most are inclined to think of politics as an essential bore or an unavoidable obstacle to economic progress. To them, homeland politics means a request for money.

Perhaps the most interesting phenomena among all the overseas Chinese are the real old-timers, who after generations have almost lost or turned their backs upon their Chinese identity. Sometimes one must look hard to find the Chinese among Thai officials, but they are usually there. The late *dato,* Sir Tan Cheng-lock, in Malaya once exclaimed, "How can anyone call me a newcomer or an immigrant to this country! Don't they know that I now live in the same house in Malacca which my ancestors lived in when Albuquerque arrived?" Some of the distinguished old-line families in the Philippines, with names like Uichangco, Tuason, Soliangco, or Locsin, spell their names as one word so as to erase the Chinese derivation —but their Chinese origin is unmistakable. These families are now often pillars of the church, ladies of the society page, wearers of awards or medals of distinction from many governments, and the most bitter of anti-Chinese elements in local politics. They have made their peace with the local environment and have carved their niches in it. They do not wish to be challenged by newcomers who would travel the same road they traveled generations ago.

At this point in history overseas Chinese must be politically involved whether they like it or not. As a matter of fact, they were stirred out of their comfortable isolationism by the projection of Sun Yat-sen's nationalism into the political preserves of the colonial empires. The Chinese became "dangerous" when they began to identify themselves with local communities and preach the ideas of self-determination. The British and the French both outlawed the activities of the Kuomintang in their respective spheres. It was considered as dangerous then as the Communists are now. During the Japanese invasion the local Chinese were singled out for special attention, and many were put to death whether or not they professed allegiance—as many did—to Wang Ching-wei. The Kuomintang consular staff in Manila was among the earliest victims of Japanese militarism. The local Chinese were made aware of their oneness as never before, and for self-preservation were forced to take an interest in local affairs. Now the overseas Chinese are victims of xenophobic nationalism in the newly emerged states; they are constantly harassed by racial, political, economic, ideological, and cultural problems. They are furthermore entangled in the conflicting aspirations of Peking and Taipei, and they are often smoked out of a disinterested, nonaligned stance by the pressures of the Cold War.

It is not realistic to see the overseas Chinese as a built-in fifth column or as potential commissars for an aggressive Communist China. The Peking regime has its dedicated workers and possibly its vanguard cadres for any anticipated successful revolution, but these are unusual hard-core operators and not the rank and file of the ordinary overseas Chinese. Nevertheless, if the latter were forced to choose one China or two, most without hesitation would go for one. The sense of pride in China is overwhelming. I shall never forget Tan Cheng-lock, during the guerrilla war in Malaya but after the Korean War, saying to me: "I have nothing at all in common with these Chinese Communists. They brand my rubber trees and kill my friends. But I want to tell you I am proud of every drop of 'yellow' blood in my veins. With three gunboats you defeated us in 1840 and with a single division you sacked our capital city at the time of the boxer Rebellion. But with all your force you could not defeat us in Korea." Prosperous overseas Chinese hate the communism in China, but they cherish a hope for a change in ideology which would make the mainland way of life more compatible with their own.

Very few, I think, would opt for Taiwan. Taiwan is not considered as anybody's homeland or as a locale for future greatness. Sun

Yat-sen may be enshrined in the hearts of many overseas Chinese, but Chiang Kai-shek is scarcely accepted as his successor. Chiang Ching-kuo is still more a stranger. To many, the Kuomintang is a lost cause. It had its chance and failed. Not many Chinese tears would be shed in Southeast Asia if a "Republic of Taiwan" were to be formed, or if an independent Taiwan were to be reabsorbed into mainland China as was the case when Taiwan was reabsorbed into Manchu rule of mainland China after the fall of Koxinga's grandson.

## THE RECORD, COUNTRY BY COUNTRY

*Thailand.* In Thailand the imposition of controls on the overseas Chinese began before World War II. In the twenties the King himself, in spite of Chinese amnesty, was supposed to have written a pamphlet against the Chinese labeling them the Jews of the Far East. After the revolution in the thirties, *alien* Chinese were excluded from rice farming, taxi-driving, barbering, butchering, and casting the images of Buddha. The singling out of the alien Chinese was explained as a device to force the pace of assimilation. In the fifties legislative restrictions were placed on franchise and the acquisition of Thai citizenship. By 1955 Chinese were replaced on the administrative and teaching staffs of Chinese schools, and most instruction was given in the Thai language. Chinese higher schools and universities were forbidden. Governmental agencies and semigovernmental Thai enterprises entered fields previously dominated by Chinese. The Thais tried to put the Chinese out of the retail business, but they failed. (Government officials and police turned a blind eye to Chinese use of Thai wives, front men, and limited partners to control the businesses from which they were supposed to be barred. Large Chinese corporations put Thai members on boards of directors for protective purposes.) Immigration laws were tightened up and strict nationality laws were put on the books. But after the Bandung conference the Thais relaxed their stiffest anti-Chinese attitudes and became more receptive to legal and illegal "adjustments." The screws were again tightened with the outbreak of the Cultural Revolution.

The Thai government is extremely anti-Communist, and this makes for troublesome diplomatic and internal problems involving Chinese. On the diplomatic side, arguments flare between Peking and Bangkok. The Chinese blame the Thais for providing bases for Americans fighting in Vietnam. They chide the Thais for being American puppets. The Thais resent the Chinese propaganda broadcasts and the harboring of such Thai renegades as Luang Pradit on Chinese soil. The Chinese allegedly aggravate the incipient insurgency in northern Thailand and on the Malayan border. The Chinese encourage an anti-government Fatherland Front, reminiscent of the NLF in Vietnam, and speak of a possible autonomous tribal state on the Thai borderland. When the Chinese are in a tractable mood they hint at the dream of "Thailand irredenta," or a Greater Thailand which would consist of the territories in Cambodia, Laos, Burma, and Malaya, reunited at last with mother Thailand. It is all intended to embarrass relations between Thailand and her allies. Politically, the Thai government has outlawed the Communist party and keeps a close watch on suspected Chinese. The local Chinese, on their part, want nothing more than to be left alone by outside Chinese factions, and see their own future in making the best arrangements with the local Thai officials. There is no wholesale exodus to either the mainland or to Taiwan. There is not a great deal of sympathy for either, and it is doubtful if any but the most fanatical party workers would ever envisage or welcome Thailand as a falling domino to an advancing China.

*Burma.* Although nonaligned, Burma was the first state outside the Communist bloc to recognize Peking. It bore a grudge against Taipei, because of the Kuomintang assistance to Li Mi and the Nationalist stragglers who complicated life in the disputed China-Burma border regions. Burma made its peace with China on the border issue in 1960 and seems satisfied that the Chinese restrained themselves from interfering unduly in the internal quarrels which verged on civil war. The era of good feeling between Burma and mainland China came to an end in 1967 because of excessive revolutionary zeal on the part of Chinese in Burma over the Cultural Revolution. General Ne Win would not tolerate the slogan-chanting partisans of Mao Tse-tung, who called for a stepped up war of liberation within Burma itself. Ne Win sent the worst of the revolutionaries home and kept those who remained in Burma under strict martial law. Peking propaganda very understandably is anti–Ne Win.

*Malaysia.* The issues concerning overseas Chinese assume totally different proportions in Malaysia than elsewhere in Southeast Asia because of the high proportion of Chinese residents. The Chinese have been given liberal rights of citizenship but have been victimized to a certain extent by economic nationalism. The ten-year period of the Emergency led by Chinese terrorists under the banner of the Malayan Communist party has made the Malays extremely wary of Chinese leftist tendencies. Politics have a communal basis, but the major Chinese political vehicle represents the more moderate elements in the community. The Malay-Chinese-Indian Alliance is the dominant party. In education the government dislikes the Chinese schools but tolerates them in the hope that it may reduce their importance by creating better common schools in the public system. The Chinese language is no longer official and is therefore not used as a medium of instruction in the schools of the Federation. A certain percentage of jobs is reserved for the Malays in the public service, and the local Chinese realize that they suffer from political discrimination. They cannot complain too loudly because they know how much Malaysia fears the ominous presence of Singapore across the causeway.

*Singapore.* Singapore is a Chinese city, or rather, an independent state with 75 per cent of its population Chinese. It is prosperous, the fourth largest trading port in the world, and it boasts an enviable industrial growth. Its rate of population increase is the highest in Asia, but so is its per capita income. Its social services are among the best, and its leadership is highly trained and most efficient. Lee Kuan-yew is among the most capable prime ministers anywhere in the world. His policies are socialistic but not communistic. He professes nonalignment; he is basically against the Vietnam War but states publicly that he knows the policies of the United States are buying time for him and he would be a fool not to take advantage of his opportunities.

Lee Kuan-yew's ambitions transcend the narrow limits of Singapore island. He aroused the antagonism of the Tungku of Malaya by his aggressiveness and caused the Tungku to break up the Malaysia combination rather than run the risk of having it come under the control of Lee Kuan-yew. Lee and his socialistic supporters are under constant challenge from an opposition of the left. The students and the labor unions are his sources of worry, and he knows that he would be in serious trouble if Singapore were to experience economic depression.

Singapore trades with everybody and welcomes everybody's investment. It faces the economic loss which will follow the withdrawal of British forces from the Far East, but it cannot avoid a certain satisfaction in seeing the disappearance of the last glaring evidence of the age of imperialism. Although Chinese, and intellectually appreciative of changes accomplished in mainland China, Lee has made it clear in no uncertain terms that whatever China's future, he does not want it to include Singapore as a part of a possible Communist system.

*Borneo*. The overseas Chinese in the former British territories on Borneo are a microcosm of all Southeast Asia. Chinese of one sort or another dominate the agricultural production, trade, banking, supermarkets, and professions of Sarawak and Sabah. They have their own associations in opposition to their rival Malays, and yet their associations are so varied that they have monthly meetings of the "Association of Associations." Many hated to see the end of British rule, and they have had a difficult time adjusting themselves to the increased influence of Kuala Lumpur and Singapore on Borneo island. They wanted the jobs they held in government and business for themselves, and they object to those they call the carpetbaggers (even Chinese) who came to Borneo with the creation of Malaysia.

*Indo-China*. On the Indo-China peninsula, the local Chinese are individualistic lots in South Vietnam, North Vietnam, Cambodia, and Laos. Most of the Chinese in South Vietnam are congregated in Cholon, where they enjoy the usual Chinese power in the local economy. Or at least they did before the United States began to pour huge sums into South Vietnam as demanded by the hostilities. In the fall of 1956 South Vietnam launched a harsh attack on the overseas Chinese, but it was aimed at large-scale assimilation. The authorities ordered registration of all Chinese born abroad, and they confiscated the registration papers of those born in Vietnam. The local Chinese were ordered to choose between compulsory naturalization and evacuation to Taiwan. Regulations required Vietnamese language instruction in Chinese schools, the abolition of Chinese shop signs, and pressures on local-born Chinese to Vietnamize their names. Chinese nationals were barred by decree from eleven important categories of occupation, but the resulting disruption of the Vietnamese economy forced the government to retreat. In Saigon and Cholon the local Chinese rioted in retaliation; Chinese leaders swore that nothing would make them renounce their Chinese nationality. Vietnamese goods were boycotted in Hongkong and Singapore; and financial pressures abroad forced a disastrous drop in the value of the Vietnamese piaster.

At first quietly, and then openly and with official encouragement, the Chinese went back to their old trades in partnership with Vietnamese, or working under the names of their Vietnamese wives. As long as Diem was president, he tried unsuccessfully to undermine Chinese economic power, but the Chinese proved essential to the success of his economic program. The Chinese were obliged to resort to every stratagem, legal and otherwise, to keep what they considered their just rewards. The case of the Chinese businessman who was shot by Cao Ky for his alleged black marketing is indicative of the uneasy truce between the Saigon government and its Chinese constituents. Now the American presence is overwhelming and the prime factor in the formation of the attitudes of resident Chinese. It will be so as long as the war continues.

The small number of Chinese in North Vietnam may come as a surprise, but China is not popular in Hanoi. The historical memory of imperialist China weighs heavily in Hanoi, as does the more recent nightmare of the Nationalist troops who came to North Vietnam to accept the Japanese surrender. Since their coming to power in North Vietnam, the Communists have been comparatively successful in displacing Chinese from ordinary occupations. They have done it by competitive superiority as well as by government regulation. The Chinese have not been nearly so essential as commonly supposed, either for the army or for the direction of government and party. North Vietnam has demonstrated an incontestable ability to manage its own affairs. In the presence of almost continuous civil war since 1946, it has not proved to be a particularly attractive place for immigration. And the Chinese who are there are presumably more concerned about their relations with the local hierarchy and the future of North Vietnam than with potential leaders in China after Mao.

*Cambodia.* The Chinese in Cambodia until 1967 were allegedly docile and in tune with the government of Prince Sihanouk. In his public speeches he praised Peking regularly for its kind assistance to poor Cambodia and for living up to its pledge not to interfere in the internal affairs of its smaller neighbors. The Prince was never pro-Communist, although he was often castigated for being overly sympathetic with Peking. Once, in an interview with me, he said he knew very well that if the Communists were ever to come to power in Phnom Penh he would be the first to go because he was rich, royalist, and Buddhist. He excused his neutralism on the ground that the ants must beware when the elephants fight. In 1967 he became fed up with the overzealousness of the Cultural Revolution. He permitted cautious *démarches* with the United States and adopted a severe anti-Chinese tone in many of his journalistic writings. He denounced Peking for fanning the flames of opposition to the government within Cambodia and promised all sorts of dire reprisals if Peking failed to change its course. As for the local Chinese themselves, what could they do? Profit, perhaps, from the traffic with Vietnam, pay off the government in increased amounts, and take their cues for policy shifts as best they could from the zigs and zags of the changeable chief of state.

*Laos.* By the Chinese in Laos, I refer to the businessmen in Vientiane and the cities along the rivers and trails, rather than to those who live in the mountains near the border and come over to "Dr. Dooley's" hospital for treatment of their wounds. Chinese stores in Vientiane still display pictures of President Eisenhower and Sun Yat-sen. But the Chinese embassy in Laos since the Troika settlement in 1962 is that of Peking. The Chinese make their profits and find their security in the American presence, and the necessity for any choice as to the future of China will have to await some sort of turning point in the Vietnamese hostilities.

*Philippines.* The Chinese in the Philippines are the prime targets of Philippine nationalism: official relations with mainland China are nonexistent because of the temper of the Philippines and their American ally. The Philippines would like to destroy the economic power of the local Chinese, and they have proceeded by such measures as forbidding Chinese to own property for commercial purposes, curbing their financial activities, and forcing them out of the retail trade. The Philippine Chinese are friendly to Americans because of their anti-communism and because of their mutual opposition to Philippine nationalism. It is commonly believed that what the Filipinos are doing to the Chinese today, they will do to the Americans tomorrow. The Philippine Chinese are perhaps the most pro-Chiang of the overseas Chinese, but it is hard to say how much of their support comes from the heart and how much from political expediency.

Some Philippine Chinese have begun to show a new interest in mainland China, but they are cautious. One shrimp boat operator has been the go-between for the arrangement of visas for Filipino journalists who have visited mainland China. Curiously, more Filipinos than Chinese have been interested in this development. It has taken place as an echo of "anti-American" sentiments. As one editor explained it to me, "Too long we have taken our interpretations of Communist China from *Time* magazine, *Newsweek*, *Life* and the CIA—now we intend to look for ourselves." The articles in the *Free Press* and the *Manila Times* have praised more than they have criticized the Cultural Revolution. They give an entirely different picture of China than one gets from most Hong Kong China watchers. But as a Filipino reporter said, "Do not get me wrong, I want no part of China. It's all right for those who wish to be revolutionary, but it is far too austere for my fun-loving soul." And it is doubtful if journalistic accounts of China could in any way influence the hard-boiled pro-Kuomintang attitudes of the thousands of overseas Chinese who have made their home in the Philippines for generations and who have become an integral part of its political and economic life. Increasingly, the Philippine Chinese are likely to take a more active interest in Philippine national affairs and to look more and more like concerned well-wishers rather than active participants in determining the China of tomorrow.

*Indonesia.* Of all the overseas Chinese, perhaps the most tragic and uprooted today are those in Indonesia. A scant two years ago the Chinese in Indonesia drew Peking's praise and enjoyed the benevolence of the Sukarno government. Their status was apparently protected by an international treaty. Those Chinese who were capitalistically oriented seemed to be able to prosper in their Indonesian environment, and those who believed that communism was the wave of the future saw themselves as the anvil against which the last vestiges of imperialism would be hammered into nothingness. The Chinese in Indonesia felt secure in the Guided Democracy.

Their complacency was rudely shattered on the night of September 30 / October 1, 1965. In a counter-coup, the forces of government, primarily the army, swooped down on Communists, whether Indonesian or Chinese, and put between 300,000 and 500,000 to death in the bloodiest orgy in our generation in Southeast Asia. Chinese and Indonesians, accused of communism, were hunted down from Medan to Bali and slaughtered systematically in cold blood. Chinese were rounded up. Some were deported and others released to the mercy of the populace. Their property and their means of livelihood were stripped from them, and their future was turned into a question mark.

But apparently few Chinese have asked to be sent to Taiwan or to Peking. Too many have been away too long from the land of their birth. No matter how tragic, Indonesia is still their home. The Chinese of today must face the same dilemma which their ancestors must have faced as the aftermath of similar tragedies centuries ago. They do not have the power to reshape Indonesia in their own interest, but still less do they have any power or disposition to cast their lot with China.

## THE POLICIES OF TAIWAN AND MAINLAND CHINA TOWARD THE OVERSEAS CHINESE

Taiwan has more or less lost much of its initiative with the overseas Chinese, but it still professes the right of protection. Like Peking, Taipei follows the doctrine of "once a Chinese, always a Chinese," although it recognizes the right of naturalization. It has official representation in the Philippines, Thailand, and South Vietnam. It invites students and scholars to Taiwan, and makes a place for them in the government schools. The welcome mat is out for distinguished visitors, and a constant stream of propaganda from Free China keeps overseas Chinese informed of Taiwan's respectable economic advancement. Investments are solicited, and places are made for overseas representation in some of the government and party organs. Strongest appeals are based on anti-Communist ideology, and the line has not been abandoned that overseas Chinese should never flag in the sacred mission to return to the mainland.

Peking has worked energetically to attract the loyalties of the overseas Chinese, giving them representation in the People's Congress and the party hierarchy and offering special privileges to relatives at home who were engaged in social reconstruction. Remittances from overseas Chinese were important sources of foreign exchange and packages from abroad were vital in keeping many Chinese alive during the worst days after the failure of the Great Leap Forward. Peking is just as active as Taipei in the propaganda field. Party workers from mainland China were sent to infiltrate the guilds and associations of Chinese in Southeast Asia, and Communist ideology was spread through Chinese textbooks and teachers in the local schools. Through Chinese and local banks, economic and financial help was extended to those who showed themselves sympathetic with Peking. These soft, surface tactics may have camouflaged hard, covert relations on a nongovernment level.

Peking followed a line of peaceful coexistence toward the overseas Chinese between the Bandung conference and the outbreak of hostilities on the Indian border in 1962. Chou advised all overseas Chinese to be good citizens of the countries in which they lived and to contribute their wealth and loyalty to that country's progress. He announced that he would not interfere in the internal affairs of any country, even to protect the alleged rights of his own countrymen. In 1955 he concluded a nationality treaty with Indonesia which recognized that all persons of Indonesian-Chinese nationality would be considered Indonesian unless they specifically opted for China. To Chinese in Indonesia, the work of Peking seemed to promise support for them in their running battle against discrimination by the Sukarno government. All through Southeast Asia the local Chinese seemed to benefit from Chou En-lai's enlightened diplomatic offensive for peaceful coexistence.

Peking lost a great amount of power and prestige among the overseas Chinese with the wilting of the "Hundred Flowers" campaign and the failure of the Great Leap Forward. Pretensions of progress were exposed as shams, and China was shown to be deteriorating economically, while other nations, principally Japan, were marching spectacularly forward. The fiasco of the offshore islands in

1958 dimmed China's military luster. Southeast Asia's Chinese could see no earthly benefit in letting relations with India deteriorate to the point of hostilities and make a shambles of Chinese-Indian friendship and brotherhood.

The Sino-Soviet split did not affect materially most overseas Chinese' attitudes toward Communist China. Not many Chinese in Southeast Asia have any use for Russia, and the Russian association with China merely made the Communist philosophy that much more odious to those who hated it anyway, and that much more unintelligible to those who were skeptical of its alleged benefits. After the Sino-Soviet break, a certain source of pride attached itself to China's accomplishments without Russia, and this spirit of independence was climaxed by the assertion of pride in the demonstration of Chinese nuclear capacity. The new nation-states of Southeast Asia shuddered at the news of the Chinese nuclear explosion, but the Chinese elements of the population made no bones about their glee that China had joined the nuclear club. But the measure of satisfaction in no way generated a desire to go back to China or to give up their local citizenship for that of China.

The detachment of overseas Chinese from China has been reinforced by reports of chaos emanating from China during the Cultural Revolution. The sight on the screen of a propaganda film such as "The East Wind Prevails" did not strengthen an urge on the part of many overseas Chinese to identify themselves more intimately with the mainland. The deification of Mao Tse-tung and the waving of the little Red Book had little effect on the older generation in Southeast Asia. No doubt it quickened the pulses of some of the young who imbibed the philosophy of Lin Piao and caught a vision of a world revolution under China's leadership.

It would be a mistake, I think, to overlook or underestimate that segment of the Chinese population inside China and outside China which apparently has faith in total revolution, and which is dedicated to the making of a new image of man. To those Chinese, China has not suffered diplomatic setbacks as we so easily assume. What we interpret as a defeat—as, for example, when a Peking contingent is dismissed from an African state, or a break looms with Indonesia, Burma, or Cambodia—supporters of Chinese communism see as an unmasking. In their view, what difference if government relations with bourgeois governments are severed! China can then ignore ordinary diplomacy and resort to total revolution, and can thereby maintain its position as the consistent exponent of true Communist ideology without the slightest taint of revisionism. In their view also, what is happening in China is not chaos but remobilization and rededication, so that a revitalized China can be a more effective agent for total revolution and total support for all wars of liberation abroad.

I do not think many overseas Chinese buy this interpretation. For the time being they are less concerned with Taipei and Peking than they are with their own destiny. They want to be sure of their own fate before they lend their support to any side in the question of what shall become of China after Mao Tse-tung and Chiang Kai-shek. In light of the problems which beset the overseas Chinese and the limitations on their capacity to cope with them, their first concern is bound to be their own personal interest, their welfare, their homes, and the place they live. In a secondary way they may devote themselves to their Chinese homeland, but I do not see how their contributions will have any more decisive influence on tomorrow's China than the immigrants of any other country will have on the land of their birth.

These observations are in no way meant to minimize the effort that Chinese governments will expend to attract the support of the overseas Chinese. Twentieth-century China has reversed the traditional attitude that Chinese who emigrate and abandon the graves of their ancestors are to be regarded as social outcasts. Emigrants are now looked upon as assets of inestimable value, both in preserving cultural values in alien lands and in earning money which can be returned to China in the form of remittances, contributing to the support of relatives who have remained at home. Both Peking and Taipei hope the philosophy of "once a Chinese always a Chinese" will generate a sympathy for the aims and objectives of the home government. It is always worthwhile for any administration or faction to gain as many adherents as possible among the overseas Chinese, because, in theory at least, the more friends they win the better the chances for local understanding and effective promotion of diplomatic policies which either China may adopt.

# On Being Chinese: A Philosophical Reflection

Vincent Y. C. Shih

E ver since the middle of the nineteenth century, after its encounter with the West, China has been in a quagmire, an institutional as well as an intellectual quagmire. The traditional way of life, which had for so long formed around her an insulating, protecitve husk, giving her a sense of security and complacency, began to crack after the impact of Western ideas. China as a nation and the Chinese as a people have since experienced a series of shocks unlike any in Chinese history. Dislocated and lost, the Chinese began a long, difficult journey in search of self-identity. First they sought to make China wealthy and strong by grafting Western technology onto its moral and institutional base. When this failed, some sought to revitalize the country by institutional reforms, adopting selectively certain elements of Western culture. When this also failed, the Chinese realized that there was no halfway between the old and the new. A series of revolutionary movements were launched, attempting to create a new identity capable of coping with the exigencies of a modern world. But however well intentioned, none has been really successful. The latest experiment has put China in a new, ideological quagmire.

Against such a historical background, it is natural that a "Chinese," whether he lives in mainland, Taiwan, or in any other part of the world, is bound to ask: "What does it mean to be a Chinese today?" The difficulty of this question is that the term "Chinese" is used in different ways. First, it designates an ethnic group whose members have recognizable physical traits which distinguish them from other ethnic groups. Second, it refers to a number of factors or common ties less recognizable but equally or even more important than the physical traits, such as racial consciousness, nationality or culture, geographical area, and so forth. These factors are much more complex in that among the Chinese themselves there are many sub-groups, varying significantly in their intellectual attainment or emotional attachment to their national heritage. This complexity is further compounded in the case of Chinese who live either as individuals or in a community away from their homeland in an alien civilization.

Understandably, the clearest, least ambiguous identity is an ethnic one, expressed in the proposition that one is a Chinese. Whatever changes take place in one's intellectual and emotional life, whatever new patterns of behavior one might acquire by living abroad, one remains a Chinese in physical appearance. This physical identity has its emotional implications: one tends to identify himself with that geographical entity known as "China," and with the particular locality in China that one comes from. In the past such emotional identification inspired more poetry than any other single theme. Wang Ts'an's (177–217) "Teng-lou fu" is perhaps the classic example in this respect. Once, after he had fled the political chaos in the north to Ching-chou (now Hu-pei), he climbed up a high tower looking north. He was overcome by nostalgia, which inspired him to write this poetic prose. In it he refers to two incidents in history to illustrate his own nostalgic feelings: a man from Ch'u imprisoned in the north composed Ch'u music, and a man from Yüeh who became a high minister in another state

longed for Yüeh when he was ill. Wang Ts'an draws from these the
following conclusion: "A man naturally feels for his home town, no
failure [referring to the prisoner] or success [referring to the min-
ister] could change his loyal heart."

Some poets felt a subtle sense of sadness to find, upon returning
home, that things were not what they used to be. A T'ang poet, Ho
Chih-chang, wrote the following lines:

> I left home a youth, but returned an old man,
> Still speaking with the same local accent, but with hair
>   almost gone.
> Children met me but did not recognize me;
> Smiling they asked, "Stranger, where did you come from?"

Many little things we do in our lives reveal—without our ever
being aware of it—this deep attachment to our native place. Traditionally, the Chinese, even though they might have lived in other
places for one reason or another, always hoped to go home to end
their days and be buried in their native place. No doubt such a sense
of attachment to one's native place was fairly common in many
parts of the world before the modern period. But in the turbulent
era in which we live, in China as elsewhere, people no longer give a
second thought to moving from one place to another. In this respect,
my own experience may be a case in point. Although I was born
in Foochow, my real native place is a little town situated south of
Foochow, called Fu'ching, where my father and grandfather were
born. Actually, I have little feeling for my real native town, because
I moved around so much, first to Peking where I studied and was
married, then elsewhere to work. After the outbreak of the Sino-
Japanese War we were compelled to move again, and finally we
settled in North America. (The high mobility that characterizes
modern living has, among other things, resulted in the gradual disappearance of the "local accent," which was mentioned in the poem
of Ho Chih-chang.)

As for the "cultural identity" of the Chinese, it too involves
ambiguities, because in the Far East, where modernization took the
form of Westernization, various elements of culture—religious,
literary, and philosophical—have become fused with those of the
West. There remain, nonetheless, some widely accepted views about

the enduring qualities of Chinese culture. First is the notion that it
is "spiritual." Second is the so-called "intuitive" approach of the
Chinese to the problem of knowledge. Third is the family as a
uniquely Chinese form of social institution. Finally is the idea of
*jen*, variously rendered as love, benevolence, humanity, human-
heartedness, and the ideal of a world of the greatest harmony, as the
dominant motif of the Chinese cultural tradition.

The oft-repeated statement that Chinese culture is spiritual in
contradistinction with the more materialistic Western culture may
be interpreted in various ways. On a simple level it might refer to
the humanistic emphasis of traditional Chinese culture. Probably
this is what was meant by the nineteenth-century Chinese Chang
Chih-tung, who stated that "Chinese learning is the substance and
the Western learning is for application" (*Ch'üan-hsüeh p'ien*).
This formula was offered when China had to reassert her cultural
superiority after a dismal show of force against the West. It implied
that if the soul of China were still intact, technology, which seemed
to have been responsible for the military success of the West, could
be mastered in a short time. This was China's first attempt at cultural self-identity, by grafting Western technology onto the traditional Chinese world-view. The attempt was unsuccessful, because
the Chinese failed to realize that technology also had a soul of its
own.

A more refined view of the spirituality of Chinese culture is
offered by many Chinese scholars. According to this explanation,
the East emphasized moral value and the West scientific truth.
With moral value as the object of inquiry, one naturally turns his
glance inward, revealing the nature of the inner self. But with truth
as the object, truth understood to be concerned with a factual outside world, one naturally trains his intelligence outward, illuminating the objective world. Not that Chinese thinkers have no use for
truth, but they subordinate it to the training of moral character. So
instead of dubbing the East spiritual and the West materialistic, it
is far more accurate to say that the East is more ethically inclined
and the West scientifically inclined. But this too is oversimplification, because many modern Chinese intellectuals have become
more concerned with science than with ethics. For example, the

late Dr. Hu Shih, with all his enthusiasm for the Chinese cultural heritage, for more than forty years believed that science would eventually solve all problems. Besides, to say that the West is mainly scientifically inclined may be correct only if this statement does not imply an utter lack of moral values. In any case, the attempt to distinguish the Chinese cultural tradition from that of the West by the spiritual-versus-material dichotomy is not a meaningful one.

The problem of the nature of knowledge as well as that of methodology is a variant of the same view. Elsewhere I have written: "The nature of knowledge is conditioned by the nature of its object, which also determines the method employed."[1] If the objects of knowledge are moral values and not the verifiable facts of the physical world, "the method adopted . . . cannot be of the type employed in the study of facts. The characteristics of a physical fact are, among other things, its reducibility to quantitative statements amenable to exact mathematical formulation, and its verifiability by objective reference to sense-data. And these are exactly what a moral fact or value cannot have. For values are distinctly qualitative. . . . They have to be directly experienced and conveyed by means of sympathetic understanding and penetrating comprehension between minds. They are neither objectively observable, nor reducible to quantitative formulae, and one cannot subject them to quantitative manipulation without fundamentally altering their nature."[2] Knowledge so obtained was called by the Neo-Confucianists *te-hsing chih chih* (knowledge through moral living); their method would be described by us as intuitive. If this view is correct, it explains why China never paid attention to science except in its elementary level of immediate application.

F. S. C. Northrop probably had the same view in mind when, in his attempt to create a suitable terminology for comparative philosophical study, he came upon "concept by intuition," which he applied to the East, and "concept by postulation," which he applied to the West. Let me comment again: "The value of the distinction is vitiated by two considerations: first, the same distinction holds between systems within the same culture; and secondly, what Northrop called the 'undifferentiated aesthetic continuum' is but another concept by postulation, and not at all adequate to the Tao, or Nirvana or Brahman."[3]

Institutionally, Chinese culture may be distinguished by its family system. Just as Plato's *Republic* is an individual writ large, so is Chinese society a family writ large. Y. P. Mei went so far as to invent a term to characterize Chinese society—"familiocracy."

Families are the building blocks of Chinese society. Each one is a unit of social cohesion, the foundation of a larger social unit. It is a closely knit unit in which individuals are offered protection and opportunity to mature and ultimately to find self-realization. It serves as a storehouse of family as well as social values, a conservative force for stability and order. It is characterized by the power and authority of the head of the house, subordination of individuals for the good of the whole, and subordination of women and children to men and adults. But it also provides security, if only through conformity. The government is without doubt patterned after the family: the state is a family with the ruler at its head; local officials, particularly the magistrates, are called, sometimes with genuine affection and other times with satirical bitterness, "people's parents." The authority of the father is supreme.

But this system is fast disappearing. As early as the 1930's Olga Lang reported that Western ideas were forcing changes. These ideas instilled in the young people a feeling of individual, personal worth and independence. The family began to lose its status as the primary economic unit. If one thinks of the Chinese Communist effort to destroy the sanctity of the family system, it is clear that the system soon may no longer be a mark of Chinese identification. It was functional and served the people well in an agricultural society, but with advances in industrialization the old traditional system lost its *raison d'être*.

If we have so far found nothing definite to be a satisfactory identifying mark of Chinese culture, it may be because we are looking in the wrong places. Just as the soul of a person is his mind, so the essence of a culture is its ideals and ideas. They lie at the foundation of the world-view of a people, constitute their aims in life, determine the way they approach problems, and give meaning to their institutions. The concept of *jen* is not only the central theme of ethical thought as well as political and social ideals through Chinese history, but it is still an enduring mark of Chinese culture in our time.

The earliest example of an ideal socialist state that took the whole world as its province was envisaged in the *Book of Rites*, attributed to Confucius. He is supposed to have said:

> When the great principle prevails, the world will belong to the public. The virtuous and the able will be selected to rule. They will win the confidence of the people and culti- vate harmony among them. Thus the people will love not only their own parents and children [but others' parents and children as well]. The aged will have a place to com- plete their natural span of life, the able-bodied a specific function to perform; the young will have the guidance of the elders, and the widowed, orphaned, and the crippled and sick will have means of support. The men will have their part to play, and the women a home to settle down in. They will deplore wasting goods on the ground, but neither will they accumulate them for selfish purposes; they will deplore the strength of anybody not being put to use, but neither will they countenance its reservation for one's own exclusive use. For this reason the way to wickedness will be closed; there will be no robbers, thieves or rebels, and the outer gates will not need to be shut. This is *Ta-t'ung* [The Great Harmony].[4]

The ideal of this Great Harmony has been the inspiration of many writers' political movements. The concern for the unfor- tunate expressed here goes back to even earlier times. In the *Book of Songs* we find these lines:

> There stand some backward blades that were not reaped,
> Here some corn that was not garnered,
> There an unremembered sheaf,
> Here some littered grain—
> Gleanings for the widowed wife.[5]

And in the *Analects* we find one of Confucius' disciples saying, "All people within the four seas are brothers."

The Kung-yang commentary of the *Annals of Spring and Autumn*, as interpreted by Tung Chung-shu and Ho Hsiu, conceived of three stages in the evolution of the Chinese state: the period of decline and chaos, the period of relative peace (peace within China), and the period of peace prevailing throughout the world. "Hence the barbarians are promoted to receive rank; and the far and the near, the large and the small under heaven are as if one."[6] A modern student commented: "At that time, the Middle Kingdom will be one man and the world will be one family."[7] So this third period is identified with the world of Great Harmony. In the Sung period, Chang Tsai sent this idea ringing in his poetic lines:

> To institute the mind for the universe;
> To create conditions for all people to enjoy life;
> [an alternative translation of this line: To establish moral
>     principles for the people;]
> To revitalize the neglected principles of the past sages;
> And to herald in an epoch of peace for the ten generations
>     to come.[8]

This Chang Tsai conceived to be his mission. Elsewhere, in "The Western Inscription," Chang was also inspired by the ideal of the Great Harmony. Even down to the nineteenth century this Great Harmony received three separate endorsements: by the Taipings, K'ang Yu-wei, and Sun Yat-sen. The Taipings included it in their 1852 edition of "Yüan-tao Hsing-shih Hsün"; K'ang embodied it in his *Ta-t'ung shu* (*The Book of the Great Harmony*); and Sun wrote the whole piece on a scroll for his followers. When T'an Szu-t'ung interpreted *jen* to mean "a universal spirit that unites all races of men, classes, and sexes in an all-pervading harmony in which all inequalities are eliminated,"[9] he was without doubt inspired by the same ideal.

From the examples given above we can see how closely this ideal is related to the concept of *jen*, a term which sometimes means one virtue among many others, the perfect virtue comprehending all others, an emotional feeling of love, or a metaphysical basis for all acts of love. As I see it, the ideal of the Great Harmony is to be realized through *jen*. Y. P. Mei calls it "a spark of divinity planted in man." It is all of these and much more.

Metaphysically, *jen* is at the basis of the creative process of the universe. The great virtue of the universe is known as *sheng* (life, production, as opposed to destruction of life), and the universe is said to love life. That which confers life and vital force on all things is nothing other than this quality of *jen,* which makes this universe a moral order. When applied to human society, *jen* becomes the principle governing all social relations. To begin with, it is the basis for declaring human nature originally good. It is the inner spirit which inspires social institutions, generally conceived to be manifestations of the principle of social conduct or *li. Li* in the absence of *jen* (love or genuine feeling or concern for others) is hollow and cold; it becomes a soulless husk, hypocrisy without the warmth of feeling. In a true sense *jen* defines human nature, for according to this view man by nature is concerned with others; he is concerned because he cannot do otherwise.

This feeling for humanity breathes into each and every one of us a sense of solidarity for all mankind. All men share the same likes and dislikes; they are members of the same whole, living by the same moral laws. This concern for others and feeling for humanity is aptly described by the Elder Ch'eng brother of the Sung dynasty by means of a simile. In medicine, he said, paralysis is described as *pu-jen* (lacking in *jen*). This "lacking in *jen*" means unfeeling; that is, one part of the body does not feel concerned with the other parts. Applied to society, the implication is that we are all brothers to one another. There seems to be a sympathetic cord between hearts; whatever takes place in one heart affects all. So all peoples are parts of a whole, an organic whole, where one is all and all is one. "The man of *jen* is at one with all things," said Ch'eng. The same thought is expressed in Chang Tsai's "Western Inscription." The following is an excerpt from that work:

> Heaven is my father and Earth my mother, and I, though an unworthy creature, find myself a natural place in their midst. Thus that which fills heaven and earth forms my body, and that which takes the commanding role becomes my nature. All people are my brothers and sisters, and all things my comrades. The great ruler and ministers are Son and stewards of my parents [Heaven and Earth]. Respect the elders, following the principle [Mencius enunciated] in

> treating the elders as they should be treated. Love the
> orphaned and the weak following the principle [Mencius
> enunciated] in treating the young as they should be
> treated. . . . All those who are tired, infirm, crippled, or
> sick; all those who have no brothers, or children, who have
> lost their wives or husbands, are all my brothers in dis-
> tress and have no one to turn to. . . .[10]

Ch'eng described the "Western Inscription" as "the substance of
*jen*," because Chang Tsai here not only makes *jen* the governing
principle of human society but also unequivocally affirms for the
first time both its metaphysical reality and its universal scope,
culminating in the complete identity of the individual and the
universe.

To affirm *jen* as a principle is of course not the same as to act
according to that principle. How is one to discover the pattern of
behavior that would accord with *jen?* Here another Neo-Confucian-
ist (Chou Tun-i) supplies the hint. It is through absence of desires,
selfish desires, or desires in any form, including prejudice, precon-
ceived ideas, biases and bigotry, or even the idols Francis Bacon
thought of long ago. Chou indicates two lines of development from
this absence of desires: (1) In acquiescence it leads to open-mind-
edness, to an ability to see things in their own light without distortion, and to a real comprehension of the nature of things. (2) In
activity it leads to straightforwardness, to impartiality, and finally to
spontaneous action with universal validity.

To insure that the absence of desire is genuine, to be sure that
there is absolutely no ulterior motive in our action, one must, every
so often, investigate himself with complete sincerity. This state of
mind known as sincerity guarantees the validity of the voice of one's
conscience; for however clever one is at deceiving others, one can
never deceive oneself. In a state of sincerity one confronts his own
conscience, the God who is in him. In this sense sincerity is a religious concept, as Whitehead has noted in his *Religion in the Making:* "Religion is the force of belief cleansing the inward parts. For
this reason the primary religious virtue is sincerity, a penetrating
sincerity."[11]

Here, then, is the fundamental characteristic of Chinese culture

—a world of Great Harmony to be achieved through a life of *jen*. Moreover, the Great Harmony and *jen* have universal validity. Tragically, however, these are the very principles rejected today by Chinese Communism, which advocates a philosophy of hate and struggle. I had once thought that, even though life under Communism might be obnoxious, suffocating, and unbearable to some who are used to breathing in free air, it could be a blessing to the Chinese people at large, a people who had suffered untold misery in muted silence for thousands of years. But even this faint hope was dashed by the policies and behavior of the Peking regime. The Cultural Revolution clearly reveals that the Chinese Communists, cutting each other's throats for power in the name of ideological purity, are not even serious about their own goals. In the end it is the people who must suffer for all their follies.

What, then, does it mean to be a "Chinese" today? For me personally, it implies an identification with the noble heritage of the great Chinese culture as well as a faith in its ultimate triumph. Dynasties rise and fall, governments come and go, but the Chinese people live on. We live on because of the great ideas and ideals which were conceived in antiquity, modified, enriched, and crystallized into values and norms of conduct across the ages, and have proven effective in shaping the course of Chinese history and molding the way of life of the Chinese people. For those who consider such a view naive in the age of *Realpolitik,* let me quote a fable from *Chuang Tzu:*

> The Yellow Emperor took a trip to the north of Red Water. He ascended to the height of K'un-lun. After having looked south he returned. He found that he had lost his mysterious pearl [or black pearl]. He sent Knowledge to look for it. Knowledge could not find it. He sent Li-chu [one who is keen of eye] to look for it. Li-chu too could not find it. He sent Chieh-kou [one who is fond of arguing] to look for it. He again could not find it. Finally, he sent Naiveté to look for it. And Naiveté found the pearl. The Yellow Emperor exclaimed, "How strange that Naiveté should be able to find it."[12]

The unique vocation of being a "Chinese" in our time may well be to develop a capacity to gaze far and wide, not just decades or even hundreds of years away. Individuals come and go, but life moves on. Some day, no matter how distant the future, these ideals will become reality, if some of us, however insignificant either in number or in stature, try hard to keep them alive. For two thousand years Christianity has been teaching love and forgiveness. Has it been discredited simply because what it preaches has not come to pass? Some Chinese are in a similar position, holding fast to their ideals, and making every effort to keep them alive for future generations.

NOTES

1. See my article "The Mind and the Moral Order," *Mélanges chinois et bouddhiques,* Dixième volume (Juillet 1955), p. 357.

2. *Ibid.,* p. 358.

3. *Far Eastern Quarterly,* XII (May 1953), 316.

4. *The Book of Rites,* Shih-san ching chu-su edition, chüan 21, 3-a-b.

5. Arthur Waley, *The Book of Songs* (London, 1954). No. 162—Mao, p. 212.

6. Ho Hsiu, *Ch'un-ch'iu Kung-yang chuan chu-shu,* Su-pu pei-yao edition (Shanghai, n.d.), p. 13.

7. Ching Po-ch'ien, *Shih-san-ching kai-lun* (Shanghai, 1944), p. 459.

8. Chang Tsai, *Chang-tzu ch'un-shi,* Su-pu pei-yao edition, 14/132.

9. Clarence Burton Day, *The Philosophers of China* (New York, 1962), p. 255.

10. Chang Tsai, *Chang Tzu ch'uan-shu,* Chuan 1, pp. 1–5.

11. Alfred North Whitehead, *Religion in the Making* (New York, 1926), p. 15.

12. James Legge, *The Texts of Taoism* (New York, 1962 [1891]), Part I, p. 311.

# China
in Asia

Joseph M. Kitagawa

Today many people think of China as an enigmatic monster, whose next move is bound to be totally irrational and unpredictable even to professional China-watchers. Cartoonists portray Chairman Mao as a Chinese counterpart of General de Gaulle, only with a flat nose and pudgy figure, who uses the bizarre words of wall posters in Peking to talk to the outside world. Such oversimplifications ignore the fact that China is sensitive to the actions and policies of other nations, not only those of the United States and Soviet Russia but also to those of other Asian nations and peoples. That is to say, China not only *acts* but *reacts,* and her behavior is not so incomprehensible as our current "cultural myopia" leads us to believe.

China's long and glorious history includes extraordinary variations of advance and subsidence, and contemporary China can usefully be viewed in a larger historical perspective. The late Robert

Redfield advocated, in this sense, the importance of "thinking about a civilization." In his own words: "To think about a civilization is something different from getting information and acquaintance, though this third activity requires and is guided by the first two. It is to develop formed and nameable thoughts about the civilization. It is to conceive it, to make of it a mental artifact, a shaped work of the intellect."[1] More concretely, "to think about the Chinese civilization" does not mean to see it as a dead scaffolding of social, economic, and political institutions, languages, customs, philosophies, moralities, and religions. Chinese civilization, like other great civilizations, is an enduring and ever-growing way of life, which is basically the working and unfolding of the human spirit.

Every civilization, every culture, and every nation has a characteristic mental outlook toward the recollection of past experiences (anamnesis), the delineation of the meaning of present existence, and the anticipation of the future. These three foci are intricately interwoven in a kind of "mental prism," which sorts out significant items from a mass of data and relates historical realities to the realm of fantasy and imagination. The prism also has the built-in self-protection of forgetfulness and optical illusion. The power of the mental prism is forcefully demonstrated by the Middle East conflicts between the Jews and the Arabs, who are first cousins, so to speak, in terms of blood and religious heritage. Their conflicting views are based on two different ways of recollecting the presumably historical event recorded in Genesis (XV:18), according to which Abraham received divine assurance for the territory between the river of Egypt and the Euphrates as the promised land for his descendants. Fortunately or unfortunately, Abraham had two sons, Isaac, the ancestor of the Jews, and Ishmael, the legendary ancestor of the Arabs, who have been living in this territory for many generations. Seen through the Jewish prism, "the establishment of Israel was a Return, with all the mystical significance the capital R. implies, [whereas] for the Arabs it was another invasion,"[2] as I. F. Stone has succinctly pointed out. Thus, it is not a question of which group should occupy this small piece of real estate. The real issue is that for Jews and Arabs sacred memories of the past, the meaning of present existence, and the hopes and fears for the future are rooted in the land of Palestine. Likewise, every group, whether ethnic, national, cultural, or religious, has its own mental prism which conditions its range of understanding. In the West, thinking about "China in Asia" involves the effort to comprehend the nature of the mental prisms of the Chinese and other Asian peoples, as well as the mental prism through which Westerners have been conditioned to view China and the rest of Asia.

To a person like myself who was born and raised in Japan, or in any other part of Asia for that matter, the existence of China is a part of his thinking and being. After all, China was a great empire long before Japan and other Asian nations emerged from the state of prehistory. We can imagine, for example, when Japan first came in direct contact with Chinese civilization during the fifth and sixth centuries A.D., the early Japanese must have been dazzled by the greatness and sophistication of Chinese art, architecture, philosophy, religion, ethics, and commerce, as well as by the techniques of organizing various aspects of society and the nation. In this respect, Langdon Warner's description of the eighth-century Japan applies also to the historic relation of China with all her neighboring nations: ". . . China was hanging like a brilliant brocaded background against which we must look at Japan and its capital city of Nara to watch the eighth century, while the Japanese were at work weaving their own brocade *on patterns similar but not the same.*"[3] Historically, China extended her hegemony not so much by conquering other territories militarily but by exerting cultural and economic influence over her less civilized neighbors. In short, China provided the cultural model, so that others could develop their own cultures "on patterns similar but not the same." In the course of time China came to take for granted her role as cultural leader and model for the world known to her. And as this conviction became firmly established, China, at least until the last century, looked at the rest of the world through this mental prism. Thus China saw herself as a self-sufficient nation, and she saw foreign relations and foreign trade as acts of "tribute bearing" by others, as "an overt recognition of the overlordship of the Son of Heaven."[4]

Meanwhile, China's neighbors also developed their own mental prisms. This is one reason why it was possible for the two great civilizations of India and China to exist side by side for thousands of years in virtual ignorance of each other, for they were separated not only by mountains and deserts but by different outlooks. As far as India is concerned, the Sino-Indian relationship has been a one-way traffic with India as the giver and China the receiver of Buddhism. Other than this Buddhist expansion from India to China, there was no cultural or political rapprochement between the two countries, for both claimed exclusive greatness based on different metaphysical premises and historical memories. Other Asian peoples, of course, acknowledged their great indebtedness to Chinese and Indian civilizations, and none could match their cultural achievements. Nevertheless, they also had their own mental traits and resources which were not replaced by Chinese and Indian features. Rather, what developed was a series of Asian cultural traditions which combined, in different ways and to different degrees, the three major components, namely, the indigenous, the Chinese, and the Indian (Buddhist). Even when certain elements appear to be predominant, such as the Buddhist influence on Southeast Asia or the Chinese influence on Korea and Japan, "what matters in all such cases," to quote Oswald Spengler, "is not the original meaning of the forms, but the forms themselves, as disclosing to the native sensibility and understanding of the observer potential modes of his own creativeness . . . The same words, the same rites, the same symbol—but . . . different souls, each going its way."[5] This is another way of saying that in Asia different ethnic and cultural groups, despite the fact that they shared some common cultural and religious traits, actually lived in different "worlds of meaning."

But Asian peoples and cultures were not so hopelessly divided that there was no basis for communication and understanding among them. For example, even though China and India were historically separated by natural and mental barriers, they could have found many things in common if they had wanted to. As Prabodh Chandra Bagchi once pointed out: "It is possible to discover a community between the two amidst the great diversities of expressions. The same reliance on some heavenly order, the same force of tradition, and similar social ideals characterized the two civilizations in the past."[6] And Professor Bagchi tries to show the affinities between the Chinese idea of Heaven (T'ien) and the Vedic deity, Varuna; between Chinese and Indian views on ancestor worship, family, and kinship systems; and between Chinese Taoism and

Indian mysticism. Despite these formal similarities, however, there are basic differences in outlook. At the expense of oversimplification, we might characterize the Indian approach as metaphysical, mystical, and cosmic-centered, and the Chinese approach as ethical, rational, and this-world-centered. Granted that both accept the world as having neither chronological beginning nor end, and that both accept man as an integral part of the world of nature, still the mental prisms through which the Indians and the Chinese see everything are quite different.

There is much truth in Betty Heimann's observation that the term "metaphysics" has never acquired the significance of "beyond physical facts" in India. "If then," she says, "Indian Metaphysics is concerned with problems centering on the conception of God . . . , Metaphysics may be called 'a second Physics,' since God is the heavenly counterpart of earthly physical beings. If applied, again, to cosmic primeval Physics, or to Ontology, then the meaning becomes 'extended Physics,' while when it deals with the fate of Man after death, it is a 'renewed Physics,' simply because India's ideas of life after death, of the Hereafter, are those of another 'here,' of a new life on earth in reincarnation."[7] The Indian approach to metaphysics is not one of analytical discrimination as in the Greek tradition. Rather, it aims at contemplation and meditation of ultimate reality, which may be more akin to the spirit of mysticism. The Hindus, through the long journey of the chain of life and death, seek to attain immortality and freedom, or the "cosmicization" of the phenomenal world order. In the poetic words of Rabindranath Tagore:

In this beautiful world I have no desire to die;
I wish to live in the midst of men.
In this sunlight, in the flowering forests,
    in the heart of all living beings, may I find a place.
Incessant is the play of Life across the earth,
        with its perennial waves
        of union and separation, laughter and tears,
Weaving songs from the sorrow and happiness of Man
I wish I might build an immortal realm.
Or, failing this, I hope I can claim a seat

  amongst you for as long as I live,
  composing songs like flowers that blossom ever afresh
  for you to gather in the morning and noon.
Accept those flowers with a smile, and then alas!
  cast them aside again as they fade and die.[8]

Even Buddhism, which rejects the traditional Hindu notion of the caste system and the four stages of life, shares the longing for the "cosmicization" of man in the state of Nirvana.

In sharp contrast to the Hindu tradition, with its metaphysical, mystical traits and cosmic-centeredness, the Chinese emphasizes an ethical, rationalistic, and this-world-centered approach. To be sure, the Chinese have their share of metaphysical speculations and mystical insights, and they certainly are keenly aware of the mysterious world of nature. Nevertheless, their mental prism is securely focused on this world and the here-and-now. As Lin Yutang once stated: ". . . the Chinese are in love with life, in love with this earth, and will not forsake it for an invisible heaven. They are in love with life, which is so sad and yet so beautiful, and in which moments of happiness are so precious because they are so transient. They are in love with life, with its kings and beggars, robbers and monks, funerals and weddings and childbirths and sicknesses and glowing sunsets and rainy nights and feasting days and wine-shop fracas."[9]

Historically, the Chinese love of life found its expression in what is known as "family-ism," which is built on reciprocal prerogatives and duties both for living and for dead ancestors. Indeed, the Chinese views the nation and the whole world through the model of the family. Thus in the Great Learning we read: "If there is righteousness in the heart, there will be beauty in the character; if there is beauty in the character, there will be harmony in the home; if there is harmony in the home, there will be order in society; and when there is order in society, there will be peace in the world." The genius of the Chinese is not so much abstract theoretical thinking but a sophisticated commonsense approach to social, economic, ethical, philosophical, and religious issues. For instance, the classics of the two main philosophical schools in China, Confucianism and Taoism, are very different from Western philosophical works. They are full of dialogues, anecdotes, and homey chit-chats which display a great sense of humor and insight. In other words, Chinese philosophy, ethics, and religion, to quote Wing-tsit Chan, "support a way of life the conclusions and convictions of which are arrived at not through idle speculation but through actual handling of human affairs."[10] A similar matter-of-fact spirit is evident in Ch'an or Zen Buddhism, which is probably the most characteristically Chinese form of Buddhism. In short, the persistent thread of Chinese civilization is the intelligent management of human and social affairs based on a cultivated sense of comprehensive harmony.

Other Asian traditions are less grandiose than those of China and India. All of them are nonrational, nonmetaphysical, and ethnocentric, lacking the concept of a universal or cosmic principle. The mental prism of the Japanese, for example, is an intricate homology of two components, the artistic and the material—or the "chrysanthemum and the sword," to use Ruth Benedict's expression. Contrary to many Westerners' impression of Shinto based on its modern development, Shinto has been traditionally the artist's way of life. As Langdon Warner puts it: "Natural forces are the very subject matter for those who produce artifacts from raw materials or who hunt and fish and farm. Thus Shinto taught succeeding generations of Japanese how such forces are controlled and these formulas have become embedded in Shinto liturgies."[11] The early Japanese found the existence of the sacred or *kami* nature in everything. It was taken for granted, therefore, that the emperor had to rule the nation based on the divine oracles transmitted to him through the medium of the diviners. Only after the introduction of Chinese civilization and Buddhism did the Japanese realize there were regulative principles in the universe. Even Buddhism and the Chinese classics were seen through the mental prism of the Japanese so that "the terms of Indian metaphysics became a kind of fashionable jargon, Buddhist rites a spectacle, Chinese poetry an intellectual game . . . religion became an art and art a religion."[12] And yet, the religion of art is intertwined with the art of the *samurai*. Certainly the Buddhists in India or China never said, as did the warrior in Japan:

Under the sword raised high
Is hell, making you tremble.

> But, walk on!—
> There is the Land of Bliss.[13]

Or:

> Some think that striking is to strike.
> But striking is not to strike, nor is killing to kill.
> He who strikes and he who is struck—
> They are both no more than a dream that has no reality.[14]

And a famous warrior turned poet wrote:

> My prayer is to die underneath the blossoming cherry,
> In that Spring month of flowers,
> When the moon is full.[15]

In scanning the development of Asia during the past 450 years, we have to be all the more conscious of our own mental prisms through which we look at the meeting of Asia and the West. It has become a popular pastime in Asia to blame all the troubles of contemporary Asian societies on the evils of Western colonialism, and one can document ample evidence of economic and political exploitation of Asia by Western powers from the time of Vasco da Gama to the present. The internal development of various Asian cultural traditions is a more difficult problem to ascertain. Stated in its simplest terms, my thesis is: The decline of Asia during the past 450 years was caused initially by an internal cultural erosion characterized by overgrown bureaucracies and empty forms. The "oriental stagnation" which the West, upon initial contact, found in China, was therefore not an *essential* aspect of Chinese culture but an unhappy *historical fact*. This fact allowed the West to penetrate deeply into Asia, and, by so doing, accelerate still further the cultural disintegration already at work.

Like other peoples, Asians are susceptible to a nostalgia for the remote past, which becomes sentimentalized and idealized. There are some Asians even today who feel that if the West had not encroached on Asia, Chinese, Indian, and Japanese cultures, for example, would have grown uninterruptedly and would have unfolded values worthy of their past. But this view is based on a short memory and little knowledge of Asian cultural history. If we must pinpoint convenient dates, we might depict the establishment of (a) the Mogul empire in India (1526), (b) the Tokugawa feudal regime in Japan (1603), and (c) the Manchu (Ch'ing) dynasty in China (1644) as marking the beginning of cultural stagnation in these areas. All three regimes had many remarkable qualities, and none of them attempted to destroy the traditional culture.

The Mogul monarchs, the descendants of Genghis Khan and Timurlane, were a highly cultured people, unlike their bloody ancestors, and though they were Muslims they had profound respect for the Hindu religious and cultural heritage. Emperor Akbar (r., 1556–1605), the greatest Mogul sovereign, abolished the hated poll tax (*jizya*) on non-Muslims, enlisted Hindus in his armed forces, and befriended Hindu rajas. He even rejected the exclusive claim of Islam and advocated the doctrine of universal tolerance. His Hall of Worship welcomed not only Muslims and Hindus, but Jains, Zoroastrians, and Christians.

The Tokugawa rulers in Japan also attempted to preserve the art and culture, beliefs and practices of traditional Japan. The first Tokugawa *shogun* was fond of saying: "Shinto is the way of inner truth and of inner purity; Confucianism is the way of sincerity, love and benevolence; Buddhism emphasizes selflessness and desirelessness, teaching forebearance and compassion." Ostensibly to safeguard the integrity of the traditional culture from the encroachment of Catholicism, the Tokugawa rulers took the extreme measure of "national seclusion," forbidding all contact with the outside world with the exception of the Chinese and the Dutch.

The Manchu rulers accepted *in toto* the traditional culture of China, including the system of administration. They regarded the Confucian bureaucracy as the backbone of the central government, and the family system as the unit of social cohesion. The Manchu monarch considered himself the Son of Heaven and offered the traditional sacrifice to Heaven. The state cult of Confucius was promoted, and it was a Manchu emperor who conferred the supreme posthumous honor upon Confucius by offering the same sacrifice to him as to the heavenly deity (*Shang Ti*).

In spite of all these measures taken by the Mogul dynasty in India, the Tokugawa rulers in Japan, and the Manchu dynasty in China, cultural life and creativity were stifled. These societies were regimented by a top-heavy administrative bureaucracy which managed to preserve the forms but not nurture the spirit of the culture. For example, in traditional China government was sufficiently flexible to allow social change and individual initiative, depending more on moral persuasion than legal enforcement. But the Manchu rulers assumed that morality could be realized automatically through proclamation and edict, with little consideration for the life of common people. Thus they built gigantic palaces, full of rich furniture and decorations, but there was no room for the everyday life of the people to be elevated and refined. The lifeblood of culture was cut off. The tragedy of Asia in the past 450 years is that rulers, who had no mean talents in other ways, failed to comprehend the simple principle that "culture is a product of the human spirit, and that particular sort of product which is never finally produced; that is, culture is nothing but the *life* of human beings, and for culture to be alive means that actual human beings live in it."[16] The cultural stagnation that developed in Asia became an easy prey of the commercial, political, and cultural encroachment of the West. Asia's age-old belief in the self-sufficiency of its cultures was shattered by technologically superior Western civilization, motivated by its messianic complex, which was characterized by William Haas as "a strange compound of genuine idealistic responsibility, blindness and hypocrisy, with a strong dose of will-to-power as the basic component."[17]

The massive influence of the West did not destroy the cultural integrity of Asia but fragmented the mental prisms of Asians. In the last two centuries there has been no one characteristic Indian, Chinese, or Japanese mode of thinking. Instead, within each culture there have been those who clung to the traditional way of life and those who appropriated certain aspects of Western culture. The masses felt bewildered and uprooted in the face of rapid social and cultural change. Furthermore, different parts of Asia came under the influence of different Western nations, such as India, Ceylon, and Burma under the British, Indonesia under the Dutch, Indo-China under the French, and the Philippines under first the Spanish and later the Americans. Only Thailand, China, and Japan escaped direct colonial rule, but they too felt the strong impact of Western civilization. In every case the West came to know Asians through their Westernized segments, which inevitably presented to the West one-sided pictures of Asia. Through the mental prism thus formed, the West saw the eventual Westernization of Asia. Even today the West assumes subconsciously that through industrialization and modern education Asians will be emancipated from the dead weight of traditional culture and obscurantist magico-religion; that increasing economic and military aid will solve all the problems of the non-Western world. More than a decade ago Arnold Toynbee observed that the non-Western world is no longer simply the spectator of ongoing history but is an actor on the stage. "The West's alarm and anger at recent acts of Russian and Chinese aggression at the West's expense are evidence that, for us Westerners, it is today still a strange experience to be suffering at the hands of the world what the world has been suffering at Western hands for a number of centuries past."[18] Obviously, many individuals and nations in the West still find it difficult to adjust their mental prisms to the new realities of the modern world.

As for the Asians, their adjustment to the modern world is equally painful, if not more so, because they are still inclined to see everything through the humiliating experience of the immediate past. Intellectually, they may realize that the Western influence has brought some benefits to Asia, but psychologically they are in no mood to acknowledge it. Practically, the old pattern of cultural insularity coupled with the recent division of Asia into different Western spheres of interest makes it extremely difficult for Asian nations to develop regional communities, which must emerge if Asia is to survive at all. But it would take supreme efforts on all sides to overcome the emotional distance between China and India, China and Japan, China and Vietnam, Vietnam and Cambodia, Cambodia and Thailand, and so on down the line. And the concept of the modern nation state, which has been passionately espoused by Asia, has not resolved the persistent communalism in India, China, and other nations. This is particularly true in Vietnam, which was an artificial construct of the French, where people from northern and southern regions have little in common except mutual suspicion and hostility.[19]

Fundamentally, Asians must realize that it is impossible to turn the clock backward. They have been emancipated from the colonial rule of the West, but they cannot shake off the spirit of the modern world—modernity—which they have inhaled. Just as many Westerners confuse Westernization and modernization simply because modernity emerged in the West, so Asians find misguided consolation in thinking that all the problems caused by the modern world were created by the encroachment of the West into Asia. European colonial empires were shattered by World War II, and European military domination in Asia ended with the withdrawal of British forces from India in 1947 and of the European navies from China in 1949. But the Asians, through their mental prism, now see a sinister omen in the rise of the United States as a new Western power in the Pacific. The United States *is* a most powerful and extravagant country, which controls directly or indirectly an extraordinary percentage of the world's wealth. And, as a report of the International Missionary Council stated in 1952: "This privileged position creates suspicion, fear, envy and hate even among beneficiaries of its use of power, as well as real gratitude among many of them. No person or nation enjoys or feels secure in a situation where livelihood and welfare are largely dependent on the good will of another, however well-intentioned that other may claim to be and often demonstrates itself to be."[20] Asians are not living in fear of another Hiroshima. But we must not forget that the presence of American military forces in Asia, however important it is from the American perspective, does not help to correct the Asian vision.

More important and far reaching, I think, is the cultural dimension. I agree with F. S. C. Northrop that there are different components in "imperialism"—political, economic, and cultural. While most Asians realize that the day of political imperialism is over and that economic domination of Asia by the West may wane in the course of time, most Westerners have no appreciation for Asia's fear of the cultural component of Western imperialism. In Northrop's words:

> Witness General MacArthur's suggestion of the Christianization of Japan. Recall the public demand for a "hard-hitting Voice of America" which will convert the rest of the world to the American way of life. All such suggestions strike the Asians as demonstrating that America and the

West are withholding a political imperialism and slightly restraining an economic one merely to impose an even more dangerous cultural one.[21]

It would be wrong to infer from this observation that the cultural crisis of Asia is caused only by the attitudes and actions of the West. The structure of Asian culture is also to blame. We must remind ourselves that the traditional culture of Asia was transmitted and monopolized by the elite—the Brahmans in India, the gentry in China, and the *samurais* in Japan, for example—so that there was a great gulf between the cultured elite and the common people. What was rejected during the period of transition from the pre-modern to the modern period in Asia were the prerogatives of the traditional elite and the metaphysical-social principle implicit in the age-old cultural framework. The impact of the West helped to accelerate this process, and it continued even after the influence of the West began to diminish.

It is extremely difficult to untangle the cultural development of China and other Asian nations during the last hundred years. The combined effects of rivalry and cooperation between the old elite and the Westernized intelligentsia, conflicting views between the elite and the common people, and the varied forms of response by different Asian peoples to the challenge of the West have produced a fascinating and melancholy drama. The significance of China in the modern history of Asia lies in the fact that she, more than any other nation, epitomizes the agony of the adjustment of the proud old culture to the modern world. From the latter days of the Manchu rule, China suffered at the hands of Western powers, Russia, and Japan. The ambitious effort of Sun Yat-sen and his followers to reform China was inhibited and aborted by reactionary elements at home and by the unfriendly policies of foreign nations. Soon the high idealism generated in the initial stage of Sun Yat-sen's revolution was diverted by the conservative wing of the Kuomintang, which eventually was driven to Formosa by the Communist regime. Undoubtedly there were many forces at work. Nevertheless it is likely that the Kuomintang failed, as Northrop says, "not because it was corrupt but because it was moral in the [traditional Chinese] meaning of the word moral."[22] Today the Peking regime too appears to be having a series of internal troubles and dissensions, since it too has to come to terms with traditional Chinese values, morality, and cultural traits.

There is, unfortunately, no simple formula which explains the complex situation of China and other parts of Asia in our own time. The dynamic tempo of cultural change in Asia may be illustrated by the fact that the sacred images of modern Asian nations—Gandhi and Nehru in India, Sun Yat-sen in China, and Emperor Meiji in Japan—venerated though they are in official circles, no longer stir the imagination of the people. More recent events, such as the rise of Muslim youths in Indonesia, restlessness manifested by the students in India, Pakistan, Korea, and Japan, as well as the fierce activities of the Vietcong and Red Guards, seem to indicate that the new generations in Asia, like their counterparts in other parts of the world, are rebelling against the world order they inherited from previous generations. The future of Asia depends largely on what kind of mental prism the coming generations will adopt.

NOTES

1. Robert Redfield, "Thinking About a Civilization," in Milton Singer, ed., *Introducing India in Liberal Education* (Chicago, 1957), p. 3.

2. I. F. Stone, "Holy War" (review of "Le conflit israélo-arabe"), in *Les Temps Modernes,* Paris, June 1967, in *New York Review of Books,* IX, No. 2 (August 3, 1967), 6.

3. Langdon Warner, *The Enduring Art of Japan* (Cambridge, Mass., 1952), p. 6, italics added.

4. Adda B. Bozeman, *Politics and Culture in International History* (Princeton, 1960), p. 146.

5. Oswald Spengler, *The Decline of the West,* trans. Charles Francis Atkinson (New York, 1929), II, *Perspectives of World History,* 57.

6. Prabodh Chandra Bagchi, *India and China: A Thousand Years of Cultural Relations* (New York, 1951), p. 174.

7. Betty Heimann, *Indian and Western Philosophy: A Study in Contrasts* (London, 1937), pp. 29–30.

8. Indu Dutt (trans.), *A Tagore Testament* (New York, 1954), p. ix.

9. Lin Yutang, *My Country and My People* (New York, 1935), pp. 103–104.

10. Wing-tsit Chan, "Chinese Philosophy and Religion," in H. G. Creel, ed., *Chinese Civilization in Liberal Education* (Chicago, 1959), p. 123.

11. Warner, *Enduring Art of Japan,* p. 18.

12. Statement by George B. Sansom, quoted in *ibid.,* p. 32.

13. Cited in Alan W. Watts, *The Spirit of Zen* (London, 1955, 2nd ed.), p. 110. Translation by D. T. Suzuki.

14. Cited in D. T. Suzuki, *Zen and Japanese Culture* (New York, 1959), p. 123.

15. *Ibid.,* p. 392.

16. William Earle, "Notes on the Death of Culture," *Noonday*, I (1958), 4.

17. William S. Haas, *The Destiny of the Mind—East and West* (London, 1956), p. 303.

18. Arnold Toynbee, *The World and the West* (New York, 1953), p. 4.

19. This is undoubtedly one of the basic problems for South Vietnam today, where the main core of present political and military leadership comes from those who migrated from the north, because they are not so readily accepted by the southern Vietnamese as they are by Washington.

20. Report of Commission IV, compiled by Wynn C. Fairfield (New York, February 1952), pp. 3–4.

21. F. S. C. Northrop, *The Taming of the Nations* (New York, 1952), p. 67.

22. *Ibid.*, p. 119.

# Two Realities          Mark Mancall

Nowadays the American press is agreed that the United States, the bloc we euphemistically call "The Free World" (which evidently includes such free and democratic countries as Greece, Spain, Taiwan, and South Vietnam), and even the Soviet bloc face a "China problem." The problem reflects more than a clash between foreign policies. It is a confrontation between two realities. Each side is trapped in its own view of reality which relates man and the universe and acts as a structure within which human beings interact. Foreign policies arise from these realities and embrace all the inconsistencies of the American perspective toward China. These inconsistencies must be explored before alternatives can be suggested which might bring China and the United States closer to peaceful coexistence.

Impossible as it may be to define clearly the exact content of this problem, the tenets of the American approach at present may be conveniently summarized in a series of syllogisms:

(1) Large and strong nations are aggressive. China is a large and strong nation. China is aggressive.

(2) Nations armed with nuclear armaments and missile delivery systems are more dangerous than conventionally armed nations. China is arming herself with nuclear armaments and may have a missile delivery system sometime in the 1970's. China may be more aggressive and dangerous in the 1970's than she is today.

(3) Large and potentially aggressive nations in a state of turmoil are a threat to world peace. China is currently in a state of turmoil. China is a threat to world peace.

(4) Potentially aggressive nations must be contained. China is a potentially aggressive nation. China must be contained.

(5) The Free World must be defended against communism. Taiwan is a part of the Free World. Taiwan must be defended against communism.

(6) Stability is a defense against communism. The current situation in the Taiwan Straits is stable. The maintenance of the current situation in the Taiwan Straits is a defense against communism.

(7) A successful China policy requires both military containment and constructive forms of political and economic suasion. Our present China policy is based almost solely on military containment. Our present China policy cannot be either successful or constructive.

(8) More constructive forms of political and economic suasion depend on increased contacts and the information and diplomatic leverage that can be derived therefrom. The United States needs a more constructive China policy. The United States needs increased contacts with and information about China.

If these syllogisms are acceptable as statements of the premises underlying current thinking about China policy in the United States, it quickly becomes apparent that this thinking envisages a policy that, to borrow a phrase from Chairman Mao Tse-tung, "proceeds on two legs," namely containment and integration. At the same time, the problems and contradictions inherent in that policy are immediately clear.

The concept of "containment" is ill-defined and perhaps incapable of a definition sufficiently refined to permit it to serve as the basis of anything more than an unconstructive, obstinate international position. Currently it has led to several distinct but related policies, all subsumed under the expression "holding the line." It is readily admitted by many official spokesmen and by scholars and observers that the Vietnam War is as much a struggle to contain China as it is to create a "free and democratic" South Vietnam. In the United Nations and throughout the structure of international organizations, the policy of containing China has meant continued American sponsorship of the exclusion of Peking from participation in international bodies and unstinting support of Chiang Kai-shek's government in Taipei as the sole legitimate representative of China. Containment has included the imposition of an embargo on trade of all kinds with China and an American effort to inhibit the growth of commercial contacts between its allies and the People's Republic of China. In many instances this has strained Washington's relations with nations otherwise friendly to the United States.

"Containment," as defined both verbally and in the context of particular policies, stands in direct contradiction to the other "leg" of United States policy toward China, which is the "building of bridges" to China. On all sides—from the universities, the press, Congress, political candidates—the call is for opening new avenues of communication with the Chinese Communists. An exchange of journalists, scholars, professional men, and students is one such proposal. The admission of China into the United Nations is a second, which goes further than the first. A third proposal is immediate American diplomatic recognition of Peking. Proponents of these steps hope for reciprocity by Peking but are often prepared to pursue them, particularly the second and third, unilaterally, in the hope that the further involvement of Peking in international relations would force China to abandon some of her more aggressive intentions and lead her to become a "responsible" member of the family of nations. These "bridges" would also add to American knowledge and understanding of China, it is argued, thus enabling Washington to develop a constructive policy of peaceful coexistence with an increasingly cooperative China.

Such a two-legged China policy may appear attractive to some Americans for a variety of reasons: to diplomats, because their basic concern is with the maintenance of peace with honor; to politicians, because it enables them to appeal simultaneously to the prideful American self-images of might and magnanimity; to scholars, because it holds out the hope of advancing their special intellectual concerns; to journalists, because access to China will give them one of the greatest stories of this century; and to large sections of the general public, because it lessens the liberal American's guilt that arises from relying on the fundamentally militaristic principle that "might makes right."

This line of thought is buttressed by the concept of "two Chinas," one of them non-Communist. It permits the development and continuation of the myth that no surrender to communism in China has really taken place, that we are helping to keep open to the Chinese people a truly Chinese alternative, that we have not abandoned that people to the fate of a communism that will destroy the freedom of traditional or modern liberal institutions. The need to maintain the fiction of a Formosan China as truly Chinese as the mainland explains in part the great financial support given often third-rate Chinese Nationalist scholarship and academic institutions on Taiwan. The half-hearted hope is that a new liberal Chinese voice may emerge from the death rattle of a moribund Chinese traditional culture, thus salving our historical conscience (guilt-ridden because of Western imperialism's contribution to the rise of communism in China and because of the American "loss" of China).

The Two Chinas concept has been given two comparatively imprecise definitions. First, the Republic of China (Taiwan) and the People's Republic of China (Peking) are separate entities which may coexist, if necessary, in a state of mutual hostility so long as neither infringes militarily on the other. In this definition it is assumed that eventually both states will be represented in the United Nations, with the question of China's permanent Security Council seat a matter for negotiation. Second, Taiwan may recognize Peking's suzerainty while maintaining complete internal and international autonomy, in which case China's U.N. seat may have to go to Communist China.

Whatever the definition given the Two Chinas concept, it is an integral part of the two-legged policy approach to Communist China, because it assumes the possibility, and even the necessity, of establishing some kind of positive American relationship with Peking and of bringing Communist China into the United Nations. Unfortunately, the two-legged policy is faulted by an internal contradiction which lays the United States open to an accusation—often made by Peking and others, like Hanoi—of duplicity. One of America's leading China specialists has written, "Toward China a balance of containment and contact—informational, commercial, cultural, and diplomatic—may take years to achieve. But one will avail little without the other."[1] But *contact* is not always *communication,* or at least not positive communication.

To be sure, informational, commercial, cultural, and diplomatic contacts are all vehicles for communication; more than that, they are communications themselves. But so are the various forms for implementing a policy of containment. Thus a statement that "we must maintain an American presence in Southeast Asia as we do in other key areas, necessarily an armed presence, ready to fight if need be, somewhere, sometime," is a direct communication of hostility to any other power that may have an interest in Southeast Asia, namely China.[2] And the actual presence of American troops in Southeast Asia is understood by Peking not simply as a "safeguard" against future Chinese aggression or as a "threat" to her interests but as an act of aggression itself. An American military presence is *ipso facto* an act, in the same way as the writing of a letter by hand is a different act, conveying a different meaning, from a letter typed by machine. Hence the contradiction in a "containment and contact" policy: a simultaneous communication of active hostility and a willingness to coexist.

These opposite messages must bewilder China's leaders, unless one assumes that by some magical action of dialectical reasoning Peking's policy-makers will understand that we do not mean to communicate aggression by acting aggressively. Certainly they permit Communist China a very limited number of responses. By ignoring American acts of "aggression," Peking would in effect accept the United States' definition of China's political and historical interests. This would be tantamount to accepting an inferior position on the international scene; the acceptance of someone else's definition of one's self is part of the definition of inferiority. On the other hand, if China accepts American threats at face value, the danger of conflict between the two powers is greatly increased. Actions may speak louder than words, but the fact is that actions are words and words are actions. The message is muddled by the contradiction.

By the same reasoning, a policy of Two Chinas is also a contradiction. While any nation may be brought to accept, however unwillingly, the alienation of part of its territory, it can hardly accept the existence of another state that claims the *whole* of its territory. Moreover, American support of Chiang Kai-shek, who claims the whole of China, cannot be understood by Peking except as a threat to the existence of the People's Republic. Therefore, while the United States may someday wish to recognize two Chinas, American military support of one now appears as a threat to the other. This contradiction can be resolved only by total incorporation of Taiwan within the People's Republic, or by the establishment in Taipei of a government that is Taiwanese, not Chinese, and that renounces all claims to Chinese Communist territory, including those offshore islands currently in Nationalist hands but part of provinces now almost wholly within Communist China. This latter position, while not necessarily acceptable to Peking, is perhaps more feasible and certainly is more reasonable than a Two Chinas policy.

A Two Chinas policy bears little relation to the interests of either Peking or Taipei, and neither is willing to consider the idea. Both Chinas insist that there is only one China, which must be reunited.[3] On certain occasions, such as the Sino-Indian border conflict in 1962, the Nationalist government has made it clear that while it does not support Chinese Communism, its interpretation of China's interests is the same as Peking's.[4] The legitimacy of Chiang Kai-shek's regime on Taiwan rests largely on its insistence that it represents all of China, both historically and today. A Two Chinas policy questions that regime's legitimacy, as the Generalissimo quite clearly recognizes. To develop an alternative source of legitimacy, other than the *de facto* existence of a regime kept in power by fascist or quasi-fascist police methods as is currently the case, would require a democratic plebiscite. Most observers agree that Chiang and his Nationalist party could not survive any reasonably democratic elections in a nation where five-sixths of the population considers itself either non-Chinese or, at least, disaffected. Consequently, the possibility of Two Chinas is reduced to a myth which is acceptable to neither of the parties involved.

The "containment and contact" policy is, as all foreign policies probably are, fundamentally manipulative. More important, however, it is manipulation based primarily on force and only secondarily on the politics of peaceful suasion. The greater reliance on military over political suasion is not the product of some militaristic streak in the American character. Rather, it is the result of the failure of policy assumptions, leading to the conclusion that "the only thing they understand is force." The ultimate assumption behind our present China policy is that both the United States and China are parts of an international "system," resembling, but different from, a nation's social system. Attaining objectives through the system involves certain policy "inputs" which are intended to elicit predictable responses from the Chinese. The system is conceived as a model of reality in international politics, of "the way things are"; strategy and tactics evolve logically from the structure of the system and government's stated objectives.

Our behavioralist social scientists have brought these assumptions to the policy-making process. Indeed, since World War II the policy-maker and the social scientist have come to have more and more in common. In some cases they have even been the same individual. Great institutions of social science research, such as the Rand Corporation and the Stanford Research Institute, have developed in close cooperation with the government.[5] In some instances important policies can be traced to the social scientists working in such institutions. For example, Eugene Staley, an economist at Stanford Research Institute, was primarily responsible for the development of the disastrous "agroville" plan for the relocation of South Vietnamese peasants in fortified villages. Ultimately the work of these men presumes that there is a political, social, economic, historical, and intellectual reality that is not only knowable by all men, given the proper tools, but, moreover, that once known can be used to promote American policy objectives. Furthermore, it is assumed that there is a close relationship between science and reason, and that "reasonableness" can be used to arrive at accommodations between contending parties.

Leaving aside the question of the existence of a reality knowable by all men, the point is that different cultures and traditions do not necessarily perceive that reality in the same way. For instance, American policy-makers, and Americans in general, pride themselves on being "reasonable." They think of themselves as representing the correct view of reality, based on science, logic, and humanitarian instincts. The others—in this case the Chinese Communists—are unreasonable; because they do not agree with us they are somehow less logical, less scientific. They are ideological; we are practical. For example, the "Freedom House" statement on American Far Eastern policy, subscribed to by a large number of the United States' leading Asia specialists, declared, in analyzing the origins of the Cultural Revolution in China:

> But the most important cause of the Great Cultural Revolution was failure. . . . The crucial issue was economic policy—how China might best develop. A subsidiary and related issue was relations with the Soviet Union. The "Maoists" have supported mobilization politics—the appeal to sacrifice, loyalty and patriotism to the Communist cause. Opponents have called for more rational economic policies—functional specialization and economic incentives. Coupled with this has been the recurrent issue of whether it is not better to approach relations with the USSR in the framework of united action, with imperative economic and military interests in mind rather than to determine Chinese foreign policies primarily on the basis of ideology, nationalism and xenophobia.[6]

The implications are obvious, and while it is doubtful that the signers of the statement—all respected scholars—would consider an appeal to "sacrifice, loyalty and patriotism" unreasonable in the United States, it is clear they do so in China.

In fact, what is happening here is that our conception of reality is challenged by another, which we think dangerous and which makes us exceedingly uncomfortable. It suggests that our view of reality is inevitably subjective, a challenge to the whole popular Western belief today in "science," social or otherwise. Again, the West, particularly the United States, prides itself on being "civilized." The Chinese are "blue ants," who fight with techniques such as "the human wave." Secretary of State Dean Rusk, in a news conference on October 12, 1967, said, "Within the next decade or two, there will be a billion Chinese on the mainland, armed with nuclear weapons, with no certainty about what their attitude toward the rest of Asia will be."[7] The image of the hordes of Genghis Khan is obvious.

It is just possible that the Chinese do not see us as civilized as we like to think we are, that in *Chinese reality* we are not what we think we are within our own reality. How might a Chinese historian today, neither a Communist nor one seeking American foundation support by writing slavishly about the United States, briefly summarize the changing Chinese view of us? At the turn of this century, forward-looking Chinese intellectuals turned toward the West, more particularly toward the United States, for sources of inspiration and ideas that would contribute to the transformation of China. Hundreds and thousands of Chinese studied abroad, many in the United States, beginning first at Yale University; and gradually they perceived Anglo-Saxon liberalism as the hope for China's future. But during World War I they began to doubt this. They witnessed Westerners killing Westerners with weapons far more "advanced" but also infinitely more "barbarous" than any the Chinese had ever turned against each other or against foreigners. What is more, Westerners used their weapons against the masses of people who were not directly involved in formal military combat, as a means of bringing the foe to its knees. Certainly this was a form of uncivilized behavior unknown in the history of Chinese warfare. If Westerners were so barbaric, perhaps Western ideas were not as relevant to China as they had at first appeared.

On top of this, Westerners were dishonest. The American President, Woodrow Wilson, who spoke everywhere about the self-determination of peoples, agreed with England and France at Versailles in 1919 to turn over to Japan all of Germany's former interests in China's Shantung province. In short, the history of the West written by a Chinese historian would differ drastically from one written by a professor at an American University. Yet can we seriously presume to suggest that this hypothetical Chinese history of the West is less "realistic" than an American version? Isn't it obvious that the West so described is as much "reality" for a Chinese as one which we describe for ourselves?

In an article in the *New York Review of Books,* Mary McCarthy explored the role of intellectuals and of social science in the Vietnam War, and she discussed the danger inherent in assuming our understanding of reality to be universally valid and of basing a particular policy on it.[8] To overstate the case only slightly, the American social scientist is as a beast in the jungle, lurking in the foliage to lure us as we pass by with sugar plums of "truth" and policy which, when we bite into them, we find are poison. Nothing, after all, has been more poisonous or more deadly in the last half-decade than the Vietnam War. And this has been the social scientists' war *par excellence.* The Bundys, the Pyes, the Scalapinos, the Rostows, social scientists all, have, like wizards of yore, beguiled us with their magic formulae and have conjured up visions which have enticed us deeper and deeper into the jungle quagmire of Southeast Asia.

The danger in the development of American policy toward China today is that we assume that we are both operating within the same reality, that if we can only determine which button to push we will obtain the desired response from the other side. In fact, however, the United States and China perceive each other only dimly, through a glass darkly. What follows is an attempt to present, impressionistically, some of the fundamental differences between American and Chinese perceptions, differences that contribute more than a little to the problems of formulating policy toward China.

Americans, liberal or conservative, and Chinese, Communist or traditionalist, disagree on where good and evil are located in the universe. Our contemporary individualism, real or imagined, is at least in part derived from the belief that each of us has in us the divine spark. God operates within each person. Therefore, even in a secularized society, Americans are concerned with saving the individual and speak about individual dignity, raising the standard of living of individuals, individual opportunity, and the like. The Chinese, on the other hand, see good and evil operating in and through man, to be sure, but located somewhere outside of man, in the universe, in history, in the larger reality that is the cosmos. Confucius said in his autobiography, "At forty, I had no more doubts. At fifty, I knew the will of Heaven. At sixty, I was ready to listen to it. At seventy, I could follow my heart's desire without transgressing what was right."[9] In other words, Confucius had educated himself to the point where he could act in complete accordance with the will of "Heaven," or the universe. Man was part of a larger cosmos; the cosmos was not inside each man. To jump through time to the present, the same basic assumption persists: the revolutionary Chinese Communist sees the problem of the location of good and evil in much the same way. Good is located in history, and man has identity and value and is good only insofar as he acts so as to permit history to operate through him; conversely, he is evil if he turns against the stream of history or tries to hold it back. But man may be saved by changing his viewpoint. This is what gives rise to such phenomena as "brainwashing" and the "educational" aspects of the Great Cultural Revolution.

In the West, until recently—and many Westerners still accept this —it was widely held that evil men had to be destroyed. Criminals who committed certain heinous crimes were destroyed by the state. Capital punishment is the logical development, within our legal structure and penal system, of the idea that men who are evil must be destroyed, a conception necessary if we believe that evil, like good, is located inside man. Communist Chinese, believing that men who have associated with evil can transform themselves and associate with good, have tended not to destroy men physically but rather to "re-educate" them. At the highest level of the society, Liu Shao-ch'i was excoriated by various dominant factions in the Cultural Revolution and still remained as head of state, because his opponents believed that he had erred in his perceptions and must be brought to see the errors of those perceptions. His consciousness had not developed sufficiently to permit him to see the good or the truth that is in history; given time, he would come around or history would leave him behind, as it had Chiang Kai-shek.

The problem of the location of good and evil directly influences the perceptions China and the United States have of each other and, therefore, the kind of behavior they direct at each other. From the other's point of view, each society is evil. The Chinese view the United States as guilty of falsehood and of championing historical evil by fighting against history's inexorable march toward communism, by fighting the harbinger of the future, Communist China. Americans are not evil in and of themselves, but they have chosen to struggle against good. The American view of man in history (and politics) is the opposite: it centers on the dichotomies of cowboys and Indians, cops and robbers, democrats and communists. In each case the structural relationship between opposites is the same, and children who play cops and robbers grow up to play democrats and Communists. Americans see historical actors not as agents of social forces who are capable of changing allegiances but, rather, as good guys against bad guys. The good guys will win inevitably, if only the bad guys can be held down long enough or destroyed. As a rule, the good cowboy wins the girl and leaves dead Indians strewn on the field of battle. In the satiric film *Dr. Strangelove,* the ultimate cowboy rides a nuclear bomb into the Soviet Union shouting the equivalent of "Hi-ho Silver, away!" These are not simply popular representations of American culture myths. There is ample evidence that they are conceptualizations of reality which inform not only the behavior of our soldiers in Vietnam but even the world perceptions of some of our highest policy planners. In Vietnam, for example, we built stockades and called them "agrovilles," to physically divide the good Vietnamese from the bad in the tradition of the Old West, where the white settlers lived in stockades while the Indians and the outlaws lived outside. Just as the only good Indian was a dead Indian, that is, someone whose evil had been killed with his body, so the only good Vietcong is a dead Vietcong, and the government keeps weekly body counts to measure scientifically and statistically the victory of good over evil.

This dichotomy between good and evil, whether held *consciously* by a great many Americans or not, forms the American perception of the Chinese. They represent those values of nationalism, chauvinism, or, worse yet, racism, that Americans define today as evil, as a threat to democracy and the American way of life. Perhaps the Chinese see themselves differently, not as the center of the universe but as the carriers of historical truth, which is very different from chauvinism or even nationalism. As early as 1938 Mao Tse-tung wrote, "Can a Communist, who is an internationalist, at the same time be a patriot? We hold that he not only can be but must be. The specific content of patriotism is determined by historical conditions. . . . The victory of China and the defeat of the invading [Japanese] imperialists will help the people of other countries. Thus in wars of national liberation patriotism is applied internationalism."[10] Because we perceive ourselves as good and China as evil, China frightens us: good always fears evil even while it is convinced of its own inevitable victory.

Within the category "good," democracy and the bourgeois class are linked concepts in the broad mainstream of American thought. The middle class created democracy or democratic institutions, we are taught in our textbooks on history or political science, and democracy is the highest stage of the political development of man. The linking of the two leads directly to the conclusion that if the United States wants friendly democratic societies in other countries, it must encourage in them the development of the middle class and the urbanization of rural societies—since cities are the locus of the bourgeoisie and urbanization is the *sine qua non* for modernization, itself another "good." As a result of this view, American aid programs have usually encouraged the growth of private enterprise and an urban middle class, regardless of the historical, social, or economic bases for such developments. This strong commitment, which is nothing short of ideological, has sometimes inhibited the United States in its competition with the Soviet Union. In India, for instance, the U.S.S.R. supported the construction of the great Bokaro steel mill complex, a state-owned enterprise, when the United States refused, insisting on channeling its aid into the economy's private sector.

The modern American bourgeois is, as the daily torrent of television commercials alone testifies, consumption-oriented, and from his own experience he apparently concludes that consumer goods are the primary desire of all men. The problem is to get a radio into every house, a mirror on every wall, a washcloth on every face, a toothbrush in every mouth. Eventually the people of the underdeveloped, revolutionary, anti-democratic countries will acquire automobiles and television sets, which somehow contribute to the growth of middle-class democracy. Thus, for example, the gradual liberalization of the Soviet Union and the growth of an American-Soviet détente is linked with the *embourgeoisement* of the U.S.S.R. that results from a rising standard of living and more consumer goods.

The close relationship between urbanization, a rising standard of living, and the kind of social change in the "third world" that would be welcomed by the United States has been stressed by Professor Samuel P. Huntington, chairman of the Department of Government at Harvard University. Arguing that "the massive American effort is producing a *social* revolution in the Vietnamese way of life," Professor Huntington finds that urbanization has been "the most dramatic and far-reaching impact of the war in South Viet Nam . . ." In fact, as a result of the influx into the cities of refugees seeking security and peasants desiring a higher standard of living, South Vietnam is now, according to Professor Huntington, "more urban than Sweden, Canada, the Soviet Union, Poland, Austria, Switzerland and Italy (according to early 1960s data)." While admitting that the major cause of urbanization has been flight from the dangers of war, with resulting refugee camps in which conditions "have at times been horrendous," Huntington argues:

> The immediate economic effects of urbanization are somewhat more mixed. Those who were well-off in the countryside often suffer serious losses in the move to the city. The rural poor, on the other hand, may well find life in the city more attractive and comfortable than their previous existence in the countryside. The urban slum, which seems so horrible to middle-class Americans, often becomes for the poor peasant a gateway to a new and better way of life. For some poor migrants, the wartime urban boom has made possible incomes five times those which they had in the countryside. In one Saigon slum, Xom Chua, in early 1965 before the American build-up, the people lived at a depressed level, with 33 percent of the adult males unemployed. Eighteen months later, as a result of the military escalation, the total population of the slum had increased by 30 percent, but the unemployment rate had dropped to 5 percent and average incomes had doubled. In several cases urban refugees from the war refused to return to their villages once security was restored because of the higher

level of economic well-being which they could attain in the city. The pull of urban prosperity has been a secondary but not insignificant factor in attracting people into the city.[11]

Implicit in Professor Huntington's argument is a class-based materialist view of history and of man that is equivalent to, but obviously quite different from, the Marxist argument that the proletariat is the carrier of social virtue at this stage in history. Ambassador Henry Cabot Lodge set forth this same materialist view of man, less elegantly and without any specific class reference, in a speech at the Oxford Union on June 16, 1965, when he defined victory: "When a young Vietcong soldier, waking up, says, 'I'm not going back today'—because he would get killed and because he saw around him 'the rice and the fish and the ducks and the pineapples and the American aid coming in'—and life looked 'pretty good right there.' "[12] In other words, human happiness depends primarily on consumption.

The sense of desperation that has characterized the almost unbending stubbornness of American policy toward China, and the war in Vietnam as well, is the product of that view of history which holds the bourgeois class to be the highest development of man. The relatively strict categories of Good (in social terms: the middle class) and Evil (the enemies of the middle class), and the belief that once the "bad guys" are vanquished, the good will triumph, limits conceptions of the future to extrapolations from contemporary technology and social structure. History, as the evolution of new social structures or of a New Man, ends with the middle class. While the ideological American can foresee the development of new forms of business organization and management, for instance, or an increasingly computerized economy, or a society living at a much higher standard of living, he evidently cannot entertain the serious possibility that the middle class too may pass from the historical scene, just as the European feudal land-owning class did, and that some quite different form of society may emerge. Given certain assumptions, a post-bourgeois stage of history is practically inconceivable. Consequently, American security is challenged at a profound psychological and intellectual level by the Chinese, who predict with great confidence the death of the middle class and who are actively encouraging its passing. We may co-exist with the Soviets, who are not only becoming more bourgeois but whose standards of taste and excellence resemble our own, but the Chinese Communists are a different matter altogether. This, in part, is what lies behind the slogan "Better dead than red," which many Americans not only apply to themselves and to the Vietnamese but, were the cost not as great as it seems, would apply to the Chinese as well.

The Chinese Communists view history differently, both as Marxists and as Chinese. Precisely because they see socialism as the next stage of history and are struggling to build it, they conceive of the present only as a prelude to a future that will deny the present. A social class, depending on its relations with other classes in a particular historical period, and, therefore, its relationship with the future, may be either progressive or reactionary. The bourgeoisie was progressive in its struggle against feudalism, reactionary in its oppression of the workers and peasants and its fight against socialism. This same reasoning is applied to individuals, whose evaluation proceeds from an analysis of their role in the process of change. For instance, a bourgeois businessman who contributes to the construction of the nation and does not rely on foreign capital is termed a "national bourgeois," and is more progressive, or at least less reactionary, than one whose primary activity is cooperation with foreign capitalists. This is far more than a theoretical matter, because the former will be treated differently than the latter. In the same way, countries change their position in the flow of history; national policy reflects a perception of history in political terms, and changes in policy reflect changes in historical roles and perceptions. France, for instance, formerly considered an uncompromising member of the imperialist camp, improved, from the Chinese viewpoint, with her recognition of Peking and her opposition to American policy in Southeast Asia. This was not because she became China's "friend," but because she brought herself into line with history itself, in which China is the harbinger of the future.

Paradoxically, China accepts the American position that democracy, as the United States describes and practices it, is historically linked with the bourgeois class. In fact, it is the tool of that class and therefore evil to the same extent that the bourgeoisie is historically reactionary. Man, not institutions, is the primary factor in social and political organization; consequently, "democracy" is a matter of personal orientation and behavior rather than of institutions or law. This same emphasis on man is a characteristic of Chinese conceptions of economic development, which stress not just capital accumulation and investment but, fundamentally, human will. This is the significance of the story of the old man who moved mountains, which has been used by Mao to illustrate the centrality of Man:

> There is an ancient Chinese fable called "The Foolish Old Man Who Removed the Mountains." It tells of an old man who lived in northern China long, long ago and was known as the Foolish Old Man of North Mountain. His house faced south and beyond his doorway stood the two great peaks, Taihang and Wangwu, obstructing the way. With great determination, he led his sons in digging up these mountains hoe in hand. Another greybeard, known as the Wise Old Man, saw them and said derisively, "How silly of you to do this! It is quite impossible for you few to dig up these two huge mountains." The Foolish Old Man replied, "When I die, my sons will carry on; when they die, there will be my grandsons, and then their sons and grandsons, and so on, to infinity. High as they are, the mountains cannot grow any higher and with every bit we dig, they will be that much lower. Why can't we clear them away?" Having refuted the Wise Old Man's wrong view, he went on digging every day, unshaken in his conviction. God was moved by this and he sent down two angels, who carried the mountains away on their backs. Today, two big mountains lie like a dead weight on the Chinese people. One is imperialism, the other is feudalism. The Chinese Communist Party has long made up its mind to dig them up. We must persevere and work unceasingly, and we, too, will touch God's heart. Our God is none other than the masses of the Chinese people. If they stand up and dig together with us, why can't these two mountains be cleared away?[13]

This emphasis on Man in economic development is associated

with the view that man's greatest need and desire are not consumption but the overcoming of alienation. Alienation is not a dissatisfaction born of an insufficiency of consumer goods or low standards of living. It is the state of being separated from the progressive forces of history, the inability to participate in the essential project of man, which is the making of the world. The good society is the society that permits man to participate to the fullest in the project of history, which is the overcoming of alienation through the creation of a new man and new social environments.

The emphasis on man in history and in economic development has a further consequence: because man never ends (leaving aside the possibility of his disappearance in a nuclear holocaust), history never ends.[14] Man is in constant struggle with the past, with nature, with the contradictions that are a part of the human condition, such as distinctions between old and young, male and female, coastal environment and the interior. And because struggle is a constant, victory, as a final solution to any problem, is only transitory, or better, transitional. Victory, within the structure of dialectical thinking, will inevitably produce its own opposite; there are no solutions, only resolutions that give rise to new problems. Nothing is final, including victory and defeat. This helps to explain the difference between American and Chinese views of international agreements and treaties. The United States considers treaties as final solutions or, at least, as documents laying the groundwork for final solutions. Treaties have status in law and are thus part of a stable universe of statements that are supposed to govern man's behavior. But from Peking's point of view treaties are only moments in a process. There is no end in time and no final solution, so each treaty will ultimately confront its own negation. Americans accuse them of "betraying" international agreements when they do not obey treaties. They do not perceive their behavior as betrayal, only as a move to the next stage in history.

The contemporary French philosopher Lucien Goldmann has suggested that "if philosophy is more than a simple conceptual expression of different views of the world, if, beyond its *ideological* character, it also conveys certain *fundamental truths* concerning the *relations of man with other men and of men with the universe,* then these truths should be found at the very base of the human sciences and especially in their methods."[15] The structure and content of human consciousness and of ideology, which may be understood as the conscious expression of those fundamental principles which organize human thought and, therefore, which structure the reality within which human beings act, are themselves part of reality. Individual men, groups, and nations act toward one another and re-act to each other in the real world, but one aspect of that real world is consciousness, which structures it and gives its parts form and meaning. Thus there is a kind of identity between the subject and the object of consciousness, between the actor and the world within which and on which he acts. That is to say, an individual acts in a world that is the sum of his perceptions of the real world. Those forms of conflict we call "cultural" or "ideological" are not simply conflicts of different assumptions concerning reality; they are, in fact, conflicts between the realities within which the contending parties exist and act.

Further, the structure of reality as perceived by an individual or a group is part of that individual's or group's identity structure; the formation of that identity "employs a process of simultaneous re-flection and observation, a process taking place on all levels of mental functioning . . ." Moreover, "we deal with a process 'located' *in the core of the individual* and yet also *in the core of his communal culture,* a process which establishes, in fact, the identity of those two identities."[16] This creates a serious problem in cross-cultural or international understanding. The United States and China per-ceive, and act upon, each other not in a real world that is the same for both; rather, each perceives and acts upon the other within its own reality. When either nation challenges the other, it is challeng-ing not simply a political position or an action within a common international social system; it is challenging the other's identity. The moves and statements made by one side are refracted through the other's reality structure.

Chinese development of nuclear weapons affords an example of the conflict of realities. The "bomb" has become, by the common assent of the Western powers (which now include, according to Chinese definition, the Soviet Union), not just the symbol of great-power status but part of the very definition of that status. Charles de

Gaulle, recognizing this, insisted upon France's development of nuclear power and weaponry, not because he intended to atomize Moscow, Washington, or London, but because it had been made a necessary component of great-power status, which was his image of France. Without the bomb, France's pretensions to great-power status would collapse, not only in the eyes of the atomic powers but in its own eyes as well. But because of other powers' perceptions of France, neither the United States nor the Soviet Union hindered or countered French efforts. While some mild discomfort was experienced in Washington and Moscow at the thought of the spread of such weapons, there was no noticeable fear—despite the fact that France has been one of the more aggressive nations in the world since the end of the Second World War. (One need only note the French war in Indo-China, the French struggle against Algerian independence, French cooperation with England and Israel in the attack on Egypt in 1956, French interventions in the internal affairs of some of the former French colonies in Africa, and General de Gaulle's verbal and even political encouragement of the movement for the division of Canada and the virtual independence of Quebec. Nor have France's relations with the United States been particularly friendly in recent years.)

In the case of China, as with France, her own great-power status is an intrinsic part of the reality within which she exists, and her image of her own history supports this assumption. While verbally China has been perhaps one of the most aggressive nations in the world over the last decade and a half, her behavior has been certainly no more aggressive than that of France. Except for the Korean War and the remarkably restrained Sino-Indian conflict, and occasional symbolic bombings of the islands of Quemoy and Matsu, China has engaged in no major conflicts with other nations. Even her "invasion" and "occupation" of Tibet was, when all is said and done, an "internal affair," since the United States, for instance, has never questioned the validity of China's claims to Tibet, and refused to sponsor a Tibetan appeal to the United Nations in 1948 for recognition. China's participation in the Indo-Chinese and Vietnamese wars has been miniscule compared to French and American activities in that area. China's foreign economic aid programs and foreign political activities in support of revolutionary movements or friendly governments have been much more restricted than American support of counterrevolutionary regimes. On no occasion has China intervened militarily in the domestic affairs of another nation as the United States did in the Dominican Republic. And yet, unlike France, China, in America's reality structure, plays the role of "aggressor." This leads to great American fears of growing Chinese nuclear power, validates for many policy-makers and citizens the assumption that China will use her weapons against the United States or its friends, and results in such armament policies as the development of a limited anti-missile missile system aimed at China.

Only the most strenuous intellectual exercise will permit either party in Sino-American relations to understand the other's reality and thus to act not just in terms of its own assumptions but in terms of the other's as well. Even then, it may not be possible to look forward to a world in which both nations live in peace and friendship. The construction of a common perception of the world may be far beyond our capabilities now or in the foreseeable future. In the meantime, if coexistence is preferable to war, it must be pursued on a far more profound level than at present. It will require recognition by each side that it lives in quite a different reality than the other. Boldness in the search for peace must be defined not in terms of the exertion of power but as caution and respect for the integrity of *both* sides.

NOTES

   1. John K. Fairbank, *China: The People's Middle Kingdom and the U.S.A.* (Cambridge, Mass., 1967), p. 145.
   2. John K. Fairbank, "Perspective on Vietnam," *New Republic*, January 20, 1968, p. 17.
   3. See, for instance, "Stopping New Tricks in the Game of Creating Two Chinas," *Lien Ho Pao* (Taipei, November 2, 1963), as translated in United States Information Service, Taipei, *Press and Publications Summary*, PPS 63–1551 (November 13, 1963), pp. 16–17; "The Chinese People Will Surely Liberate Taiwan," an editorial from Peking *People's Daily* as broadcast by the English Service of the New China News Agency and translated in United States Consulate General, Hong Kong, *Survey of the China Mainland Press*, No. 3489 (July 2, 1965), pp. 19–20.
   4. Compare, for instance, "Peiping-Indian Border Clashes," *Chung Hua Jih Pao* (Taipei, October 16, 1962), as translated in United States Information Service, Taipei, *Press and Publications Service*, PPS 62–1292 (October 17, 1962), pp. 13–14; "Chedong Belongs to China, Says Penchen Erdeni," New China News Agency,

Lhasa, September 29, 1962, as published by United States Consulate General, Hong Kong, *Survey of the China Mainland Press,* No. 2832 (October 4, 1962), pp. 23–24.

5. See, for instance, Bruce L. R. Smith, *The Rand Corporation: A Case Study of a Nonprofit Advisory Corporation* (Cambridge, Mass., 1966).

6. *New York Times,* December 20, 1967, p. 14.

7. Transcript of Dean Rusk's press conference of October 12, 1967, in *New York Times,* October 13, 1967, p. 15.

8. Mary McCarthy, "Report from Vietnam III: Intellectuals," *New York Review of Books,* May 18, 1967, pp. 4–11.

9. Wm. Theodore de Bary, Wing-tsit Chan, and Burton Watson, eds., *Sources of Chinese Tradition* (New York, 1960), p. 24.

10. Mao Tse-tung, *Quotations from Chairman Mao Tse-tung* (Peking, 1966), pp. 175–176.

11. Samuel P. Huntington, "The Bases of Accommodation," *Foreign Affairs,* XLVI (July 1968), p. 649. Italics in original.

12. "Are the Vietnamese Relevant?," *Manchester Guardian,* June 17, 1965, p. 10.

13. Mao Tse-tung, *Quotations,* pp. 201–202.

14. See, for instance, Edgar Snow's paraphrase of Mao Tse-tung's remarks on his own position in history: "From the long-range view, future generations ought to be more knowledgeable than we are, just as men of the bourgeois-democratic era were more knowledgeable than those of the feudal ages. Their judgment would prevail, not ours. . . . Man's condition in this era is changing with ever increasing rapidity. A thousand years from now all of them, he said, even Marx, Engels, and Lenin, would possibly appear rather ridiculous." Edgar Snow, "Interview with Mao," *New Republic,* February 27, 1965, pp. 17–23.

15. Lucien Goldmann, *Sciences humaines et philosophie* (Paris, 1966), p. 17. Italics in original.

16. Erik H. Erikson, *Identity: Youth and Crisis* (New York, 1968), p. 22. Italics in original.

# American Perceptions of China

Seth Tillman

W hen *I* use a word," Humpty Dumpty told Alice, "it means just what I choose it to mean—neither more nor less." Like the meaning of a word, a perception is the product of an interaction between the viewer and the view, with the viewer usually in command. We see one another, as Professor Kitagawa points out, through "mental prisms" shaped out of our experiences and expectations, our fears and our hopes.

Perfect objectivity about people and ideas is probably beyond human capacity, but an approach toward objectivity is not. It begins with awareness of the imperfection of our own mental processes, and from this awareness skepticism must flow—not so much as to principles as to our perceptions of things. The educated mind is skeptical of itself, as conscious of its own prismatic distortions as it is of the images beyond. It cannot free itself of the built-in prism—

we are all, to one degree or another, captives of our experience—but it can, by awareness, allow for the distortion, and in so doing approach objectivity. To make the point simply: we cannot hope to progress very far in our study of others unless, at the same time, we study ourselves.

## AMERICAN PERSPECTIVES

Neglect of the study of ourselves is the single most important failing in the scholarship of American foreign policy. Fueled by enormous transfusions of government money, social science seeks assiduously to know the motives and "multipliers" of alien societies. But we do not seem to be interested in uncovering the motives of the motivators. We ask what "they" are likely to do, but we do not ask why we are so anxious to know, and what we will do with the knowledge when we get it. We ask how we can influence someone's behavior toward "desirable" ends, but we do not ask why we wish to influence the behavior of others, whether indeed we need to or ought to, or by what right we claim the privilege of deciding what are and what are not "desirable" ends.

Perhaps the answers to these questions about ourselves are considered self-evident, to which I can only reply that they are not self-evident to me. Nor, lest suspicions of "neo-isolationism" be aroused, do I suggest for a moment that we ought to study the Americans to the exclusion of the Chinese and the Russians and the Vietnamese. I suggest only that we not study the Chinese, Russians, and Vietnamese to the exclusion of the Americans—not only because our first and principal responsibility is to our own people (as I do strongly believe), but because only the knowledge of our own prejudices and predilections can allow us insight into the beliefs and behavior of others.

For a start we might consider that most of the ideological convictions held by most of the people on earth are the result not of a rational intellectual process but of accidents of birth. Before launching forth on crusades, or even on tirades, about China's revolutionary extremism, we might ponder the probability that almost any one of us, had he been born in China, would endorse the Lin Piao doctrine as vehemently as an American opposes and fears it. In the most fundamental sense, a war between China and the United States would be a conflict not between two great "philosophies," with all that that word implies of coherent and rational thought, but between two imperfect pictures of the world, each the product of a unique synthesis of experience, accident, *and* rational thought.

This is not to say that values are relative, that one ideology is as good as another. My point is a different one: it is that a foreign ideology *may* be as good as our own *although we do not think so,* and that an ideology that suits our society well may be unsuited to another. My premise is that, for reasons beyond our understanding, man was vouchsafed only an imperfect knowledge of his own best interests and very limited knowledge indeed of the best interests of others, making it, as Professor Pulleyblank says in his discussion of the prospects for reunion between mainland China and Taiwan, "an impertinence for foreigners to interfere."[1]

Among the prismatic distortions that affect the American view of the world, the one which seems most to reduce our capacity for insight and empathy toward a great number of countries, including China, is our deep abhorrence of revolution. It is complicated by the fact that we do not know we abhor revolution, that indeed we think we approve of it, even regarding ourselves, erroneously, as the "most revolutionary society in the world."

Part of the problem is semantic imprecision. When the same word is used to identify different things, one supposes they are the same thing when in fact they have little more in common than their name. One hears it argued, for example, that Latin Americans do not truly object to "intervention" inasmuch as their dislike of interference by the Marines is not matched by a comparable distaste for economic aid, although both may be characterized as "intervention." The inference is a fallacious one, drawn from the supposition that two different things are really one and the same thing because they happen to be called by the same name. Similarly, the term "revolutionary" is used to describe events ranging from Robespierre's terror to the marketing of a new laundry soap. In American usage the term "revolutionary" means little more than "new" or "different" or "markedly changed." It is indeed in this sense—and this sense only—that America is a revolutionary society: we tear down buildings and put up new ones and alter—or desolate—our landscape at a rate and on a scale unprecedented in human history.

Social revolution is something different. Almost always violent and sometimes extremely violent, its essence is the destruction of existing institutions and social fabric and the attempt, not necessarily successful, to create a new society with new values and new institutions. The only elements of this kind of revolution in the United States are the student and Negro rebellions and, isolated and undisciplined though their current manifestations are, they are scaring the daylights out of us. Our heritage otherwise in conservative and unrevolutionary, a fact in which we ought to take satisfaction because it indicates that our institutions by and large have proven themselves durable and adaptable as our country has grown from an isolated agrarian republic to a world industrial power.

As Louis Hartz has pointed out, Americans substituted migration for revolution. From the Mayflower to the covered wagon, Americans simply moved away from those relics of medievalism that people less fortunately situated had either to endure or overthrow. Not only is the Revolution of 1776 remote and ritualized in the national memory; it was not nearly the kind of violent social upheaval that was subsequently to occur in France and, in this century, in Russia and China. American society was already largely self-governing and democratic when her colonial grievances against Great Britain erupted into violence. Quite obviously, both the Revolution and the Civil War altered the course of American history, but neither involved the total destruction of an existing social order; on the contrary, they served to accelerate the democratic evolution which had preceded them.[2]

The effect of the unique American experience has been an ambivalent attitude toward social revolution. Welcoming a country's initial struggle for democracy and independence, we turn away in mounting horror as the revolution becomes violent in method and socialist in objective, Cuba being an almost perfect case in point. As Hartz puts it, "From the French Revolution onward the American response to revolution abroad is like a love affair which is constantly turning sour, like an infatuation which is forever ending in disenchantment."[3] Generalizing from the particular, as human beings are prone to do, Americans have bemused themselves with the notion that the American Revolution was prototypical, the model against which all other revolutions are to be judged as good or bad, legitimate or illegitimate. Few have passed this impossible test, with the result that America, the champion of revolution in principle, has become in practice the foremost opponent of the great, violent, socialist revolutions of the twentieth century.

There is nothing wrong with the American perspective except its claim of universal applicability. Ethically, the American dislike of revolutionary terror and totalitarianism is highly defensible; it is the presumption of a right to judge others in terms of a unique national experience that is intellectually indefensible. Even when the presumption takes on the highly sophisticated forms of modern social science, we are still looking at the world through the distorting prism of our own experience. It is for this reason that there can be no understanding of others unless the effort to gain it is accompanied, indeed preceded, by no less an effort to understand ourselves.

## CHINA THROUGH THE PRISM

Not entirely without justification, Americans feel indignant that the most venomous epithets of the Chinese are directed at the United States. To be sure, the West has earned China's hostility, but America, after all, was the least voracious of the Western imperialists and had always regarded itself as China's true friend. Did we not return a part of our share of the Boxer indemnity to finance scholarships for Chinese students to study in the United States? Did we not proclaim the "Open Door" in order to secure equal commercial access to China and, incidentally, to preserve China's territorial integrity? Did we not try to uphold Chinese independence and territorial integrity after the First World War and subsequently express our opposition to the Japanese incursions? Did we not fight as China's ally in World War II, voluntarily repudiate the privileges of the "unequal treaties," sponsor China as a great power with a permanent seat on the United Nations Security Council, and then, after the war, even try to win for the Communists a position of equality in a coalition government with Chiang Kai-shek's Nationalists?

Though natural enough, our sense of injury in the face of Peking's execrations is based in large part on a sentimentalized view of the history of America's relations with China. Shaped by the merchants, missionaries, and diplomats who represented the United States in China for a hundred years before the Communist revolution, our national outlook toward China is marked by certain illusions. As enumerated by Professor James Thomson of Harvard University, these include: the illusion of America's special moral status as against the Europeans'—an illusion fostered by the fact that we abstained from most of the foreign military encroachments into China although we stood ready to share in their benefits under the "most-favored-nation" principle; the illusion of China's "special responsiveness" to us—fostered, says Thomson, "by the hopes of our missionaries and entrepreneurs, who offered a vision of 400 million converts and 400 million customers"; the illusion of America's special role as protector of China on the basis of the "Open Door" and our often stated but unenforced pronouncements in support of China's "territorial integrity"; and, finally, what Thomson calls "the sentimental and condescending illusion of Chinese weakness, Chinese gentleness, Chinese passivity, and, most serious of all, China's patent incapacity for self-government."[4]

These perceptions and judgments provide the background for America's current perspective of China. They do not of course in themselves prove that any of the attitudes we now hold toward China are wrong, but they do strongly suggest that our attitudes have almost certainly been influenced in some degree by historical distortions.

The extent of the discrepancy between American perceptions and present Chinese reality can only be judged with authority by specialists in Chinese affairs (provided, of course, that their absorption in the study of Chinese behavior has not caused them to neglect the study of American behavior). There are, however, certain salient facts available to the nonexpert observer—facts which cast doubt upon the theory of a Chinese design for the conquest of Asia. Among these are the following:

As of the spring of 1969 the United States had half a million troops in Vietnam; China had some work teams in North Vietnam engaged in the maintenance of railroads and other transport, but, to the best of our knowledge, no combat troops. There are reports that some or all of these Chinese were removed after the cessation of the American bombing.

India fought a border war with China in 1962 and, although the Chinese army could probably have marched to Calcutta and Bombay, it stopped after gaining the disputed borderlands—territory, incidentally, which even the Chiang Kai-shek government on Taiwan claimed to be Chinese.

When the Korean War ended in 1953, there were close to a million Chinese soldiers on Korean territory, with nothing to stop them from remaining there to annex, subjugate, or do what they wished with North Korea. But in 1958 the entire Chinese army withdrew, and since then North Korea has governed itself as an independent Communist state. In 1966 North Korea's leaders announced their intention to build communism neither on the Chinese nor Soviet model but in their own "Korean" way.

There is little doubt but that China wishes her neighbors to be "friendly" in somewhat the same way the United States insists upon "friendly" neighbors in Latin America. We all know how the United States feels about Cuba and how it reacted when the Russians tried to establish missile bases there. Is it astonishing that the Chinese lack enthusiasm for a powerful American military bastion in South Vietnam, in addition to America's unchallenged sea power and its ring of air bases on the islands off China's coast? Is it incomprehensible that China wants its neighbors to be as friendly to it as, say, Mexico is to the United States, and especially that they not allow themselves, like Thailand, to be used as powerful American military bases?

The possibility cannot be overlooked that at least some part of the evil is in the eye of the beholder. Professor Pulleyblank suggests that prevailing fears of a direct Chinese military threat against China's neighbors derive largely from a projection of Western attitudes onto the Chinese, particularly the Western assumption that great powers are by nature expansive.[5] Is it not possible that such a projection—with the violent language of the Chinese leaders, our own ingrained tendency to regard Communist countries as aggressive by definition, and the sense of injury and betrayal arising out of our sentimentalized view of America's past relations with China— has had something to do with the development of the theory of a Chinese design for the conquest of Asia?

In addition to seeking insight into our own predilections, it is important for us to recognize that China is in an abnormal state of mind. It is a nation which, as U Thant has put it, has had a kind of "nervous breakdown." Or, as Professor John Fairbank has written, "Peking is, to say the least, maladjusted, rebellious against the whole world, Russia as well as America. We are Peking's principal enemy because we happen now to be the biggest outside power trying to foster world stability."[6] We are, in addition, the dominant power of the West and, as such, inevitably if unjustly, we are the principal object of China's historically based anger.

Even more important than the intellectual analysis of behavior is the essentially nonintellectual task of learning to think of the Chinese as members with ourselves in a common humanity. Antagonists usually dehumanize each other, and when antagonism is compounded by distance, by lack of historical familiarity, and by that disease of the Western mind, racism, it becomes possible to think of China not as a society of over 700 million individual human beings, every one of whom has fears and hopes and feelings just as individual Americans do, but rather as a kind of terrifying abstraction. When Chinese soldiers are described—as I have heard them described—as "hordes of Chinese coolies," it is clear that they are being thought of not as human but as something inanimate and menacing, like lava flowing out of a volcano.

Dehumanization, which enables people who may be decent and kind in their personal relations to destroy each other with a clear conscience, is the basic deformation in the prism through which Americans view Chinese. Kenneth Boulding writes of the young man who dropped the first atomic bomb:

> . . . If he had been ordered to go and drop it on Milwaukee, he almost certainly would have refused. . . . Because he was asked to drop it on Hiroshima, he not only consented but he became something of a hero for it. . . . Of course, I don't quite see the distinction between dropping it on Milwaukee and dropping it on Hiroshima. The difference is a "we" difference. The people in Milwaukee, though we don't know any of them, are "we," and the people in Hiroshima are "they," and the great psychological problem is how to make everybody "we," at least in some small degree.[7]

CHINA AND THE WEST: "WE" AND "THEY"

Someday—it is inconceivable that it will be soon—the fatal gap may be bridged between the Western "we" and the Chinese "they." Someday, we hope, the bombardier will be as unwilling to drop his bomb on Hiroshima as on Milwaukee, as unwilling to drop it on Peking as on Washington, or on Washington as Peking. What are required, fundamentally, are not arrangements but attitudes, most particularly the extension of that attitude of "we" which the bombardier felt toward Americans whom he did not know but which he did not feel toward foreigners whom he also did not know. The feeling of "they" was the death sentence for eighty thousand people in Hiroshima; the feeling of "they," as between Chinese and Americans, may one day be the death sentence for the human species. We cannot overcome it easily or soon; we may not be able to overcome it at all. It seems salutary, however, if there is to be any chance at all of overcoming it, that we begin by recalling to ourselves, as accurately as we can, exactly how China became alienated from the West.

A great and ancient empire, feeling itself to be a self-contained civilization rather than a nation-state in the Western sense, traditional China asked nothing of the outside world except to be let alone. Proud and parochial, the "Celestial Empire" accepted tribute from its Korean and Vietnamese vassals, and occasionally from the outer "barbarians." But the idea of engaging in international relations on the European model was alien and uninteresting. When King George III of England proposed in 1793 to send a permanent Ambassador to Peking to take care of England's trade with China, he was advised by the Emperor that the proposal was "not in harmony with the state system of our dynasty and will definitely not be permitted," because, the Emperor pointed out, "there is nothing that we lack. . . . We have never set much store on strange or ingenious objects, nor do we need any more of your country's manufactures."[8]

But, as the Chinese were soon to find out, there was something which they lacked: they lacked guns and ships and trained armies, and, for lack of them, this ancient civilization was to be reduced in the course of the nineteenth century to a semi-colonial domain for Western exploitation.

First came the British, then at the peak of their imperial power, the most democratic nation in Europe and also the proudest. When in 1839 the Chinese took steps to suppress the smuggling of opium, which was destroying the health of a great number of Chinese but which was also a major source of revenue for the imperial government of India, England made war on China. When the Opium War was won, England compelled China to cede Hong Kong, open up five treaty ports for British trade, accept tariffs which could not be changed without Britain's consent, and, in addition, pay an indemnity to compensate British merchants for confiscated opium. ". . . A war more unjust in its origin," said Gladstone, "a war more calculated in its progress to cover this country with permanent disgrace, I do not know and I have not read of."[9]

British incursions on the decaying Chinese empire were followed by those of other European powers. New concessions and indemnities were exacted by the British and French in the 1850's. In 1860 the British burned the imperial summer palace in Peking and forced the Chinese to cede Kowloon to Great Britain. The Russians also fell upon China in the fifties and forced China to yield first the territory north of the Amur River and then the maritime territory where the port of Vladivostok was later established. Japan attacked China in 1894 and extracted extensive trading privileges as well as cession of the island of Taiwan. Germany, coming late on the scene, then forced China to yield a leasehold on the port of Kiaochow and commercial privileges on the Shantung peninsula. Russia seized Port Arthur and Dairen, and France exacted an extensive sphere of influence in South China, including a leasehold on Kwangchow Bay. When the Boxer rebels rose against the foreigners in 1900, an international "rescue force," which included Americans, was sent to Peking. The commander of the Allied force, a German, was under instructions from the Kaiser "to give no quarter and to take no prisoners" so that "no Chinese will ever dare to look askance at a German."

Largely precipitated by the ravages of the West, there began in 1911 an era of revolution in China. In the course of almost forty years of foreign war and domestic turmoil, China's ancient institutions and values were shattered. Only when the Communists took control in 1949 was China again unified, but the Communist phase of China's great revolution is still, in the late 1960's, at flood tide. China has really had two revolutions, one against the foreign "barbarians" who fell upon China and humiliated her, the other against the ancient customs and institutions which, in their parochialism and decay, proved so brittle under the foreign onslaught.

Both revolutions, the foreign and domestic, are still in progress, and their outcome can only be guessed at, but there seems to be agreement among the experts on China that the emphasis is on domestic change, on converting this vast and populous land into a strong, modern nation. As one specialist suggested to the Senate Foreign Relations Committee, China's leaders seem "anxious to turn in and focus their efforts even more than they have in the past on the domestic concerns of the Chinese revolution. . . . If the Chinese can become convinced that they do not face imminent threat of an American nuclear attack, they are likely to withdraw even more from the world while continuing to issue revolutionary proclamations and concentrate on their internal difficulties and opportunities."[10]

There is further understanding to be gained from some perspective on what Crane Brinton calls "the anatomy of revolution." Great revolutions unfold according to a more or less common, though by no means a preordained, pattern.[11] Preceded by the decay of a traditional ruling class, such as the Russian tsars or the Manchu emperors, the revolution is characterized first by the rule of moderates, such as the Russian provisional government of 1917 or the Chinese republic of Sun Yat-sen. The moderates tend to be overwhelmed by the violence which they themselves have set loose; they are replaced by extremists, whose extremism degenerates into terror, such as the Stalin purges or Mao Tse-tung's Cultural Revolution. Finally, the extremists give way to more practical men, such as Khrushchev or Kosygin; under their rule the flames of revolution are allowed to abate and life becomes more normal and behavior more conventional. Only in this stage is the revolution consummated; permanent and unalterable changes have been wrought, but revolutionary doctrine gradually passes into the patriotic liturgy, no longer a program of immediate action but now a statement of ideals to be realized only at some unspecified time in the future.

China undoubtedly is still in the extremist stage of her revolution.

It is conceivable that she will remain there forever, but that seems unlikely. History suggests as the greater likelihood that someday, perhaps when a new generation of leaders comes to power, perhaps only after several generations, China will pass out of the stage of extremism into a post-revolutionary normalcy, both in her domestic life and in her foreign relations.

Until that transition occurs, the danger of war between China and the United States is likely to remain acute. It is sometimes suggested, by people who judge that China's hostility to America is permanent and unalterable, that the United States ought to initiate a "preventive" war against China in order to destroy her nuclear capacity before it becomes a major threat to us. Such a war would be a strategic nightmare. As General Ridgway wrote in his memoirs:

> . . . I challenge any thesis that destroying the military might of Red China would be in our own long-range interest. We could create there, by military means, a great power vacuum. Then we would have to go in there with hundreds of thousands of men to fill that vacuum—which would bring us face to face with Russia along a 7000-mile frontier. If we failed to go in, then Russia herself would fill it, and the threat to our own security would not have abated one iota.[12]

At best a strategic futility, a pre-emptive war against China would be a moral disaster. Inevitably killing millions of innocent people, it would shock the conscience of all decent human beings, branding America as the most barbarous of nations, as the perpetrator of an unprecedented act of mass violence. We simply could not initiate such a war and still be ourselves; such an act would tear our country apart, giving rise to a wave of revulsion among our own people that would make the debate over Vietnam seem trivial by comparison. We are, so we believe, a decent society; that being so, no act involving the destruction of decency can be included among our options.

Such hope as there is for an abatement of the danger of war and for the gradual rehabilitation of China to a more or less normal role in the world lies in the prospect of change within China and of American patience and understanding. Experience suggests that the abatement of revolutionary fervor is a natural tendency. No special effort is required to slow down a revolution; on the contrary, a concerted effort must be mounted to sustain it at a high peak of intensity.

The latter is exactly what China's leaders are trying to do, and *we may be helping them*. Nothing serves better to keep a population mobilized to the high state of discipline and dedication necessary for the momentous tasks of modernization than the existence of a foreign enemy who can be characterized as enormously powerful and threatening. That is the purpose we may be serving for China's extremist leaders; that is the basis of what one scholar, Richard H. Solomon, calls "America's revolutionary alliance with Communist China." From the viewpoint of the Chinese leadership, he writes: ". . . 'U.S. imperialism' is an enemy allied in the cause of uniting and motivating the Chinese people, through tension and hatred, for the cause of creating a new society."[13]

Professor Solomon quotes an editorial from the Chinese Communist party paper, *People's Daily*:

> The Chinese people's great enemy is U.S. imperialism. This enemy is indeed most hateful and harmful to us; but we must see that its existence also has a beneficial effect on us. To have a ferocious enemy like U.S. imperialism glowering at us and threatening us day and night will make us Chinese people always bear in mind the danger of war while living in peace and raise our vigilance a hundred fold; will keep us always on the alert and enable our enthusiasm to burst forth; can help the Chinese people always to maintain preparedness and sharpen our fighting spirit. Wanton U.S. imperialist aggression and intimidation can further raise our political consciousness, strengthen our unity and enhance our combat readiness.[14]

If this analysis is valid, it seems clear that the Chinese leaders wish the United States to be hostile because they are able to use that hostility for *domestic* purposes, essentially for the purpose of trying to freeze the Chinese Revolution in its extremist stage. If that indeed is the case, then the first, extremely important conclusion to be drawn, from the viewpoint of American policy, is that China's hostility toward us is not in itself indicative of a program for the conquest of Asia.

The second, equally important inference to be drawn is that there is no reason at all why we must continue to play Mao's game, no reason at all why we cannot withdraw from our "revolutionary alliance" with Communist China. There is nothing to stop us from refusing to confirm the Chinese image of our "aggressive imperialism," nothing to stop us from calling off the dragon-baiting and offering to China the hand of our friendship, knowing that it is likely to be rejected for the foreseeable future but knowing as well that an honest, standing offer of peaceful coexistence, not too importunately pressed, will gradually weaken the Chinese image of a hostile America and perhaps serve the equally salutary purpose of gradually breaking down the American image of China as a menacing abstraction.

Something more is required of us than "reciprocity" in the churlish sense in which conventional diplomacy might require it. We are called upon to show empathy and generosity toward a great and ancient civilization which, as U Thant put it, has suffered a kind of "nervous breakdown." "Magnanimity in politics," said Burke, "is not seldom the truest wisdom; and a great empire and little minds go ill together."[15]

Despite the unlikelihood of an early favorable response, there are certain specific steps that can and, in my opinion, should be taken by the United States to make its friendship available to the Chinese without trying to force it upon them. We can, for example, remove existing prohibitions on travel between China and the United States, remove the embargo on trade in nonstrategic commodities, drop our opposition to Chinese membership in the United Nations provided that a place is retained for Taiwan, and offer to open up diplomatic relations on any level agreeable to the Chinese. Most or all of these offers would probably be rejected, but at least we could show China that there is an alternative to eternal hostility and that we do not intend to remain bound to her in baneful "revolutionary alliance." The only caution I would offer is that, in making these proposals for improved relations, we resist the temptation to make a propaganda festival by pressing our proposals too eagerly and too often, lest their quite probable rejection result in a reinforcement of hostile attitudes on both sides and a consequent setback to the long-term prospect for improved relations.

For a long time to come, the single most constructive thing we can do in our relations with China is, to the greatest possible extent, to leave her alone. China has had a shattering experience in her relations with the West; she needs time to recover her pride and strength and, until she does, she cannot be expected to seek or accept friendly associations with her recent tormentors. China has experienced what is probably the greatest and most thoroughgoing revolution of modern times; she—and we—need time for it to run its course.

In practice, "leaving China alone" implies the creation of *strategic distance* between the United States and China by means of the neutralization of Southeast Asia, either *de facto* or by general or piecemeal agreements in the wake of some kind of settlement of the Vietnam War. The critical question to be asked in considering such a strategy for Asia, besides its desirability, is whether we *can* leave China alone, whether China will leave us alone. Obviously we do not know. There are no certainties in planning policies for the future, and all that one can say about any proposed course of action is that it seems like a good bet. As long as China continues to be concerned primarily with her internal affairs, only secondarily with encouraging foreign revolutions, and apparently not at all with plans for the direct military conquest of Asia, then neutralization seems the best bet we have.

There remains the question of what we might do, after neutralization, if China should after all try to overrun its neighbors, and whether America can be secure without powerful military bases on the Asian mainland. With our highly mobile striking force, our chain of island bases in the western Pacific, and our deterrent missile and air power, we have no need of bases on the Asian mainland in order to bring requisite power speedily to bear against an act of aggression. Indeed, insofar as our presence invites countervailing measures, our military withdrawal from the mainland would probably reduce the danger of Chinese attack upon or subversion of her neighbors. I think it is more than coincidence that the only Southeast Asian countries which have been troubled by domestic insurgencies supported by China have been those countries—Vietnam, Laos, and Thailand—which are supported militarily by the United States.

Whatever strategic threat China poses to the United States itself is posed by her incipient nuclear and missile power. American capacity to meet that threat is its vastly superior nuclear deterrent power—the same power that is relied on to deter the formidable nuclear capacity of the Soviet Union. Our ability to deter or retaliate against a Chinese attack does not require military bases in Vietnam. We can readily attack or threaten China with our ICBM's, our Polaris submarines, our island bases, and our unchallenged sea and air power in the western Pacific.

Besides a strategy of "strategic distance"—and in the long run more important—it would profit us greatly to adopt some new attitudes as well: a new attitude toward China, a great nation torn by revolution, but also a great civilization deserving of a respected place in the world community; a new attitude toward the force of Asian nationalism, which, whatever ideological form it takes, has shown itself to be the strongest barrier to subversion, and therefore —whatever ideological form it takes—a powerful ally of American interests; and finally, a new attitude toward communism itself, which, despite its liturgy, is neither unified nor uniform, and which, like every universalist doctrine that has preceded it, has shown patent incapacity—and, as time goes on, even a flagging will—for ruling the world.

OUR "VITAL INTERESTS"

Connoting as it does the question of life or death for the nation, the concept of "vital interest" has a ring of no-nonsense about it. Its very sound is of something certain, clear-cut, coldly calculated, and critically important—the very opposite of the sentimental visions of idealists. As commonly used, however, its purpose is to justify some policy, almost always a policy with military or strategic implications such as the Monroe Doctrine, the "Open Door," or the Vietnam War.

Obscured by the concept of "vital interest" is the question of values. What is vital to us in our foreign relations is the by-product of what is valuable to us in our own society. One cannot talk meaningfully about our "vital interests" in relation to China or anyone else without first being clear about our concept of ourselves, about the kind of country we want America to be and the kind of role we want it to play in the world. Our national security is or is not at stake in Asia depending on what it is we hope to secure.

In a report on "National Commitments" issued in 1969, the Senate Foreign Relations Committee commented on the basic purpose of our foreign policy: "Foreign policy is not an end in itself. We do not have a foreign policy because it is interesting or fun, or because it satisfies some basic human need; we conduct foreign policy for a purpose external to itself, the purpose of securing democratic values in our own country."[16]

Implicit in the committee's words is the idea that the nation's vital interests—perhaps one should say "ultimate interests" in order clearly to indicate the teleological sense in which the term is being used—are essentially *domestic* in character, that it is our own democracy that is to be defended, that our proper basic concern is not with what we might wish to make of the world but what we wish to make of ourselves and, secondarily, with what we need to do in the world in order to be free to make what we want of ourselves. This definition of "vital interest" can be called "neo-isolationism," but its essence is *selectivity* in our international commitments—selectivity according to our own needs, our own capacities, and a healthy respect for the right of others to make comparable judgments for themselves. If accepted, this general view of our vital interests must lead us to a re-evaluation of our attitude toward China.

As to ourselves, the concept of vital interest as essentially domestic implies attitudes of modesty in our aspirations and skepticism as to our own motives, especially those we consider our "best" motives. If this be thought selfish or timid, the answer, I think, is that awareness of one's own limitations is not only the beginning but the indispensable precondition for generous and even courageous action. The experience of nations leaves little doubt about the mischief which is wrought by those who, with good motives or bad, take it on themselves to remake the world or even to bring unqualified blessings to an unenthusiastic beneficiary.

To speak of the "duty" of America, acting alone, to perform this service or that for humanity or for any one of its benighted branches, is more *irrelevant* than anything else, because such services are largely beyond our capacity. Among nations, as between individuals, the greatest generosity is respect for another's autonomy and the acceptance of individual differences, even when—especially when—these differences are distasteful or incomprehensible. Beyond that, our duty to the world beyond our borders is a duty of *partnership,* through the United Nations and other multilateral arrangements for the maintenance of peace, through the World Bank and international financial institutions for the support of economic development. The attitude implicit in this approach is recognition of the limits of human capacity, material, moral, and intellectual. It is a melancholy fact, but a fact of experience nonetheless, that most men simply do not know what is best for other men, and incalculable harm is wrought when they act on the supposition that they do.

The premise is exactly that which is written into the Constitution of the United States. The essence of that document is the restriction of political power—not, presumably, because of a malign desire on the part of the framers to deny our government the authority to perform useful services for the people, but because of their desire to protect the people, and our leaders too, from the human susceptibility to misuse power. If it is wisdom to restrict the power of a government over its own people, how can it be regarded as a failure of moral or political responsibility to apply comparable restrictions in our dealings with people of whom we know very little, or of whom, as in the case of the Chinese, we are not only ignorant but fearful as well?

In our relations with China, the concept of "vital interest" as essentially domestic implies an effort to allow for, if not actually to overcome, the distortions caused by the mental prism through which we look at Asian societies. Even today, as Professor Kitagawa points out, we foresee Asia's future in terms of industrialization, technical education, and democratization—which is to say, Westernization.[17] What we do not consider, and cannot consider as long as we look at Asia through the prism of our own values and preferences, is that the tide of Asian revolution may be moving toward forms of life and political organization quite dissimilar from those known or favored in the West.

To anticipate the emergence and prevalence of strange and, to us, incomprehensible social forms requires the transcending of parochialism; to anticipate them with reasonable equanimity requires the overcoming of arrogance; to contemplate them with friendly curiosity rather than instinctive hostility requires genuine magnanimity. All of these are required for a mutual respectful relationship between the United States and China. None is likely to be attained except on the basis of a concept of "vital interest" as *domestic* in its ultimate aspirations, because only when we have made a clear, conscious decision that our "vital interests" have to do with the kind of society *we* live in, and not with the kinds of society other people live in, will it be possible to be comfortable in the face of diversity and to distinguish clearly between that which is menacing and that which is merely unfamiliar.

For these reasons it seems clear that, for the expert and non-expert alike, the study of China must begin with the study of America. Only if we know ourselves can we hope to learn what most needs to be learned about China: that the Chinese have been, remain, and will surely continue to be different from us in culture, tradition, and political values, but that, nonetheless, they share with us those essential needs, spiritual and material, which bind all men together in a common humanity. Knowing these things, we should be able to take the news calmly when we are told that the Chinese are embarked upon a campaign to create a "new man" with a new human nature; we might even wish them well in a worthy but hopeless undertaking.

NOTES

1. See p. 93 above.

2. Louis Hartz, "The Basis of the American Response," in *The Nature of Revolution*, Hearings Before the Committee on Foreign Relations, U.S. Senate, 90th Cong., 2nd sess. (Washington, D.C., 1968), pp. 109–120; see also *The Liberal Tradition in America* (New York, 1955).

3. *The Nature of Revolution*, p. 115.

4. James Thomson, in *The Nature of Revolution*, pp. 67–68.

5. See pp. 82–83 above.

6. John K. Fairbank, "How To Deal with the Chinese Revolution," *New York Review of Books*, February 17, 1966, p. 16.

7. Kenneth Boulding, "World Economic Contacts and National Policies," in Quincy Wright, ed., *The World Community* (Chicago, 1948), pp. 101–102.

8. Quoted in Ssu-Yu Teng and John K. Fairbank, eds., *China's Response to the West: A Documentary Survey, 1839–1923* (New York, 1965), p. 19.

9. Quoted by Maurice Collis, in *Foreign Mud* (New York, 1947), p. 269.

10. Morton Halperin, *U.S. Policy with Respect to Mainland China*, Hearings Before the Committee on Foreign Relations, U.S. Senate, 89th Cong., 2nd sess. (Washington, D.C., 1966), p. 287.

11. Crane Brinton, *The Anatomy of Revolution* (New York, 1965).

12. Matthew B. Ridgway, *Soldier: Memoirs of Matthew B. Ridgway* (New York, 1956), p. 279.

13. Richard H. Solomon, "Parochialism and Paradox in Sino-American Relations," *Asian Survey,* VII (December 1967), 833.

14. *People's Daily,* February 20, 1966.

15. Edmund Burke, Second Speech on Conciliation with America.

16. *National Commitments,* Report of the Committee on Foreign Relations on S. Res. 85, 91st Cong., 1st sess. (Washington, D.C., 1969), p. 9.

17. See p. 38 above.

# A Note on Further Reading

Books on China are many and varied. We have selected a limited number of reliable and easily accessible books which can provide a general background about China. Most of the books cited here are available in paperback.

GENERAL INTRODUCTION

All the standard encyclopedias carry useful articles on China. Probably the most comprehensive introductory work is Chang-tu Hu, *China: Its People, Its Society, Its Culture,* edited by Hsiao Hsia (New Haven: HRAF Press, 1960). Ping-chia Kuo, *China* (New York: Oxford, rev. ed., 1965), and Kenneth Scott Latourette, *China* (Englewood Cliffs, N.J.: Prentice-Hall, 1964), are both brief and well written. Harley F. MacNair, ed., *China* (Berkeley: University of California Press, 1946), though dated, is still a useful introduction to China. More elementary but up-to-date are Hyman Kublin, *China,* and its companion volume, *China: Selected Reading,* edited by the same author (both Boston: Houghton Mifflin, 1968).

Some readers prefer literary works about China instead of the usual introductory materials. For example, many Westerners have been introduced to China by a series of works by Pearl S. Buck (all New York: John Day), i.e., *Dragon Seed* (1942, 1966), *The Good Earth* (1931, 1939), *The Hidden Flower* (1952, 1954), and *My Several Worlds* (1954, 1956). Also, Han Suyin, *A Many-Splendored Thing* (New York: New American Library, 1952, 1955); George N. Kates, *The Years That Were Fat: The Last of Old China* (Cambridge: MIT Press, 1952, 1967); Ida Pruitt, *A Daughter of Han: The Autobiography of a Chinese Working Woman* (Stanford: Stanford University Press, 1945, 1967); Yee Chiang, *A Chinese Childhood* (New York: Norton, 1963); and Lin Yutang's essays, especially *My Country and My People* (New York: John Day, 1935), have been read profitably by many.

## GEOGRAPHY

The most widely used book on the subject is George B. Cressey, *Land of the 500 Million: A Geography of China* (New York: McGraw Hill, 1955). Norton S. Ginsburg, ed., *The Pattern of Asia* (Englewood Cliffs, N.J.: Prentice-Hall, 1958), deals with China in a larger canvas of Asia. Hsieh Chiao-Min, *China: Ageless Land and Countless People* (Princeton: Van Nostrand, 1967); Victor P. Petrov, *China: Emerging World Power* (Princeton: Van Nostrand, 1967); and Theodore Shabad, *China's Changing Map: Political and Economic Geography of the Chinese People's Republic* (New York: Praeger, 1956), stress human, political, and economic factors.

## HISTORY

There is no one definitive theory about the origin and formative period of Chinese civilization. Nevertheless, Li Chi, *The Beginnings of Chinese Civilization* (Seattle: University of Washington Press, 1957); Herrlee G. Creel, *The Birth of China* (London: Jonathan, 1936; New York: Frederick Ungar, 1961); and William Watson, *Early Civilization in China* (New York: McGraw-Hill, 1966), are illuminating. (Pierre Teilhard de Chardin, whose cosmic vision has stimulated much speculation and discussion in recent years, was a competent archaeologist, as evidenced by his *Le Néolithique de la Chine,* co-authored with Pei Wen-chung [Peking: Institut de géobiologie, 1944].)

Books dealing with various aspects and epochs of the long and colorful history of China are too numerous to be cited. A novice in this field will benefit more by reading such general works as Charles P. Fitz-Gerald, *China: A Short Cultural History* (New York: Praeger, 4th ed., 1962); L. Carrington Goodrich, *A Short History of the Chinese People* (New York: Harper, 3rd ed., 1959); René Grousset's now slightly dated *The Rise and Splendour of the Chinese Empire,* trans. by A. Wat-son-Gandy and T. Gordon (Berkeley: University of California Press, 1952, 1959); and Dun J. Li, *The Ageless Chinese: A History* (New York: Scribner's, 1965). More comprehensive is Kenneth Scott La-tourette, *The Chinese: Their History and Culture* (New York: Macmil-lan, 3rd ed., 1956), which combines the account of Chinese history with general discussions on specific topics, e.g., the government, eco-nomic life and organization, religion, social life, language, literature, and education. The history of China is prominently dealt with in Edwin O. Reischauer and John K. Fairbank, *A History of East Asian Civilization,* Vol. I, *East Asia: The Great Tradition* (Boston: Houghton Mifflin, 1960). It is fortunate that we now have in paperback editions such important works as Etienne Balazs, *Chinese Civilization and Bureaucracy; Variations on a Theme,* trans. by H. M. Wright (New Haven: Yale University Press, 1964), which is a collection of the author's stimulating essays; G. F. Hudson, *Europe and Asia: A Survey of Their Relations from the Earliest Times to 1800* (Boston: Beacon, 1931, 1961); and Owen Lattimore, *Inner Asian Frontiers of China* (Boston: Beacon, 1940, 1962), which offers an historical account of China's relations with her frontiers and immediate neighbors.

Understandably, the modern history of China has received close attention by many competent scholars. The following are but a small sample of growing literature in this area: Chang Chung-li, *The Chinese Gentry: Studies on Their Role in Nineteenth-Century Chinese Society* (Seattle: University of Washington Press, 1955); John K. Fairbank, Edwin O. Reischauer, and Albert M. Craig, *A History of East Asian Civilization,* Vol. II, *East Asia: The Modern Transformation* (Boston: Houghton Mifflin, 1965); John K. Fairbank, *The United States and China* (New York: Viking, rev. ed., 1962); Charles P. FitzGerald, *The Birth of Communist China* (Baltimore: Penguin, 1964); John A. Harrison, *China Since 1800* (New York: Harcourt Brace, 1967); Chien-Nung Li, *The Political History of China, 1840–1928,* trans. and ed. by Ssu-Yu Teng and J. Ingalls (Stanford: Stanford University Press, 1956, 1967); C. T. Liang, *The Chinese Revolution of 1911* (Jamaica, N.Y.: St. John's University Press, 1962); Henry McAleavy, *The Modern History of China* (New York: Praeger, 1967); David N.

Rowe, *Modern China: A Brief History* (Princeton: Van Nostrand, 1959); Vera Simone, ed., *China in Revolution: History, Documents, and Analyses* (Greenwich, Conn.: Fawcett, 1968); Ssu-yu Teng and John K. Fairbank, eds., *China's Response to the West: A Documentary Survey, 1893–1923* (New York: Atheneum, 1954, 1963); Arthur Waley, *The Opium War Through Chinese Eyes* (Stanford: Stanford University Press, 1958, 1968); Allen S. Whiting, *Soviet Policies in China, 1917–1924* (Stanford: Stanford University Press, 1958, 1968).

CONTEMPORARY SCENE

For the most part, books on China's contemporary development are written by specialists in various fields, such as economics, politics, and international relations. Here again we can only mention a few essentials among a wide variety of books that are available: A. Doak Barnett, *China After Mao: With Selected Documents* (Princeton: Princeton University Press, 1967); Derk Bodde, *Peking Diary: 1948–1949, A Year of Revolution* (Greenwich, Conn.: Fawcett, 1950, 1967); Conrad Brandt, *et al., A Documentary History of Chinese Communism* (New York: Atheneum, 1952, 1966); Claude A. Buss, *The People's Republic of China* (Princeton: Van Nostrand, 1962); Ch'u Chai and W. Chai, *The Changing Society of China* (New York: New American Library, 1962); S. Chandrasekhar, *China's Population: Census and Vital Statistics* (New York: Oxford, 1960); Jerome Ch'en, *Mao and the Chinese Revolution* (New York: Oxford, 1967); Vidya Prakash Dutt, *China and the World: An Analysis of Communist China's Foreign Policy* (New York: Praeger, 1966); Stewart Fraser, ed., *Chinese Communist Education: Records of the First Decade* (New York: John Wiley, 1965); Morton H. Halperin, *China and the Bomb* (New York: Praeger, 1965); Francis L. K. Hsu, *Under the Ancestor's Shadow: Kinship, Personality, and Social Mobility in Village China* (Garden City, N.Y.: Doubleday, rev. ed., 1967); Dan N. Jacobs and Hans H. Baerwald, eds., *Chinese Communism: Selected Documents* (New York: Harper, 1963); George P. Jan, ed., *Government of Communist China* (San Francisco: Chandler, 1966); John W. Lewis, *Leadership in Communist China* (Ithaca: Cornell University Press, 1963, 1966); Robert Jay Lifton, *Thought Reform and the Psychology of Totalism* (New York: Norton, 1961); Hugo Potisch, *Red China Today*, trans. by Heinz von Koschembahr (Chicago: Quadrangle, 1966); Stuart Schram, *Mao Tse-tung* (Baltimore: Penguin, 1967); Tang Tsou, *America's Failure in China, 1941–50*, 2 Vols. (Chicago: University of Chicago Press, 1963, 1967); Yuan-li Wu, *The Economy of Communist China: An Introduction* (New York: Praeger, 1965); and C. K. Yang, *Chinese Communist*

*Society: The Family and the Village* (Cambridge: MIT Press, 1959, 1965).

## CULTURE, THOUGHT, AND RELIGION

Inasmuch as the Chinese have always viewed life as an integrated whole and not as a composite of separate departments, the usual modern Western categories such as culture, thought, ethics, philosophy, and religion may not fully apply. For example, scholarly opinions vary as to whether Confucianism is a philosophy, ethics, religion, or all of them rolled into one. Similar questions may be raised about many other aspects of Chinese tradition. Thus, while many of the books cited in this section deal primarily with specific topics, we trust that the readers will try to see the inner unity underlying various facets of Chinese life.

John Blofeld, *The Jewel in the Lotus: An Outline of Present Day Buddhism in China* (London: Buddhist Society, 1948), is a good introductory reading on the subject. Derk Bodde, *China's Cultural Tradition* (New York: Holt, Rinehart, 1957), succinctly discusses the genius of Chinese tradition. O. Brière, *Fifty Years of Chinese Philosophy, 1898–1950* (London: Allen & Unwin, 1956; New York, Praeger, 1965), is a very good survey of the crucial phase of Chinese philosophical development. Among Wing-tsit Chan's many scholarly works, *Religious Trends in Modern China* (New York: Columbia University Press, 1953), *An Outline and An Annotated Bibliography of Chinese Philosophy* (New Haven: Yale University Press, 1961), *A Source Book in Chinese Philosophy* (Princeton: Princeton University Press), and *Chinese Philosophy, 1949–1963: An Annotated Bibliography of Mainland China Publications* (Honolulu: East-West Center Press, 1967), are pertinent. Chen-chi Chang, *The Practice of Zen* (London: Rider, 1960), and Kenneth K. S. Ch'en, *Buddhism in China: A Historical Survey* (Princeton: Princeton University Press, 1964), are important contributions to the study of Chinese Buddhism, while H. G. Creel, *Chinese Thought: From Confucius to Mao Tse-tung* (New York: New American Library, 1953, 1960) and his *Confucius and the Chinese Way* (New York: Harper, 1949, 1960), stress the centrality of Confucian tradition. Those interested in the Buddhist influence on Chinese art are strongly advised to read J. LeRoy Davidson, *The Lotus Sutra in Chinese Art* (New Haven: Yale University Press, 1954). Clarence B. Day, *Chinese Peasant Cults, Being a Study of Chinese Paper Gods* (Shanghai: Kelley & Walsh, 1940), is a rare book which deals with folk religion in China. William Theodore de Bary, *et al.*, comp., *Sources of Chinese Tradition*, is now available in a two-volume paperback edition (New York: Columbia University Press, 1964). Amaury de Riencourt,

*The Soul of China: An Interpretation of Chinese History* (New York: Harper, 1965), delineates the philosophical underpinning of Chinese history. Wolfram Eberhard, *Guilt and Sin in Traditional China* (Berkeley: University of California Press, 1967), is a penetrating study of Chinese concepts of sin and retribution. John K. Fairbank, ed., *Chinese Thought and Institutions* (Chicago: University of Chicago Press, 1957, 1967), and Albert Feuerwerker, ed., *Modern China* (Englewood Cliffs, N.J.: Prentice-Hall, 1964), are both collections of informative and thought-provoking essays. Thomé H. Fang, *The Chinese View of Life* (Hong Kong: Union Press, 1957), unfortunately little known in the West, is a penetrating book on the traditional notion of "comprehensive harmony," whereas Charles P. FitzGerald, *The Chinese View of Their Place in the World* (New York: Oxford, 1964), interprets how the traditional outlook has been modified by the present Communist regime.

A noted Chinese philosopher, Fung Yu-lan, publicly repudiated his earlier writings after he became "enlightened" by communism, but his *The Spirit of Chinese Philosophy* (Boston: Beacon, 1947, 1962) and *A Short History of Chinese Philosophy* (New York: Macmillan, 1948, 1966), are still important books for the edification of Westerners. E. R. Hughes, *The Invasion of China by the Western World* (London: Black, 1937), is a sober analysis of this important subject, while E. R. and K. Hughes, *Religion in China* (London: Hutchinson, 1950), is a well-balanced description of traditional religions. Also, E. R. Hughes, ed. and trans., *Chinese Philosophy in Classical Times* (New York: Dutton, 1942), is in itself a small classic. Those who are concerned with recent ideological developments in China might profitably turn to Joseph R. Levenson, *Modern China and Its Confucian Past: The Problem of Intellectual Continuity* (Garden City, N.Y.: Doubleday, 1964), and John W. Wilson, ed., *Major Doctrines of Communist China* (New York: Norton, 1964). Many of the excellent papers on Chinese philosophy presented at the East-West philosophers' conferences are now collected in Charles A. Moore, ed., *The Chinese Mind: Essentials of Chinese Philosophy and Culture* (Honolulu: East-West Center Press, 1967). John K. Shryock, *The Origin and Development of the State Cult of Confucius* (New York: Century, 1932), is the only work available on this important phenomenon. Laurence G. Thompson, *Chinese Religion: An Introduction* (Belmont, Calif.: Dickenson, 1969), is a handy and reliable work, stressing the social function of religion in China. Max Weber, *The Religion of China: Confucianism and Taoism*, trans. and ed. by H. H. Gerth (New York: Macmillan, 1964), though dated, is still "must" reading because of the author's keen sociological insight. Holmes H. Welch, who earlier published *Taoism: The Parting of the Way* (Boston: Beacon, 1957, 1966), has recently contributed two important works on modern Chinese Buddhism entitled *The Practice of Chinese Buddhism, 1900–1950* (1967) and *The Buddhist Revival in China* (1968), both published by Harvard University Press. Arthur F. Wright, *Buddhism in Chinese History* (Stanford: Stanford University Press, 1959; New York: Atheneum, 1965), gives a lucid narrative of the complex history of Chinese Buddhism. Finally, C. K. Yang, *Religion in Chinese Society: A Study of Contemporary Social Functions of Religion and Some of Their Historical Factors* (Berkeley: University of California Press, 1961, 1967), should be read by all who are concerned with Chinese religion and society.

## LITERATURE AND ART

Many works of Chinese literature and poetry have been translated into Western languages with varying degrees of success and are now available in paperback editions. While we cannot cite these specific works, we can suggest some of the general works on literature and art, such as Laurence Binyon, *Painting in the Far East: An Introduction to the History of Pictorial Art in Asia, Especially China and Japan* (New York: Dover, 1959); Cyril Birch, ed., *Anthology of Chinese Literature: From Early Times to the Fourteenth Century* (New York: Grove, 1967); Cyril Birch, ed. and trans., *Stories from a Ming Collection* (New York: Grove, 1968); René Grousset, *Chinese Art and Culture,* trans. by H. Chevalier (New York: Grove, 1959); Kai-Yu Hsu, trans. and ed., *Twentieth Century Chinese Poetry: An Anthology* (Garden City, N.Y.: Doubleday, 1963, 1964); Soame Jenyns, *A Background to Chinese Painting* (New York: Schocken, 1935, 1966); Lin Yu-tang, ed., *Famous Chinese Short Stories* (New York: Simon and Schuster, 1948, 1954); James J. Y. Liu, *The Art of Chinese Poetry* (Chicago: University of Chicago Press, 1962, 1966); Hugh Munsterberg, *The Art of the Chinese Sculptor* (Tokyo and Rutland, Vt.: Tuttle, 1960); Robert Payne, ed., *The White Pony: An Anthology of Chinese Poetry* (New York: New American Library, 1947, 1960); Shio Sakanishi, trans., *The Spirit of the Brush* (Wisdom of the East Series, New York: Paragon, 1939); A. C. Scott, *An Introduction to the Chinese Theater* (New York: Theatre Arts Books, 1958); Michael Sullivan, *A Short History of Chinese Art* (Berkeley: University of California Press, 1967); Peter Swann, *Art of China, Korea, and Japan* (New York: Praeger, 1963); Sze Mai-mai, *The Way of Chinese Painting: Its Ideas and Technique* (New York: Random House, 1956, 1959); and Chi-Yuan Wang, *Oriental Brushwork* (New York: Pitman, 1964).

# A Note on
the Contributors

CLAUDE A. BUSS, Professor of History at Stanford University, previously served as a language officer in China, as executive assistant to the U.S. High Commissioner to the Philippines, and as a specialist on Southeast Asia with the U.S. Embassy in Japan. He is the author of *Asia and the Modern World, War and Diplomacy in Eastern Asia, The People's Republic of China, The Far East,* and *Southeast Asia and the World Today.*

NORTON GINSBURG is Professor of Geography and Associate Dean of the Division of Social Sciences at the University of Chicago. Formerly secretary of the Joint Committee on Contemporary China and now chairman of the Social Science Group of the U.S. National Commission for UNESCO, he is a specialist in the geography of Eastern Asia. He is the author of *An Atlas of Economic Development* and co-author of *Malaya.*

MELVIN GURTOV is a staff member in the Social Science Department at The Rand Corporation, concentrating on Communist China and Southeast Asia. He is the author of *The First Vietnam Crisis: Chinese Communist Strategy and U. S. Involvement, 1953–54;* "Hanoi on War and Peace," in John Boettiger, ed., *Vietnam and American Diplomacy;* and articles in *Current History, Asian Survey,* and *The China Quarterly.*

JOSEPH M. KITAGAWA is Professor of History of Religions, The University of Chicago. He is the author of *Religions of the East, Gibt es ein Verstehen fremder Religionen?,* and *Religion in Japanese History,* and editor of *The Comparative Study of Religions, Modern Trends in World Religions, History of Religions: Essays on the Problem of Understanding,* and *Modern Buddhist Classics.*

MARK MANCALL, Associate Professor of History at Stanford University, previously taught at Harvard and El Colegio de Mexico, and was editor of *Formosa Today.* He has contributed to C. D. Cowan, ed., *The Economic Development of China and Japan;* John Keep, ed., *Contemporary History in the Soviet Mirror;* and Thomas T. Hammond, ed., *Soviet Foreign Relations and World Communism.*

E. G. PULLEYBLANK, Professor and head of the Department of Asian Studies at the University of British Columbia, previously taught at the School of Oriental and African Studies, London, and at Cambridge University. He is the author of *The Background of the Rebellion of An Lu-shan* and many articles on the history of the T'ang dynasty (618–906) and on Chinese historical linguistics.

HENRY G. SCHWARZ is Professor of Political Science and History at Western Washington State College. He specializes in contemporary Chinese government and politics and in Chinese Central Asia, and is the author of *Leadership Patterns in China's Frontier Regions, China: Three Faces of a Giant, Liu Shao-ch'i and "People's War,"* and several articles.

VINCENT Y. C. SHIH is Professor of Chinese Philosophy and Literature at the University of Washington, Seattle. He has written *The Taiping Ideology: Its Sources, Interpretations and Influences; The Literary Mind and the Carving of Dragons; Religious and Philosophical Concepts in Ancient China; Prolegomena to Metaphysics* (in Chinese); and *Descartes, Spinoza and Leipnitz* (in Chinese).

SETH TILLMAN, consultant to the Senate Committee on Foreign Relations, previously taught Political Science at Massachusetts Institute of Technology and served in the offices of then Representative John Lindsay of New York and Senator J. William Fulbright. He is the author of *Anglo-American Relations at the Paris Peace Conference of 1919.*

STEPHEN UHALLEY, JR., is Associate Professor of History at Duke University. He taught previously at the University of Arizona, served on the staff of the Asia Foundation, and edited *The Journal of the Hong Kong Branch of the Royal Asiatic Society.* He has contributed to Chun-tu Hsueh, ed., *Revolutionary Leadership in Modern China,* and the *Journal of Asian Studies,* the *China Mainland Review,* the *China Quarterly,* and *Asian Survey.*

YUAN-LI WU is Professor of International Business at the University of San Francisco and a consultant to the Hoover Institution on War, Revolution, and Peace, Stanford University. He is the author of *The Economy of Communist China: An Introduction; Economic Warfare; An Economic Survey of Communist China;* and *China's Economic Policy: Planning or Free Enterprise?*

# Index